Carnegie Commission on Higher Education

Sponsored Research Reports

COLLEGES OF THE FORGOTTEN AMERICANS:
A PROFILE OF STATE COLLEGES AND
REGIONAL UNIVERSITIES
E. Alden Dunham

FROM BACKWATER TO MAINSTREAM:
A PROFILE OF CATHOLIC HIGHER
EDUCATION
Andrew M. Greeley

THE ECONOMICS OF THE MAJOR PRIVATE
UNIVERSITIES
William G. Bowen
(Out of print, but available from University Microfilms.)

THE FINANCE OF HIGHER EDUCATION
Howard R. Bowen
(Out of print, but available from University Microfilms.)

ALTERNATIVE METHODS OF FEDERAL
FUNDING FOR HIGHER EDUCATION
Ron Wolk

INVENTORY OF CURRENT RESEARCH ON
HIGHER EDUCATION 1968
Dale M. Heckman and Warren Bryan Martin

The following reprints and technical reports are available from the Carnegie Commission on Higher Education, 1947 Center Street, Berkeley, California 94704.

RESOURCE USE IN HIGHER EDUCATION: TRENDS IN OUTPUT AND INPUTS, 1930–1967, *by June O'Neill, published by Carnegie Commission, Berkeley, 1971 ($5.75).*

ACCELERATED PROGRAM OF MEDICAL EDUCATION, *by Mark S. Blumberg, reprinted from* JOURNAL OF MEDICAL EDUCATION, *vol. 46, no. 8, August 1971.*

SCIENTIFIC MANPOWER FOR 1970–1985, *by Allan M. Cartter, reprinted from* SCIENCE, *vol. 172, no. 3979, pp. 132–140, April 9, 1971.*

A NEW METHOD OF MEASURING STATES' HIGHER EDUCATION BURDEN, *by Neil Timm, reprinted from* THE JOURNAL OF HIGHER EDUCATION, *vol. 42, no. 1, pp. 27–33, January 1971.*

REGENT WATCHING, *by Earl F. Cheit, reprinted from* AGB REPORTS, *vol. 13, pp. 4–13, no. 6, March 1971.*

WHAT HAPPENS TO COLLEGE GENERATIONS POLITICALLY?, *by Seymour M. Lipset and Everett C. Ladd, Jr., reprinted from* THE PUBLIC INTEREST, *no. 24, Summer 1971.*

AMERICAN SOCIAL SCIENTISTS AND THE GROWTH OF CAMPUS POLITICAL ACTIVISM IN THE 1960s, *by Everett C. Ladd, Jr., and Seymour M. Lipset, reprinted from* SOCIAL SCIENCES INFORMATION, *vol. 10, no. 2, April 1971.*

THE POLITICS OF AMERICAN POLITICAL SCIENTISTS, *by Everett C. Ladd, Jr., and Seymour M. Lipset, reprinted from* PS, *vol. 4, no. 2, Spring 1971.*

THE DIVIDED PROFESSORIATE, *by Seymour M. Lipset and Everett C. Ladd, Jr., reprinted from* CHANGE, *vol. 3, no. 3, pp. 54–60, May 1971.*

JEWISH AND GENTILE ACADEMICS IN THE UNITED STATES: ACHIEVEMENTS, CULTURES AND

POLITICS, by Seymour M. Lipset and Everett C. Ladd, Jr., reprinted from AMERICAN JEWISH YEAR BOOK, 1971.

THE UNHOLY ALLIANCE AGAINST THE CAMPUS, by Kenneth Keniston and Michael Lerner, reprinted from NEW YORK TIMES MAGAZINE, November 8, 1970 .

PRECARIOUS PROFESSORS: NEW PATTERNS OF REPRESENTATION, by Joseph W. Garbarino, reprinted from INDUSTRIAL RELATIONS, vol. 10, no. 1, February 1971.

. . . AND WHAT PROFESSORS THINK: ABOUT STUDENT PROTEST AND MANNERS, MORALS, POLITICS, AND CHAOS ON THE CAMPUS, by Seymour Martin Lipset and Everett Carll Ladd, Jr., reprinted from PSYCHOLOGY TODAY, November 1970. (Out of print.)*

DEMAND AND SUPPLY IN U.S. HIGHER EDUCATION: A PROGRESS REPORT, by Roy Radner and Leonard S. Miller, reprinted from AMERICAN ECONOMIC REVIEW, May 1970. (Out of print.)*

RESOURCES FOR HIGHER EDUCATION: AN ECONOMIST'S VIEW, by Theodore W. Schultz, reprinted from JOURNAL OF POLITICAL ECONOMY, vol. 76, no. 3, University of Chicago, May/June 1968. (Out of print.)*

INDUSTRIAL RELATIONS AND UNIVERSITY RELATIONS, by Clark Kerr, reprinted from PROCEEDINGS OF THE 21ST ANNUAL WINTER MEETING OF THE INDUSTRIAL RELATIONS RESEARCH ASSOCIATION, pp. 15–25. (Out of print.)*

NEW CHALLENGES TO THE COLLEGE AND UNIVERSITY, by Clark Kerr, reprinted from Kermit Gordon (ed.), AGENDA FOR THE NATION, The Brookings Institution, Washington, D.C., 1968. (Out of print.)*

PRESIDENTIAL DISCONTENT, by Clark Kerr, reprinted from David C. Nichols (ed.), PERSPECTIVES ON CAMPUS TENSIONS: PAPERS PREPARED FOR THE SPECIAL COMMITTEE ON CAMPUS TENSIONS, American Council on Education, Washington, D.C., September 1970. (Out of print.)*

STUDENT PROTEST—AN INSTITUTIONAL AND NATIONAL PROFILE, by Harold Hodgkinson, reprinted from THE RECORD, vol. 71, no. 4, May 1970. (Out of print.)*

WHAT'S BUGGING THE STUDENTS?, by Kenneth Keniston, reprinted from EDUCATIONAL RECORD, American Council on Education, Washington, D.C., Spring 1970. (Out of print.)*

THE POLITICS OF ACADEMIA, by Seymour Martin Lipset, reprinted from David C. Nichols (ed.), PERSPECTIVES ON CAMPUS TENSIONS: PAPERS PREPARED FOR THE SPECIAL COMMITTEE ON CAMPUS TENSIONS, American Council on Education, Washington, D.C., September 1970. (Out of print.)*

*The Commission's stock of this reprint has been exhausted.

Institutions in Transition

Institutions in Transition

A PROFILE OF CHANGE IN HIGHER EDUCATION
(INCORPORATING THE 1970 STATISTICAL REPORT)

by *Harold L. Hodgkinson*

Research Educator,
Center for Research and Development in Higher Education,
University of California, Berkeley

with a commentary by *Stanley J. Heywood*

Seventh of a Series of Profiles Sponsored by
The Carnegie Commission on Higher Education

MCGRAW-HILL BOOK COMPANY

New York   St. Louis   San Francisco   Düsseldorf
London   Sydney   Toronto   Mexico   Panama
Johannesburg   Kuala Lumpur   Montreal
New Delhi   Rio de Janeiro   Singapore

The Carnegie Commission on Higher Education,
1947 Center Street, Berkeley, California 94704,
has sponsored the preparation of this profile as
part of a continuing effort to obtain and present
significant information for public discussion.
The views expressed are those of the author.

INSTITUTIONS IN TRANSITION
A Profile of Change in Higher Education
(Incorporating the 1970 Statistical Report)

Copyright © 1971 by The Carnegie Foundation for
the Advancement of Teaching. All rights reserved.
Printed in the United States of America.

Library of Congress catalog card number 76-165254

123456789MAMM7987654321

07-010033-0

Contents

Foreword

The most comprehensive study ever made of changes in higher education in the United States was undertaken by Dr. Harold L. Hodgkinson at the request of the Carnegie Commission on Higher Education. We wanted to learn more about the dynamics of recent changes: what changes have been made, who initiates change and who supports or resists it, how the campus community interacts under stress of change, and what are the major consequences of change. In addition to recent changes, we wanted to learn more about the longer-term transition of colleges and universities.

With his colleagues at the Center for Research and Development in Higher Education at the University of California, Berkeley, Dr. Hodgkinson first obtained a perspective of institutional change over the past three decades by assembling a longitudinal statistical history. The researchers then sent questionnaires to college and university presidents, which resulted in detailed responses from more than half of the nation's centers of higher learning, on the important changes of the recent past. From this material, the author produced a valuable and sometimes surprising body of information.

The Carnegie Commission released a portion of the study in 1970 as an interim statistical report. This book incorporates much of the data contained in that version with elaboration, including five case studies of institutions in transition, and some helpful interpretations of the study's findings.

Clark Kerr
Chairman
The Carnegie Commission
on Higher Education

September 1971

Preface

This is a book about change in American higher education. It attempts to state which changes have taken place, where they occurred, how they took place, and what they may mean for the future of higher education.

There are three primary data sources for dealing with these questions. The first is a "statistical history" of changes in higher education over the last two decades based on data from the U.S. Office of Education (USOE) Directories on higher education. From this history was developed a questionnaire, answered by 1,230 presidents of institutions of higher education. This questionnaire focused on specific changes that had taken place on each campus, with the president's estimate of how they took place and what they might mean. From this analysis came our third basic data source, case studies of five institutions that had gone through what our previous work indicated were major changes that other institutions might experience in the future. It is hoped that this book will fill a gap in our knowledge of where higher education is and how it got that way, in terms of changes in persons, institutions, and systems of institutions.

The study is presented here in three main parts, the first dealing with the USOE Directories analysis and the questionnaire results. The second part contains the five case studies of major institutional changes. The third part presents some special analyses of the questionnaire returns in terms of our sample of the 1,230 college and university presidents and their academic and personal backgrounds, plus an analysis of the questionnaire data as it relates to the institutional characteristics which are associated with increased frequency of student protests and demonstrations. A final chapter attempts to put this material into a central framework for purposes of generalization.

The reader is encouraged to make use of Charts 1 and 2 on pages 26–29 and 30–33 which give most of the major results of the questionnaire analysis. There are many hypotheses that can be explored using these charts, and many relationships can be developed by the reader from this data source. It is a form of "do-it-yourself" research, in which the case studies can be used to amplify hypotheses derived from the questionnaire analysis.

Certain portions of this book appeared in the technical report of the study published by the Carnegie Commission in July 1970, also entitled *Institutions in Transition*. These sections appear here because the technical report is now out of print.

MAJOR CONCLUSIONS Some major conclusions of this study are:

1   The students in American higher education have become much more diverse in terms of social and economic background, but less so in terms of age. More of them are staying through graduation; more are going on to graduate school. Students have acquired more control over institutional policies, more influence in academic decisions, and more control over the establishment and maintenance of social regulations.

2   Although the trends are stronger in large institutions offering advanced degrees, faculty are teaching fewer hours, are more interested in research, show a slightly increased interest in teaching, are much less loyal to the institution, get tenure at an earlier age, speak out more often on issues of national policy, and support students who oppose the administration. The small private colleges offering the B.A., however, do not show these trends.

3   The huge increase in college students has been handled through the public sector, by building many new community colleges and by expanding existing public colleges and universities, often to enormous size.

4   The greatest increase in institutions awarding the Ph.D. degree is in public institutions, especially state colleges that have become state universities. The trend is even stronger in degree programs than it is in institutions.

5   Almost all higher education is now coeducational.

6   In the opinion of presidents, the most important changes in their institutions (in order) have been increases in faculty and student

power, changes in academic programs, and changes in the composition of the student body.

7   Presidents estimate that by 1975 there will be over 20,000 faculty who do no teaching at all and who spend all their time on research, in over 300 institutions.

8   Size is one of the most important factors in describing an institution. Larger institutions have a more diverse student body, a more research-oriented faculty, less institutional loyalty, more transients in the student body, poorer communication, and more student protest.

9   Region of the country and control make relatively little difference in determining what changes will take place in institutions.

10   Taken as a whole, the amount of institutional diversity in American higher education is decreasing. This is due partially to the pervasive existence of a single status system in higher education, based on the prestigious university offering many graduate programs and preoccupied with research. There are few alternative models to this system now functioning.

Acknowledgments

Although the author must take responsibility for the content, a large number of people have been involved in the preparation of this report. Financial support for the project came from the Carnegie Commission through a grant to the Center for Research and Development in Higher Education, Berkeley. The Commission's chairman, Clark Kerr, was of crucial importance during the project, making several suggestions that were very helpful, as did Virginia Smith of the Commission staff. Dr. Leland Medsker, center director, was also very helpful. A center advisory committee for the project offered many good suggestions early in the project's development. This group consisted of Ernest Palola, Algo D. Henderson, Terry Lunsford, and Robert C. Wilson.

Mrs. Alice Lynn, research assistant for the project, was very helpful in setting up the questionnaire and some of the data analysis. Krystina Grycic was secretary to the project and set up many of the tables. Walter Schenkel joined the project staff in time to do some of the data analysis and wrote some of the sections describing institutional change. Tyese Flood typed portions of the final manuscript.

The case studies were done using teams of interviewers for each campus. These included G. Lester Anderson, James Fisher, David Hauser, Berkeley Eddens, David Underwood, and Terry Renolds. Particular thanks are due to G. Lester Anderson, who provided very helpful material on the case study of the State University of New York at Buffalo.

The author is particularly indebted to the following for helpful insights on institutional change: David Riesman, Patricia Cross, Warren Martin, J. B. Hefferlin, Earl McGrath, Morris Keeton, Richard Peterson, and Rensis Likert.

xvii

Institutions in Transition

Part One

Statistical History and Questionnaire Results

1. On Change in Persons

It is interesting to note that for all his vaunted intellectual powers, the human being seems virtually incapable of perceiving change until it has taken place. There are many reasons for this: Our language binds time for us—nouns, and verbs like "is," give a note of immutability and permanence, so that when we say "Jane is pretty," we tend to understand this to mean that no matter with whom she is compared during any time period, Jane will be seen as pretty, and will always remain so. In addition to language, our previous perceptions tend to build up a bank of trained incapacities on which we draw with great frequency. In the case of strip mining in Pennsylvania, the landscape had to be decimated before people were able to perceive the change, due to the pictures in their heads which blinded them to the daily accretions that eventually added up to destruction.

Means also have a tendency to become ends. We have so much ego and effort invested in the present as we see it, that we cannot abide one who tells us that where we see permanence there is only flux. (The Greeks, of course, were rather liberal in terms of freedom of speech, except for Heraclitus, who believed that only flux was real, that stability and permanence were illusions. Not even the Greeks could take *that*. And how would we respond to a man who said that order was simply chaos misunderstood?) If a clerk has been ordering pencils for a company for 20 years and is suddenly told that pencils are out and ball-point pens will be used from here on out, his response will probably be an emotional one. Pencils, which were a means for the organization, had become an end for the clerk. His life and self-image were wrapped up in the buying of pencils. Although it may seem absurd, a clerk, in at least one case, committed suicide over such an issue. Great thinkers who present us with images of a changing world—Darwin, Marx, Lincoln, Socrates, and Christ—have a very good chance of incurring physical harm. (The genius of Dostoevsky's Grand Inquisitor scene is the insight that the vision of Christ's teaching was so far from the way people were actually living that they couldn't face it— therefore the necessity for a church to protect people from Christ.) Thus we often go about with blinders on, not seeing actual transformations of our physical environment, our political and economic systems—even ourselves—until the change has completely taken place.

We also find that our perspective on change, the field within which we interpret it, is too small. In 1971, for example, people are still interpreting student protests in light of indigenous American causes and effects without seeing that the era of student protest in secondary schools and higher education is worldwide. Much of what happens to the stock market is due to international systems for the manipulation of monetary values, yet we attribute market changes to who is winning a baseball game or to weather conditions in the United States. Understanding this is important for our present endeavor, for although we are talking about change in American higher education, many of the factors which are inducing changes do not stop at our national borders. For example, The Organization for Economic Cooperation and Development (OECD), an international organization concerned with higher education, has reported that virtually all member nations have experienced the following:[1]

1 A rapidly expanding student population in higher education due to the attainment of near-universal secondary education, with a shortage of space for applicants, and little evidence that the economies can absorb these new college and university graduates (a major international source of student dissatisfaction?).

2 New mechanisms for state and national planning.

3 New kinds of institutions of higher education, especially those designed for short-term study, vocational programs, and easy reentry for adults of all ages for both technical and general training (our community college movement?).

4 Reorganization and development of older institutions, particularly in terms of decentralization and separating the teaching and research functions.

5 New structures within institutions, particularly those which stress student participation in the affairs of the institution.

[1] Author's summary from OECD, 1970.

New forms of relationship *between* institutions, such as the exchange of learning resources, joint faculty appointments, etc. (the consortium explosion in the U.S.?).

Much more diversity in the student body, by age, social class, and length of time students plan to stay. In fact, over 50 percent of the students in all the OECD nations are first-generation students whose parents did not attend college.

Changes in fields of study, particularly interdisciplinary work and problem-centered institutes and centers, often not affiliated with universities.

This should make it clear that the American agenda for higher education is not unique, although our response to some agenda items may be. (For example, we are farther down the road toward universal higher education than some nations. Also, American students can transfer from one institution to another with great ease while in other countries such opportunities are just beginning. However, American students are often penalized very severely for changing majors in terms of credits and time lost, even when staying in the same institution.) But the nature of higher education in most countries seems to be becoming more utilitarian, more egalitarian, more diverse as to students and programs, and more flexible, with more national-level planning to try to gear higher education into the economic and occupational structure in a more rational way.

The caveat is raised here because of its fundamental importance. Although in this study we will be looking at changes in American higher education, the reader should be aware that just as no man is an island, no nation is either. Our national limit on data collection and analysis is arbitrary yet necessary, as all studies must set some limits to the scope of the investigation.

The next question is one of the most fascinating ones around: How will we go about studying change in higher education? This is a topic which I have considered at length elsewhere, developing the point of view known as interactionism. This means that if one wishes to study heredity and environment, one is wise to begin not with the assumption that it is heredity *versus* environment, and research will prove which is the more important, but rather the notion that what is important is the interaction between heredity and environment, that we study the interface where the two meet.

We could, for example, limit our study to what seems to be changing within individual *institutions* of higher education. Or we could look at changes in persons in higher education, changes in state *systems* of higher education, or changes in the *nation* as a whole. We could make a better selection of the field of inquiry if there were a widely accepted theory of change, but that is not the case in contemporary social science. Some feel that a force-field model is most useful, that a change is the result of the application of certain forces of certain strengths. But this suggests that change is linear and predictable, and that is certainly not the case. As Robert Nisbitt (1968, p. 66) puts it:

Events do not marry, and have little events that grow into big events which in turn marry and have little events, etc.; small social changes do not accumulate directionally and continuously to become big changes.

Establishing causal relationships among the 2,500 institutions of higher education in the country, the millions of people who make them go, the state boards of higher education, the regional and professional accrediting agencies, the over 200 Washington-based associations dealing with higher education, the over 500 consortia of institutions, the foundations, and the state and federal governments would be a tall order for the most ambitious computer, far beyond our scope here.

Our task will be to describe the changes that have taken, and are taking place, in institutions, in individuals, and in systems. A variety of data sources will be used to establish the interrelationships between these changes, where that is possible. First, there was no extensive "statistical history" of changes in institutions of higher education over the last several decades. Since a statistical history seemed as though it would be good bedrock for the project, and a good source for hypotheses, we compiled one using the yearly statistics gathered by the U.S. Office of Education which had never been put together in a cumulative fashion. Knowing a little more, we then constructed a questionnaire, which was returned by 1,230 presidents of institutions of higher education, in order to find out what had been going on in terms of more subtle dimensions than the U.S. Office of Education statistics on enrollments, etc., could provide. We were able to sort the answers by a grid which breaks down the 1,230 institutions by a large number of categories so that we could see if certain segments of higher education were moving in different directions from others. (The overwhelming conclusion was that this is not the case.) This was particularly important to the investigation, as America has always prided itself on the diversity of its educational system. We have private as well as public institutions, colleges as well as universities; we have institutions both big and small, residential and commuter, vocational and liberal arts, community-centered and national in scope, urban and rural, etc. This should mean different faculty reward systems, different institutional goals, different student "mixes," different personnel and staffing patterns. Although we did find some differences, the directions of change were very similar, suggesting that diversity in institutions of higher education is declining.

The next step was to develop a series of case studies of institutions that had gone through changes which seemed from our research to be formative in determining what an institution will become. Unlike many case studies which provide no bases for comparison, these cases were built around a common grid so that each case presents similar characteristics. This book then presents several special analyses of the questionnaire data before the concluding section.

Before proceeding with the analyses, a few comments might be made to set the scene and provide the context. It should be clear that revolutionary changes have taken place in the last 50 years as to the nature and length of schooling. At the turn of the century, about 50 percent of the age cohort stayed in school through the eighth grade—but only *20 percent* enrolled in the ninth grade. The accepted time for leaving the system was after completing the eighth grade, although only half even got that far. Less than 15 percent of the original population finished high school, 10 percent or less began the college experience, and 4 percent graduated from college.

If one looks at the figures today, one is struck with the nature of the revolution. The pattern of leaving school after the eighth grade has all but ceased. Completion of high school has obviously become the norm, and more and more of the age cohort is moving into some sort of postsecondary education. It now appears that better than 50 percent of the high school graduating class go on to some form of further education; in California, about 80 percent are going on, especially to community colleges. In addition to looking at the "learning force" in the *core* of formal programs in colleges and universities, we may also look at the educational *periphery*—that is, education often for credit which is taking place through the surveillance of industries, the various proprietary institutions, correspondence courses, TV, etc. If we do this we run into some very interesting numbers. In 1965, there were 57 million Ameri-

TABLE 1   *The American learning force (millions), 1940–1976*

	1940	1950	1955	1960	1965	Current estimates 1970	1976
I. The educational core							
1. Preprimary	.7	1.3	2.0	2.7	3.1	4.4	5.5
2. Elementary	20.5	21.0	26.0	29.1	32.0	32.3	30.0
3. Secondary	7.1	6.5	9.3	13.0	16.8	19.8	22.1
4. Undergraduate	1.4	2.4	2.4	3.2	4.9	6.5	8.3
5. Graduate	.1	.2	.2	.4	.6	.8	1.1
SUBTOTAL	29.8	31.4	39.9	48.4	57.4	63.8	67.0
II. The educational periphery							
6. Organizational	8.2	10.2	10.9	13.0	14.5	21.7	27.4
7. Proprietary	2.5	3.5	3.5	4.0	7.8	9.6	18.1
8. Antipoverty					2.8	5.1	7.0
9. Correspondence	2.7	3.4	3.5	4.5	5.0	5.7	6.7
10. TV				.01	5.0	7.5	10.0
11. Other adult	3.9	4.8	5.1	6.8	9.1	10.7	13.2
SUBTOTAL	17.3	31.4	23.0	28.3	44.2	60.3	82.4
III. The learning force							
TOTAL	47.1	53.3	62.9	76.7	101.6	124.1	149.4

SOURCE: Moses, 1970, p. 7.

cans in some form of education from preprimary through graduate school. In that same year 44 million Americans engaged in education through one of the peripheral formats. In 1970, there were 63 million Americans in the periphery. It is thus clear that if we focus our attention only on the educational core of formal institutions, we are missing an important fact, which is that education has become a national resource and is thus being considered too important to be left entirely to the educators in the core. By putting the core and peripheral figures together, by 1976, 150 million Americans will be taking an active part in some sort of learning experience through a school or some other organization for which they may receive some sort of "credit." This sort of proportion engaged in formal education has never been attained by any other society in the history of the world.

We are clearly approaching a proletarian era in American higher education. A rough analogy could be made between contemporary undergraduate education and the American high school of 40 years ago. At that time America "decided" that eight years of education was not enough and that a high school diploma was something to which every American should be entitled. Precisely the same arguments were raised about standards, about the selective function of the high school, etc., that are now raised about undergraduate education. We also had then the evolution of a new institution—the junior high school, which was clearly a bridging institution, designed to move us from an eight-year program of education to twelve. No one expected that individuals would leave in large numbers after having completed junior high school. It was assumed that one would move on to the next level, which is precisely what happened to most people.

In the late sixties, we discovered the enormous implications of the *junior college,* another bridging institution moving us now from a high school diploma for everyone toward a college degree for everyone. The junior high school contributed enormously to America's educational repertoire, including the development of the core curriculum, the unit method, team teaching, differentiated staffing, and a number of integrated approaches to learning. The junior or community college up until this time has contributed little to general education, but has provided some excellent technical programs and precise training for lower-level technical and managerial needs. It seems quite likely that this trend will continue and that as a result the occupational and economic value of the B.A. degree will be further decreased. On the other hand, another societal trend is emerging with some force: the tendency of industries and various other institutions within the society to be willing to certify their own kinds of instruction to meet their own needs. These certifying activities are often handled outside of the college or university. (It should be pointed out here that the B.A. probably should not have any particular significance in a vocational way, as it would be very hard to argue except in certain highly specialized cases that a bachelor's degree in any liberal arts area directly qualifies anybody for anything.)

Given this move toward a proletarian view of educational functions, it is quite clear that open admissions is only the first of a number of battles which will be fought during the next decade. No faculty to my knowledge has taken a real position on a question that may become concomitant to open admissions, which is open graduation. The options here are few—either you allow the "cul-

turally different" or "disadvantaged" person a longer period of
time to reach the monolithic, unchanging requirements for graduation, or you alter those requirements for certain individuals, making
a more flexible approach both into and out of the institutions of
higher education. When we begin talking this way, we are talking
about a *genuine* pluralism, which accepts as a working principle
the 30 years of research in the psychology of individual differences.
This research all suggests that if 20 different people read *Moby
Dick,* for example, they will have 20 different educational experiences. Formal education, however, proceeds as if the outcomes of
reading a book were common to all. The job of the instructor, then,
is to put together the diverse interpretations and meanings which
the students have acquired and begin making some gains toward
a more sensitive and sophisticated interpretation on the part of
the reader of what he has read. This is a general paradigm for curriculum and program development during the next decade.

In the past, our pattern of program development was based on
the inherent morality of the straight line; that is, the system should
be planned on the assumption that the freshman, after admission,
will go straight through the program to completion. One has only
to hang around the registrar's office of any large institution to learn
that a student who wishes to deviate from the prescribed tunnel
through which he is to travel is seen often as having committed
some sort of crime. It is clear that the American system of higher
education, like most others, will have to come to terms in the next
decade with the new demands for *flexible access.* More and more
people will enter the system of formal education and leave before
the "prescribed" period is up, only to reenter the system at a later
time. (And there is no good defense of our current practice of automatically assuming that a bachelor's degree should take 4 years or
124 semester hours, no more, no less. We do know that incoming
freshmen at some institutions know more than graduating seniors
at others, proving that the B.A. does *not* represent a fixed national
standard for personal or intellectual competence; yet we often proceed as if it did.)

In the teaching situation today there is much more flexible access
to instructional tools, such as independent study, work experience,
tutorials, programmed instruction, seminars, advisee conferences,
etc. The point is that these tools can be switched on and off depending on their functional utility at any given *moment.* In adopting
a national perspective, it may be that we will have to develop the
same program flexibility that is now possible for the individual

teacher within his course structure in selecting the right *tools* to do the job. This will certainly be a major task of higher education in the seventies, and one which is bound to disturb some of the more entrenched interests. Indeed, most of our national organizational structures will have to develop more flexible and adaptive means of meeting the needs of large segments of the population as these needs surface, rather than on some arbitrary and depersonalized schedule. This represents a fragmentary and incomplete sketch of the context in which higher education is operating, and will operate in the seventies. Let us now turn to the research data on change to see what has happened during the last several decades.

In this section, we will outline the major changes that have occurred in higher education during the last two decades. These changes will be reported in four general categories — changes in students, faculty, administration–board of trustees, and the nature of the institutions themselves. The primary data sources for this report are the census study of the U.S. Office of Education and the questionnaire responses from 1,230 institutions.

CHANGES IN STUDENTS
Without any doubt, the most vital change in students during the last two decades is their very rapid increase in numbers. America, having now accepted the notion of universal secondary education, seems to be gearing up for a new push toward some sort of universal educational experience beyond high school. It is difficult to see now exactly what this pattern will be like, but the community colleges will play a vital role in the determination. Students leave our educational system at certain highly visible points — particularly after the completion of grades 8 and 12. Changes in these patterns can be seen in Figure 1.

Although the school-leaving patterns in higher education are not clear from the graph, most evidence suggests that the last two grades, 15 and 16, show relatively little attrition. The community colleges, which claim to enroll about 60 percent of their students in transfer programs, seem to produce only about half that many students who actually *do* transfer to a four-year institution. We still have great problems in developing a clearly articulated, flexible system of education which will allow for changes in students' personal and vocational goals and will not penalize them for these changes. (For example, in most large states with big populations, students from community colleges are not given equal treatment when they attempt to transfer to four-year programs, and lose course credits through minor technicalities.) At any rate, in 1970

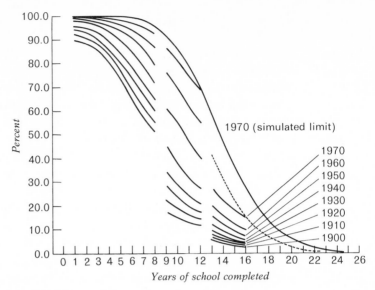

SOURCE: Byrnes, 1970, p. 3.

we had about 6.5 million undergraduates and 800,000 graduate students in American higher education.

These students are increasingly enrolling in public, rather than private, institutions. This holds true for both undergraduates and graduate students.

As one might expect, this rapid increase in raw numbers of students (now a little better than half of the youth cohort aged 18 to 21) has necessitated a marked increase in student diversity, as seen in Table 2.

Half of our 1,230 institutions reported an increase in the number of students from other states and from other colleges — indeed,

Diversity in	Percent
Ethnic composition	53
Proportion of married students	51
Proportion of transfer students	50
Proportion of out-of-state students	42
Socioeconomic background	40
Proportion of foreign students	36
Religious background	34
Political affiliation	26
Age	20

SOURCE: Author's questionnaire.

we may have the most geographically mobile student population on earth.

It is also interesting, and perhaps significant, to observe that 56 percent of the institutions report increased diversity by race, while only 40 percent report an increase in diversity of socioeconomic background. One can infer from this that higher education is still a middle-class phenomenon, and that a black middle-class youth will have a better chance of getting into college than will a lower-class young person, whatever his race. (Indeed, the recruiting efforts now being made to attract bright middle-class black and brown students resemble in no small way the energetic recruiting of high school quarterbacks for the college football team.) One of the major reasons for this discrepancy is that the income level of parents is still a very good measure of quality of education in elementary and secondary schools, where the preparation for college takes place.

The other items in Table 2 are quite obvious, although it is interesting to observe that only 20 percent of our sample indicated increasing diversity of students by age. In Europe, increasing attention is being given to college experience for *all* age levels in the population, with special attention being given to the "reentry" phenomenon of the middle-aged man or woman who now wishes to pursue some new occupational or personal goals. Although we do have many centers for continuing and adult education in this country, they tend to be seen as peripheral rather than central. The 19-year-old sophomore can transfer virtually anywhere in the country with comparative ease, but the 45-year-old woman whose children are now grown and who wishes to study for a B.A. degree will have a much more difficult time getting in, particularly if she wishes to study part time.

In addition to increased student diversity in many areas, important changes have taken place in the effectiveness of institutions of higher education, as seen in Table 3.

TABLE 3
"Effectiveness"
of institution

Effectiveness in	Percent
Proportion of graduates planning on continued education	73
Proportion of freshmen completing degree requirements	50
Proportion of graduate to undergraduate students	21
Proportion of graduate students completing degree programs	20
Proportion of dismissals for academic reasons	0

SOURCE: Author's questionnaire.

It would appear that graduate study is becoming a much more likely aspiration for the American student than has been the case. This is a matter of some seriousness for our nation, as it is not yet clear whether our labor force can digest rapidly increasing numbers of people with advanced degrees in certain areas. It is also not clear how (if at all) the system can be manipulated to pull students away from overcrowded occupational areas and toward those in which a genuine need exists for trained personnel.

Although there is great concern in many quarters for the apparently high attrition rates among American college students (a typical estimate is that for every four students admitted to B.A. study, one will graduate four years later), half of our institutions report an increase in the proportion of freshmen who graduate. Unfortunately, our data do not tell us how large this proportional increase is, but the *trend* toward improved retention may be worth some cautious optimism. Attrition figures are notoriously hard to evaluate, as an individual who takes a term off is usually listed as a casualty, even though he may come back and finish up somewhat later than he planned originally. Transfer students are also often shown as casualties. If we put together a number of studies, a rough guess would be that of all students who enroll for the B.A. degree, about half will graduate eventually. Any evaluation of the attrition phenomenon has to be made against the increased student diversity we have already mentioned, in that an institution serving students from a narrow, homogeneous range of backgrounds will generally have an easier time of it than the pluralistic "open-door" institution that tries to be all things to all students, which is almost bound to have a higher attrition rate.

About one-fifth of our institutions report an increase in the proportion of graduate students to undergraduates. This trend is particularly strong in the large public universities, often due to state funding formulas which give the institutions more money for each graduate student than they do for each undergraduate. Costs of graduate education are higher per student, but often not as much higher as the state formulas suggest. About one-fifth of our sample (presumably almost the same institutions) report an increase in proportion of graduate students who actually attain their degrees. Indeed, there seems to be a trend in much of graduate education to get students through programs at a faster rate, with more pragmatic training in their specialties and fewer niceties such as extensive foreign language training. Some graduate programs are even allowing the submission of several publishable articles in lieu of the thesis, as well as reduced residency requirements. Professional schools also seem to be moving toward shorter programs, with more emphasis on the pragmatic aspects of the profession, more exposure to the actual professional demands through internships, etc.

From Table 4 we can get some measure of the trends in the desire of many students to play an increased role in campus decision making and to be more in charge of their own activities and destinies. Note that students have been more involved in establishing standards of social conduct than in the enforcement of regulations, although about half of our institutions report an increase in the latter, which is a significant trend. Students also seem to be playing an increasing role in campuswide decision making, with a slightly less-strong trend at the departmental level on many campuses, which is to a great extent where the academic action is. They also seem to be participating in the many broadly based campus councils or senates containing student, faculty, and administration representatives, and in a large number of cases students are on presidential selection committees as well as long-range planning committees of the institution. Perhaps as a consequence of these new areas of student initiative and responsibility (and perhaps not), a little less than a third of our institutions report an increase in student protests and demonstrations. (This topic is discussed in the special chapter dealing with protests.) Underground publications and films, another area of student initiative, have increased in 16 percent of our institutions, particularly in large institutions in the East or West which offer advanced degrees.

TABLE 4
"Modernity" of student body

Modernity in	Percent
Amount of student control in establishing *regulations governing student conduct*	67
Proportion of students participating in voluntary community projects	65
Amount of student control in institutionwide policy formulation	63
Amount of student control in academic decision making	58
Amount of student control in enforcing *regulations governing student conduct*	55
Proportion of on-campus student protests	27
Underground publications and films	16
School spirit	9
Number of men joining fraternities	8
Number of women joining sororities	8

SOURCE: Author's questionnaire.

It is also interesting to look at the figures on school spirit and numbers joining fraternities and sororities, none of which show any increase worth mentioning. One could conclude from this analysis that college-aged youth are becoming more loyal to persons than they are to institutions, and that any president who tries to appeal to the students' loyalty to the institution will get no further than did the middle-class father who tried to make his children grateful because he fed and clothed them. Consistent with this position would be the argument that this college generation has little faith in the concept of representationality—I vote for Joe, and then Joe speaks for me. (Joe becomes an institutionalized me.) There is considerable evidence from other sources that the cherished institutions of politics, religion, and military, even organized big-time collegiate ahtletics, are being viewed in a rather cynical way by the young, who see in them great sources of exploitation. In the minds of many, representative government is only a cover-up for the "real" political processes—direct participation of all concerned people. Indeed, the low score on school spirit may be due to the idea that this generation of students, like the children of the middle-class father mentioned above, consider going to college, like food and clothing, as something that just happens to everyone, for which no one needs to feel gratitude or loyalty. College attendance may be shifting in its interpretation from being a distinct privilege granted to a few, to a birthright—claimed as we claim our right to breathe or walk. This will mean some very distinct changes in the leadership strategies of college administrators, and some changes in the machinery of student participation in the affairs of the institution. One small example of this redefinition can be seen in the present trend of having students present, with voice if not vote, at trustee meetings. This clearly has caused a real shift in the role of the president, who had been the chief interpreter of on-campus situations to the board. But now the students, who are getting to know the board members as human beings, are going around the president and directly to the board to get programs they want on some campuses, thus undercutting the president's authority with the board considerably.

In sum, the American student body has become more diverse in background, more transient, less willing to play higher education's games to get the gold stars that degrees represent, more politically aware and politically powerful, less easily led around by the nose, more aware of the world outside the campus, more willing to take direct action on issues they deem important to their self-interest, less willing to police their fellow students, and less loyal to abstract institutions in the same way that the American voter tends to vote for the man, not for the party. One could also postulate an increasing pragmatism and specificity in the students' attitude about higher education. This is not to say that they are gods, nor that they are always right. But this is a more sophisticated college generation, representing a larger range of background, and perhaps of ability, than higher education has ever dealt with before. Even if their SAT scores are low, they often know much about what is going on.

CHANGES IN FACULTY The rapid increase in size of student body mentioned above has necessitated a parallel increase in the size of the higher education faculty. (Actually, the ratio is not quite level, as class size is going up on most campuses, indicating that faculty growth has not kept up with student growth.) But the market for new faculty has been good; there has been a "teacher shortage" in higher education, as institutions, especially public colleges and universities, engaged in rapid expansion and sought to teach students without slowing down their growth rates. Growth, in many institutions, came to mean "excellence" in the sixties. The seventies will be different — there are more teachers than jobs, and this will continue for most of the decade. Statewide boards and planning commissions are putting enrollment ceilings on institutions of higher education, realizing perhaps too late that some of them have come to resemble dinosaurs; and the public shows less interest in continued expansion of the higher education tax base.

Some of the consequences of the sixties for faculty can be seen in Table 5.

Tenure was awarded more often and to younger men, as institutions bargained desperately to get and keep the most able younger scholars. On many campuses, the instructor rank nearly died out completely — the initial appointment was at the assistant professor level; and in the university context, the work of the instructor was carried by a new group, the teaching assistants, who often exchanged servitude for the doctorate. (At Berkeley, about half of the undergraduate teaching in arts and sciences is now carried on by teaching assistants.) There are some striking consequences of this trend to heap the younger professor with rewards in rank and tenure. Perhaps the most notable is that during the sixties it became

	Percent
TABLE 5 *"Mobility" and "commitment" of faculty*	

Mobility of faculty:

	Percent
Proportion of tenured faculty	42
Amount of faculty turnover	9
Average age when tenure is awarded	−23
Commitment of faculty:	
Commitment toward research	32
Hours spent in research	32
Commitment toward teaching	19
Commitment toward institution	− 3
Hours spent in teaching	−41

SOURCE: Author's questionnaire.

possible for a teacher to become a full professor, with tenure, by the time he was 40. The institution has cashed in its chips—there are no more rewards for it to offer. And the young full professor must survive, if he stays, for 25 years of service for which the institution has provided no reward system at all, nothing toward which he can aspire, except perhaps the inevitable gold watch on his 65th birthday. (But who would work hard for 25 years for that?)

To support this position, we refer to the surprising response to our request of the presidents to list all the faculty at their institutions whose sole activity was research, for three different time periods, and a guess for 1975. They are presented here, along with the number of institutions reporting the existence of research faculty:

TABLE 6 *Number of faculty engaged solely in research*

	1948	1958	1968	1975*
Faculty	1,305	2,065	5,567	10,810
Number of institutions reporting	36	47	138	178

*Estimated.
SOURCE: Author's questionnaire.

This rather striking increase in the numbers of faculty who do not teach is worth consideration. Since our sample is 50 percent of the institutions of higher education in the country, we can argue that in the United States in 1968 there were about 11,000 faculty members who did not teach, but dealt only with research, and that by 1975 there will be over 20,000 of them in 356 institutions. There are probably only 20 to 40 universities in the country that can claim to be basic research centers, and if all 178 institutions that plan on research faculty by 1975 aspire to become major research centers, it is not at all clear that the country could, or would, support so many. This set of statistics lends support for the idea that there is a monolithic status system in American higher education, and that its base is in research and in the "national reputation," both for the person and for the institution, that research (and a rapid increase in graduate programs) apparently can bring.

Given this background, the data in Table 7 on faculty commitment should not be too surprising. Faculty teach fewer hours (teaching load is often as important as salary in bargaining for a contract); spend more hours in research and are more committed to it (even in many undergraduate colleges which claim that their only business is undergraduate teaching); show a slight overall decline in institutional commitment, concentrated in the large institutions which offer advanced degrees; and show an overall increase in commitment toward teaching, which is reversed in the large universities. All of this seems consistent with our earlier statement that the institutional-reward structure for faculty has lost much of its viability, and that faculty are seeking rewards from learned societies and through research, even when such

	Percent
TABLE 7 *Modernity and autonomy of faculty*	
Modernity	
Faculty efforts to promote student-faculty discussions	68
Faculty willingness to experiment with new teaching methods	67
Faculty willingness to accept student course evaluations	38
Faculty support of students opposing administrative policies	29
Autonomy	
Faculty involvement in determining institutionwide policies	76
Proportion of faculty publicly advocating positions on national policy	41
Faculty autonomy in academic programs	29
External pressures limiting faculty freedom	−18
Faculty autonomy in grading	14

SOURCE: Author's questionnaire.

activity is not necessarily desired by the institution, or essential to its mission. Riesman and Jencks have suggested the existence of a monolithic status system in higher education, based on the "big-time" university model, and these data tend to support their position. It should also be noted that this single-status system works to homogenize higher education, to drive out the unusual programs based on unusual reward systems, and to drive out the unusual faculty and students who might be attracted by these different reward and status systems. (In an interview last year, I was told by a high administration official, "A student who came to this campus and announced that he was searching for the good life would be dispatched to the psychiatric clinic.") The community colleges provide an institution which should be able to provide an alternative reward system, but one source has indicated that over 40 percent of community college faculty would rather be teaching in a four-year college. More recent data indicate that the percentage who feel this way may be declining, which suggests that the community college may be establishing a reward system of its own.

Table 7 offers some interesting additions to our change data on faculty—first, they seem increasingly willing to get involved with students in discussions and are willing to experiment with teaching techniques, but are much less willing to accept student evaluations of faculty, which many of them clearly see as a threat to faculty prerogative. Perhaps with the security which comes with tenure, faculty are increasingly willing to support students who oppose the administration, to publicly advocate positions on national policy. (Both of these items are highly related to the incidence of student protest, as reported in the special section of this report dealing with student protest.) Faculty have clearly gained an increasing role in decision making at the institutional-policy level in most institutions. It is interesting that the items dealing with faculty autonomy in academic programs and grading are very small—one of the problems of a "trend" analysis such as this one is that if faculty autonomy in these two areas is virtually complete (as is most likely the case) then there would be no way in which to record an increase in autonomy, just as sons of upper-class fathers cannot be shown to be improved in occupational status over their fathers.

Some general problems have emerged from our analysis of faculty trends. First, during the sixties, large numbers of young faculty received tenure as a reward to keep them at the institution. On many campuses, between two-thirds and three-fourths of the faculty have tenure. Because a great many of these faculty are young, and plan to stay at the institution, and because it will become more difficult financially to justify the creation of new faculty positions, it will mean that for the next 20 years or so, almost all the nontenured faculty will have to leave the institution, as there will be no tenured position available for them. This creates two further problems:

1 If too many of the younger faculty who are denied tenure are demonstrably superior to the senior tenured faculty, very poor faculty morale may result. (Even now, it is easy to find cases of senior faculty rejecting a junior faculty for tenure when the grounds for rejection apply even more to the senior than to the junior.)

2 This bunching of faculty by age will mean that in about 20 to 25 years a large percentage of the senior faculty will retire within a very small time span, which might mean replacing half of the faculty in several years.

There is presently much consideration of the tenure issue. Little evidence can be provided that shows that the tenure system *has* protected the jobs of faculty members when pressured by political forces, and it may well be that tenure dulls the faculty members' initiative and desire to improve, although there is little evidence on that score. On the other hand, there is evidence that higher education, especially public higher education, is becoming more open to direct political intervention, due particularly to statewide centralization of higher education, governed by groups which have direct linkages into the state political structure and pressure system. Tenure is unfair, however, in providing some political immunity to only a fraction of the professoriate, rather than making it a condition which *all* higher education faculty deserve. This suggests that there are at least two tasks which must be considered soon: (1) the provision of some sort of political immunity from coercion for all faculty members, or for none; (2) a drastic overhaul of the faculty-reward structure so that a faculty member can be expected to grow and improve as a professional *throughout* his career.

As can be seen from Table 8, administrators need to be more aware
of agencies outside the campus walls than ever before. There is
now in American higher education a bewildering array of consortia
—cooperative arrangements by institution, by academic department, by region, by type (junior college associations, land-grant
colleges and universities, etc.), by state, and by city. Over three-
fourths of our presidents report an increase in the number of working relationships with other institutions. There are of course
many benefits from these arrangements—better use of specialized
resources, more contacts for faculty in other institutions, less
insularity, etc. There has been considerable concern about the
erosion of institutional autonomy by overdoing such relationships,
but at the moment that fear does not seem to be well founded.
About half of our institutions report an increase in cooperative
programs with local industry. One might have thought that this
was largely a function of the community colleges in our sample,
but the trend turns out to be widely distributed across all types
of institutions, as can be seen on the master chart. This strong
trend may foretell an era in which vocational training programs
will be of a much more collaborative nature, with work-study
programs, course work, certification of competence, and even the
award of a degree as a truly joint venture between the college or
university and the industry. We may even find a sharper distinction in the future between certification of competence and the
awarding of a degree, the former done by industry, the latter by
the college. And much could be said for a system in which most
industries, with clear performance criteria, would test anyone

TABLE 8
*"Scope" of
administrative
authority*

	Percent
Number of working relations with other colleges and universities	78
Number of cooperative programs with local industry	45
Influence of state department of education on institutional policy making	18
Number of departmental requirements for undergraduate degree	12
Alumni influence on institutional policies	7
Authority of central campus administration	− 7
Degree to which institution controls student behavior	− 35
Administrative attempts to increase student-faculty communication	88
Attempts to attract students from disadvantaged homes	62

SOURCE: Author's questionnaire.

who walked in, and hire them if they had the needed skills. (This is particularly important in interpreting the statement already made, that by 1976 there will be about 67 million Americans in schools, from kindergarten to graduate school, while 82 million Americans will be in other organized learning situations, such as TV courses; proprietary institutions; and training programs of business, industry, and the military. Thus the educational "core" may be smaller than the educational "periphery.")

Eighteen percent of our institutions report an increase in the influence of state departments of education. Surprisingly, although the trend is stronger in public institutions, it is also present in private ones. There are major differences by region of the country—in the Northeast, only 2 percent report an increase, while the Southwest reports increases in 38 percent of the institutions. It may well be that this trend will continue. It is too early to tell what the impact of state departments of education will be on institutional autonomy. It is clear that within states there is a great deal of overlap and waste by their allowing a number of institutions to offer identical programs. On the other hand, student migration being as great as it is, it is equally absurd to say that students in the institutions of state X are there to meet the manpower needs of that state only— a medical school in the Midwest may be preparing more doctors for New York and California than for the home state. There will probably be more centralization of policy formation on issues such as manpower needs in the future, simply because of the great mobility of the population across state lines, and an increasing movement across national borders.

Many of our institutions report a decrease in institutionwide requirements for the degree, and some report a small but consistent increase in the number of departmental degree requirements. In some institutions this is simply a standoff as far as the poor student is concerned—for example, several institutions voted out the foreign language requirement for all students in April, only to find in May that each *department* had just adopted the requirement that the institution rejected.

The four-year private liberal arts college has shown the largest increase in the influence of alumni on institutional policy, probably due to the fact that these institutions must rely on alumni for financial support.

There is, in almost all institutional categories, a reported small decline in authority of the central campus administration. However, there is a much larger report of a decline in the degree to which the institution controls the student body. This trend is much stronger in large institutions. One could read this trend as meaning that not only are social regulations less effective, but the faculty are less effective in their "control" of students. More independent study programs, pass-fail grading, and student participation on departmental committees and on major institutional bodies would all support the argument that students have become less controllable, if control is to mean instant obedience to orders from a superior. On the other hand, if education is becoming a more personal, intrinsic activity for students on some campuses, they may have become less controllable but more educable. If that is the case, the tradeoff might be worth it. At the moment, however, the evidence is simply not in.

Virtually all our presidents report that they have worked to increase student-faculty communication, consistent with the leadership style of the president as mediator, suggester, supporter, facilitator. From comments presidents made on the establishment of the most important change at their institution, most of them play this kind of role. (This style, for whatever else it is worth, usually has greater survival benefits than that of the "shake-'em-up" president, who usually has a brilliant but short career.)

Well over half of our presidents report that their institutions have made attempts to attract students from disadvantaged homes. Although the trend is strong throughout the sample, it increases with institutional size and with institutional complexity. (Thirty percent of the single-purpose institutions show an increase, while sixty-seven percent of the multipurpose institutions do.) One interpretation of these data would be that "disadvantaged" may mean race as often as it does economic status—we have already established that the increase in student diversity by race is greater than by social class. It is also clear that large, complex institutions usually exist in large cities, and that these institutions feel a greater obligation to do something just because of sheer proximity to the urban poor. On the other hand, the *rural* poor (both white and black) have not been recruited so energetically, even though they still represent a major American social problem. During this last year, I visited six campuses with rural locations which were vigorously recruiting black students from a major city hundreds of miles away, while virtually on their doorstep one could find large numbers of very poor rural whites, Chicanos, and American Indians!

Perhaps most important, we asked our presidents to indicate how much they thought their budgets would increase in 1975, compared to 1967–68 (the last full year before this survey was taken). Although we wanted dollar amounts, we were reluctant to ask the question directly, as our pretest showed that presidents were often unwilling to share information on operating budgets. We therefore asked presidents to estimate the amount of change in fractions, as reported in Table 9.

It would seem that, given existing market and finance conditions, many presidents were being slightly overoptimistic, particularly the 55 percent who felt that their operating budget would double or more than double. It also can be said that this is the area in which our presidents are most ego-involved. On the last page of the questionnaire we asked for a number of open-ended responses from the presidents, one being, "What MAJOR PROBLEMS that you are currently facing are of most concern to you?" A clear majority of the respondents indicated that their most important problem was that of financing the program. This was true even in a number of institutions which had had an increase in student protests and demonstrations! The reason for this is obvious — one has a chance of coming out ahead when there are protests on campus, but if the budget is not capable of paying salaries, then failure is inevitable. (However, having said this, it must also be said that a number of institutions have become thoroughly familiar with deficit financing during 1970–71, and many seem to be surviving rather well. One of the problems is that the faculty, accustomed to relative affluence, may find it difficult to adapt to a financial situation in which their every need will *not* be met, and their criteria for extra positions and equipment requests will have to be much more carefully weighed. In this situation, the president

TABLE 9 President's estimate of budget increase for 1975, based on 1967–68 operating budget	Increase	Number of presidents	Percentage of response
	Less than half	124	10
	Half	173	14
	Three-quarters	154	13
	Double	448	36
	Triple	140	11
	More than triple	100	8
	No response	91	8

SOURCE: Author's questionnaire.

must again be the chief teacher of the institution, in communicating financial necessities to the faculty and students.)

In the write-in section, we also asked the presidents about where they thought their institutions were heading, and where they ought to be headed. We can present the questions and rough categories of answers here:

1 *Specifically, what future change(s) do you expect to occur at your school?*
Most frequently listed was a more involved and restive student body, followed by a larger, more intellectually and socially involved faculty, and then by expansion of facilities. Further down the list were more remedial and vocational programs, serving more disadvantaged, and more interinstitutional programs.

2 *Please give us your best estimate of the fundamental changes you would LIKE to see occur at your campus in the next five to ten years.*
We got fewer responses to this item, which may be significant. The most frequent answers were to become more relevant to society, to get better funding, and to improve the quality of teaching. There was less clustering of the answers, suggesting that presidents are more alike in their estimates of what will be than they are about what ought to be.

3 *If you are currently involved in planning or investigating future changes, which ONE do you feel will have greatest impact on your campus?*
The responses to question 3 were less frequent than were the answers to question 1 and showed very little clustering. Mention was made of new buildings, greater financial stability, use of teaching technology, and greater involvement with the community. One gets the idea that 1968–69 was not a vintage year for the development of dynamic plans.

4 *What MAJOR PROBLEMS that you are currently facing are of the most concern to you?*
Here, the number of answers perked up, and also clustered magnificently around the problem of getting adequate funding to keep the program going. (About 75 percent of the presidents responded this way.) Far back on the list came the acquisition of faculty, sometimes "well qualified," sometimes just faculty.

Looking at all the write-in answers to these four questions, there are certain common themes. In addition to funding, there is an enormous concern with *growth*. Almost every questionnaire mentioned the word—more students, more faculty, more facilities. A very poor second was the concern for more student and faculty participation in governance, either as a need or as an anticipated development. The growth statements are fascinating, in that *growth is always seen as a solution, never as a creator of problems.* More is always assumed to be better. Presidents say that they would like to have even more students, more faculty, and more buildings—they also expect more student protest, lack of communication, and often poor morale, but they seldom if ever relate growth as a possible cause of these problems.

Although we have little data in our study dealing directly with the composition of boards of trustees, Rodney Hartnett has completed a restudy of trustees for Educational Testing Service, and has concluded that trustees are becoming slightly more diverse, veering away somewhat from the almost total dominance of the white-male-Republican wealthy-banker, -lawyer, or -doctor pattern. Trustees now include women, racial minorities, students, and faculty, though two such people on a thirty-member board could still be interpreted as tokenism. (One board sought, and found, a black female social worker, thereby absolving its social conscience with a single appointment, somewhat akin to our gifts to the United Fund.) But there does seem to be a shift in *access* of on-campus groups to the trustees, at least to be heard if not to vote. And many trustees are spending more time on the campus, talking with faculty and students, trying to counter the absentee landlord image. Although this may undercut the role of the president as chief interpreter of the campus to the board, it will probably increase the sympathy and respect the trustees have for the job the president has to do, and may increase their awareness of why he must play a mediator role at times, rather than a dictatorial one. In this situation, familiarity (with on-campus issues and people) will probably not bring contempt.

In this chapter we have briefly dealt with the major changes that we have found in *persons* involved with higher education. (The reader is again referred to Charts 1 and 2 if he has further hypotheses he wishes to check, as there is a great deal of interesting material in them that we have no opportunity to discuss.) Now we will look at some of the institutional characteristics which have changed during the last two decades.

CHART 1 **CHART 1** *Changes affecting the student body from 1958 to 1968 as perceived by presidents of colleges and universities, by institutional characteristics*

	N= 535	N= 392	N= 240	N= 520	N= 475	N= 128	N= 31	N= 9	N= 111	N= 224	N= 220	N= 208
Percent of schools reporting greater heterogeneity or increase (greater homogeneity or decrease) in:	Institutional control			Enrollment					Geographic area			
	P	S	N-S	S	M	L	G	S	NE	ME	SE	GL
Students:												
Ethnic composition	47	58	57	45	58	57	66	89	48	56	59	50
Religious background	22	48	37	32	37	36	29	11	30	37	39	38
Socioeconomic background	40	42	44	32	46	50	55	44	40	43	44	45
Political affiliation	24	29	24	20	29	33	39	22	22	20	32	30
Age	29	17	6	15	24	29	32	44	13	17	20	19
Percent of out-of-state students	29	53	57	40	47	45	58	22	52	46	51	38
Percent foreign students	35	35	40	29	38	49	61	44	34	35	35	40
Percent married students	52	45	45	43	52	63	55	11	47	43	51	44
Percent on-campus student protests	30	23	33	12	32	59	77	89	27	35	21	31
Quality of student preparation in high school	63	73	74	59	75	75	80	89	75	72	73	68
Percent freshmen completing degree requirements	52	47	53	43	57	59	45	78	46	44	58	55
Percent dismissals for academic reasons	(2)*	6	(9)	2	(2)	(6)	4	(33)	(10)	(3)	(1)	(3)
Percent dismissals for nonacademic reasons	(1)	(6)	(11)	(5)	(5)	(8)	(10)	(11)	(13)	(9)	(4)	(4)
Student control in academic decision making	58	64	53	52	63	69	65	89	53	56	54	66
Student control in institution-wide policies	63	68	58	59	66	77	65	78	59	63	60	68
Student control in establishing regulations	69	68	71	63	72	76	74	99	74	65	67	74
Student control in enforcing regulations	54	61	53	52	58	62	45	78	60	54	55	58
Percent graduating class planning further education	69	79	80	70	76	85	90	99	82	78	78	72
School spirit	16	6	(3)	14	7	(5)	(6)	(11)	(2)	11	24	10
Undergraduate publications and films	18	11	20	7	18	36	48	56	16	22	9	17
Percent students participating on community policies	57	75	73	61	70	70	77	89	69	74	59	71
Percent transfers entering institutions	50	50	49	46	54	57	65	78	43	54	49	48
Number of men joining fraternities	12	4	7	4	10	20	23		8	8	10	9
Number of women joining sororities	12	4	7	3	11	21	29	(11)	10	10	10	6
Percent of graduates to undergraduates	26	13	27	7	22	60	81	89	22	28	19	21
Percent of graduates completing degree requirements	26	13	21	7	21	58	65	78	21	22	17	19

*( )= decrease.

NOTE: Meaning of categories for Chart 1 above and Chart 2, pp. 30–33: Institutional control—P, public; S, sectarian; N-S, nonsectarian. Enrollment—S, small; M, medium; L, large; G, giant; S, super, Geographic area—NE, New England; ME, Mideast; SE, Southeast; GL, Great Lakes; PL, Plains; SW, Southwest; RO, Rockies; FW, Far West. Highest degree— —B.A., less than B.A. Institutional designation—2-YC, two-year college; 4-YC, four-year college; C/M.A., college offering M.A.; U/M.A., university offering M.A.; U/Ph.D., university offering Ph.D. Institutional purpose—Single, single purpose, Multi, multipurpose. Move from S to N-S, move from sectarian to nonsectarian. Move from TP to EP, move from

$N=$ 157	$N=$ 78	$N=$ 38	$N=$ 172	$N=$ 404	$N=$ 351	$N=$ 264	$N=$ 163
					Highest degree		
PL	SW	RO	FW	−B.A.	B.A.	M.A.	Ph.D.
45	55	48	54	38	55	70	59
37	29	29	26	19	45	44	32
35	39	42	40	32	42	48	50
26	27	29	23	15	33	32	31
19	33	32	24	20	15	25	25
38	41	24	42	26	56	49	44
31	41	24	41	27	36	42	52
63	59	58	39	40	48	58	58
23	16	21	34	14	22	38	58
68	54	71	60	49	79	76	82
46	50	58	49	48	53	49	55
8	8	5	(1)	4	5	(3)	(19)
(2)	3	3	(5)	(3)	(4)	(7)	(10)
60	50	68	62	49	65	63	64
67	46	74	69	57	67	69	66
68	46	68	73	67	65	74	72
54	45	61	57	51	60	58	55
72	73	76	66	58	81	84	85
8	19	(19)	(10)	18	11	(5)	(2)
14	13	10	21	8	11	26	34
61	60	47	67	52	71	75	77
56	54	58	46	34	58	63	52
12	17	8	(3)	5	7	14	8
14	21	8	(3)	6	7	13	13
15	23	18	25		2	52	73
14	26	32	26		3	49	67

teacher preparatory to expanded program. Move from Pr. to Pub., move from private to public. Move from B.A./M.A. to Ph.D., move from bachelor's or master's to Ph.D. as highest degree. Move from 2-Y to 4-Y, move from two-year programs to four-year programs. Changes in enrollment—S to L, small to large; M to G, medium to giant. Move from S-S to coed, move from single sex to coeducation—UG, undergraduate; G, graduate. Move from 4-Y to state, move from four-year programs to state control with graduate programs.

SOURCE: Author's questionnaire.

CHART 1 *(cont.)*

Percent of schools reporting greater heterogeneity or increase (greater homogeneity or decrease) in:	Institutional designation					Institutional purpose		Move from S to N-S	Move from TP to EP	Move from Pr. to Pub.
	N= 315	N= 285	N= 142	N= 61	N= 118	N= 138	N= 1043	N= 20	N= 57	N= 8
	2-YC	4-YC	C/M.A.	U/M.A.	U/Ph.D.	Single	Multi			
Students:										
Ethnic composition	38	59	74	75	65	36	55	65	66	63
Religious background	18	49	44	57	34	17	37	70	40	38
Socioeconomic background	33	46	49	55	54	24	44	55	49	37
Political affiliation	16	36	34	36	37	17	28	50	30	25
Age	24	18	24	29	31	5	22	30	28	25
Percent of out-of-state students	26	62	52	61	52	27	45	75	49	25
Percent foreign students	28	38	42	46	57	32	36	25	53	25
Percent married students	43	53	61	59	62	43	50	45	66	38
Percent on-campus student protests	15	23	38	46	67	12	30	30	35	25
Quality of student preparation in high school	45	81	83	83	90	44	71	95	89	50
Percent freshmen completing degree requirements	48	54	52	54	64	23	54	45	56	50
Percent dismissals for academic reasons	7	6	(8)	7	(20)	8	(1)	10	2	25
Percent dismissals for non-academic reasons	(2)	(6)	(10)	(11)	(13)	(1)	(5)		3	(13)
Student control in academic decision making	50	67	65	64	66	42	61	80	61	38
Student control in institution-wide policies	58	67	74	75	73	42	67	95	65	38
Student control in establishing regulations	65	65	80	75	76	62	70	70	70	63
Student control in enforcing regulations	48	60	69	57	63	46	57	60	56	63
Percent graduating class planning further education	56	83	86	93	92	67	76	90	95	63
School spirit	17	7	(3)	(2)	(3)	13	8	(5)	5	25
Undergraduate publications and films	7	12	25	34	40	5	18	25	21	25
Percent students participating on community policies	55	72	73	82	74	53	68	85	66	50
Percent transfers entering institutions	35	61	60	70	59	42	51	65	82	38
Number of men joining fraternities	5	6	12	21	13	7	9	20	32	(13)
Number of women joining sororities	5	6	10	23	18	3	9	15	36	(13)
Percent of graduates to undergraduates		1	48	60	81	18	22	15	49	
Percent of graduates completing degree requirements		2	49	57	76	14	22	10	51	

*( ) = decrease.

NOTE: Meaning of categories: Institutional control—P, public; S, sectarian; N-S, nonsectarian. Enrollment—S, small; M, medium; L, large; G, giant; S, super. Geographic area—NE, New England; ME, Mideast; SE, Southeast; GL, Great Lakes; PL, Plains; SW, Southwest; RO, Rockies; FW, Far West. Highest degree— —B.A., less than B.A. Institutional designation—2-YC, two-year college; 4-YC, four-year college; C/M.A., college offering M.A.; U/M.A., university offering M.A.; U/Ph.D., university offering Ph.D. Institutional purpose—Single, single purpose, Multi, multipurpose. Move from S to N-S, move from

N=61	N=89	N=25	N=7	N=90	N=15	N=47	N=1230
Move from B.A./M.A. to Ph.D.	*Move from 2-Y to 4-Y*	*Changes in enrollment*		*Move from S-S to coed*		*Move from 4-Y to state*	*Sample-wide trend*
		S to L	*M to G*	*UG*	*G*		
59	56	42	63	68	67	53	53
33	35	16	14	59	33	23	34
54	48	52	71	52	73	45	40
31	29	16	43	35	40	28	26
35	36	24	71	32	7	40	20
47	55	32	57	55	33	36	42
62	40	28	43	34	40	40	36
62	53	68	57	61	66	60	48
52	14	32	71	24	40	28	27
82	71	44	86	76	87	68	67
53	52	56		57	53	57	50
4	8	12	43	(11)	(20)	4	
(7)	(1)		(29)	(17)	(13)	5	(5)
59	58	68	71	66	47	57	58
70	61	84	43	72	40	70	63
72	73	88	71	77	73	77	67
61	64	64	57	62	67	53	55
85	83	56	99	83	93	53	73
7	32	(28)	14	3	7	(2)	9
26	9	20	71	10	27	19	16
74	72	72	57	78	73	62	65
67	66	52	57	66	40	58	50
18	10	12	14	4	7	7	8
23	8	16	29	4	7	7	8
75	12	28	86	16	67	9	21
75	11	28	43	14	33	13	20

sectarian to nonsectarian. Move from TP to EP, move from teacher preparatory to expanded program. Move from Pr. to Pub., move from private to public. Move from B.A./M.A. to Ph.D., move from bachelors or masters to Ph.D. as highest degree. Move from 2-Y to 4-Y, move from two-year programs to four-year programs. Changes in enrollment—S to L, small to large; M to G, medium to giant. Move from S-S to coed, move from single sex to coeducational—UG, undergraduate; G, graduate. Move from 4-Y to state, move from four-year programs to state control with graduate programs.

SOURCE: Author's questionnaire.

CHART 2 *Changes affecting faculty and administration from 1958 to 1968 as perceived by presidents of colleges and universities, by institutional characteristics*

	N= 535	N= 392	N= 240	N= 520	N= 475	N= 128	N= 31	N= 9	N= 111	N= 224	N= 220
	Institutional control			Enrollment							
Percent of schools reporting increase (or decrease) in:	P	S	N-S	S	M	L	G	S	NE	ME	SE
Faculty:											
Amount of faculty turnover	13	11	4	4	9	23	29	44	18	11	7
Percent of tenured faculty	39	48	42	44	44	37	38	44	41	42	45
Average age when tenure is awarded	(23)*	(20)	(27)	(12)	(27)	(45)	(42)	(89)	(21)	(28)	(19)
Commitment towards teaching	16	27	12	29	16	(4)	(19)	33	11	18	24
Commitment towards research	31	32	40	18	36	66	74	44	28	40	35
Commitment towards institution	(2)		(11)	15	(13)	(20)	(52)	(44)	(9)		10
Efforts to promote student/faculty discussions	63	78	69	73	67	67	51	67	66	76	68
Faculty willingness to accept study course eval.	30	49	39	43	34	35	42	33	30	43	36
Hours spent in teaching	(39)	(43)	(48)	(28)	(50)	(57)	(52)	(56)	(57)	(45)	(33)
Hours spent in research	30	34	38	18	37	63	71	56	32	34	33
External pressures limiting faculty freedom	(14)	(25)	(19)	(17)	(21)	(16)	(6)	11	(18)	(22)	(22)
Faculty support of students opposing adm. policy	31	30	29	19	34	51	61	44	33	36	22
Faculty autonomy in grading	12	16	14	13	17	11	6		9	21	11
Faculty autonomy in academic program	28	35	28	27	33	33	23	11	35	36	26
Percent of faculty advoc. positions regard. nat'l policy	40	45	42	29	50	62	55	67	46	48	31
Faculty involvement in institutionwide policies	77	80	75	72	82	80	78	33	79	82	75
Fac. willingness to express no views in stud. body	64	76	64	72	69	57	45	67	59	67	69
Administration											
Percent of total budget based on federal support	60	50	58	46	62	68	74	99	58	48	65
Percent of total budget based on alumni support	7	31	37	26	18	15	16	22	29	24	26
Alumni influence on institution policy making	2	13	11	13	4	3	(3)		4	8	7
State dept. of ed. influence on institution policies	23	14	14	19	19	11	17		2	18	19
Authority of central campus administration	(3)	(11)	(10)	(2)	(10)	(15)	4			(12)	(4)
Attempt to attract students from disadvan. homes	66	60	65	53	70	76	81	99	59	74	51
Administration attempts to increase commun.	88	92	89	85	92	95	97	99	90	93	87
Number of coop. programs with local industry	64	32	29	30	55	70	58	44	26	38	51
Number of institutionwide req. for UG degrees	8	(5)	(2)	6	(3)	3	10	(44)	(4)	(14)	14
Number of departments required for UG degrees	14	11	7	12	12	16		(11)	9	10	21
Length of service of major admin. officers	18	20	9	23	18		(6)	11	14	11	27
Number of working relations with other schools	79	84	75	73	84	81	94	89	77	79	81
Degree to which institution controls student body	(29)	(45)	(41)	(28)	(38)	(54)	(52)	(67)	(35)	(40)	(30)

*( ) = decrease.

N=208	N=157	N=78	N=38	N=172	N=404	N=351	N=264	N=163
Geographic area					Highest degree			
GL	PL	SW	RO	FW	−B.A.	B.A.	M.A.	Ph.D.
11	7	8	10	5	(2)	9	18	25
39	31	41	42	55	46	49	32	37
(29)	(16)	(21)	(27)	(22)	(13)	(21)	(26)	(49)
22	14	32	16	18	30	26	9	(4)
33	28	34	29	27	3	33	52	74
(10)	(5)	1		(9)	15	(1)	(20)	(19)
69	62	60	71	76	65	75	72	66
43	35	33	50	36	33	41	42	39
(51)	(43)	(14)	(39)	(36)	(26)	(43)	(56)	(54)
37	29	30	37	27	4	34	49	72
(13)	(22)	(18)	(18)	(11)	(13)	(21)	(25)	(15)
34	29	25	16	33	21	28	41	44
13	16	9	3	15	15	17	16	5
27	29	19	26	34	29	30	40	18
51	35	23	37	49	28	44	52	57
75	79	71	84	77	79	78	78	72
71	74	69	66	67	74	71	61	58
53	56	65	63	52	54	50	57	76
22	20	13	18	11	7	34	25	22
10	5	8	11	7	4	12	6	6
21	14	38	13	18	30	19	4	11
(6)	(10)	5	(18)	(10)	(1)	(9)	(14)	(5)
70	57	49	50	74	63	61	64	69
91	87	82	89	90	86	91	92	93
45	45	56	61	52	56	30	48	47
1	9	10	11		14		(6)	(10)
13	15	10	13	5	7	20	19	(2)
12	20	20	21	17	27	21	4	5
81	82	72	79	77	75	80	84	85
(45)	(39)	(17)	(29)	(35)	(15)	(43)	(50)	(55)

SOURCE: Author's questionnaire.

CHART 2   *(cont.)*

	N=315	N=285	N=142	N=61	N=118	N=138	N=1043	N=20	N=57	N=8
Percent of schools reporting increase (or decrease) in:			Institutional designation			Institutional purpose		Move from S to N-S	Move from TP to EP	Move from Pr. to Pub.
	2-YC	4-YC	C/M.A.	U/M.A.	U/Ph.D.	Single	Multi			
Faculty:										
Amount of faculty turnover	(7)	7	14	26	32	11	9	(15)	38	(38)
Percent of tenured faculty	44	52	34	38	37	29	44	25	5	38
Average age when tenure is awarded	(14)	(23)	(31)	(28)	(55)	(9)	(25)	(15)	(34)	(50)
Commitment towards teaching	32	24	10	3	(9)	20	20	25	5	38
Commitment towards research		34	49	67	79	29	33	35	54	38
Commitment towards institution	18	(7)	(17)	(30)	(22)	10	(4)	(30)	(34)	38
Efforts to promote student/faculty discussions	64	74	68	75	65	71	70	75	63	63
Faculty willingness to accept study course eval.	33	41	46	34	38	38	38	45	21	
Hours spent in teaching	(26)	(47)	(55)	(65)	(60)	(32)	(43)	(30)	(58)	(13)
Hours spent in research	3	37	45	60	77	28	33	35	43	13
External pressures limiting faculty freedom	(13)	(22)	(26)	(28)	(15)	(15)	(18)	(50)	(30)	(13)
Faculty support of students opposing adm. policy	20	29	41	47	46	15	32	40	49	13
Faculty autonomy in grading	16	15	18	12	5	11	15	30	10	25
Faculty autonomy in academic program	31	30	42	42	20	23	31	40	35	13
Percent of faculty advoc. positions regard. nat'l policy	30	47	47	56	62	25	44	55	58	13
Faculty involvement in institutionwide policies	83	80	80	77	73	60	80	99	84	75
Fac. willingness to express no views in stud. body	74	71	65	56	59	71	68	75	49	63
Administration:										
Percent of total budget based on federal support	57	55	64	64	80	23	61	60	65	13
Percent of total budget based on alumni support	7	37	25	28	24	23	21	35	12	(13)
Alumni influence on institution policy making	2	13	6	5	5	16	7	15	7	(13)
State dept. of ed. influence on institution policies	32	20	1	18	7	16	18	20	(3)	38
Authority of central campus administration	(1)	(12)	(18)	(10)	(5)	4	(8)	(10)	(6)	
Attempt to attract students from disadvan. homes	65	66	67	69	78	30	67	85	58	88
Administration attempts to increase commun.	86	92	92	98	97	80	91	99	86	88
Number of coop. programs with local industry	61	29	42	72	57	20	48	35	47	75
Number of institutionwide req. for UG degrees	14	(5)	(16)	8	(12)	8	1	(10)	7	(13)
Number of departments required for UG degrees	5	19	11	36	(5)	16	12		47	25
Length of service of major admin. officers	29	22		7		17	17	10	7	13
Number of working relations with other schools	76	80	84	85	86	72	81	95	79	38
Degree to which institution controls student body	(15)	(46)	(51)	(57)	(58)	(27)	(37)	(70)	(52)	(25)

*( ) = decrease.

$N=$ 61	$N=$ 89	$N=$ 25	$N=$ 7	$N=$ 90	$N=$ 15	$N=$ 47	$N=$ 1230
Move from B.A./M.A. to Ph.D.	Move from 2-Y to 4-Y	Changes in enrollment S to L	M to G	Move from S-S to coed UG	G	Move from 4-Y to state	Sample-wide trend
16	6	20	57	16	20	13	9
23	55	36	(14)	50	60	47	42
(46)	(17)	(32)	(14)	(23)	(67)	(25)	(23)
(8)	36	(8)	(29)	29	20	36	19
78	43	32	86	32	40	15	32
(18)	17	(44)	(86)	(4)	(20)	11	(3)
62	71	48	29	85	67	70	68
35	32	12	43	49	26	37	38
(57)	(37)	(48)	(43)	(47)	(46)	(32)	(41)
74	29	36	86	33	26	20	32
(21)	(22)	(16)	(14)	(36)	(33)	(19)	(18)
44	20	56	71	39	33	23	29
11	21	16		24	33	15	14
28	36	28	14	46	40	30	29
59	34	56	43	48	53	36	41
80	82	80	57	81	80	94	76
59	69	60	14	64	60	75	67
64	50	84	86	51	47	56	55
26	28	8	(14)	36	40	2	21
5	7	4		2	7		7
16	19	20	29	19	20	41	18
(12)	(6)	8	14	(6)	(20)	(7)	(7)
64	53	88	86	68	60	74	62
93	87	92	86	90	80	96	88
47	37	80	57	29	33	81	45
(8)	11			(20)	(73)	32	2
(3)	25	8		2		21	12
15	30		29	19	(6)	17	17
80	78	76	99	79	73	85	78
(45)	(28)	(40)	(43)	(48)	(73)	(13)	(35)

SOURCE: Author's questionnaire.

2. *Changes in Institutional Characteristics – USOE Data*

Two data sources will be used for this analysis: first, the compilation of yearly figures from the U.S. Office of Education Directories,[1] and then some selected institutional analyses from our questionnaire study of 1,230 institutions.

SURVEY OF INFORMATION FROM U.S. OFFICE OF EDUCATION DIRECTORIES Unfortunately, the statistical categories used by the U.S. Office of Education are not constant throughout the period, at least for some characteristics. Most of the tables, however, are continuous, and discontinuities are clearly indicated. The analysis section is rather short, and the reader is encouraged to pursue the charts and Appendix himself if he is concerned with change factors not mentioned in the text. Tables in the Appendix to this chapter are of three types. Tables 1 to 5 deal with total numbers of institutions in various categories by year. Tables 6 to 10 describe the closing or merging of institutions. Tables 11 to 15 deal with institutional migration or mobility to and from various categories. It is hoped that this summary material will be useful to those investigating change patterns in higher education.

This section presents data on the following variables:

1 Type of control

   a Private—public

   b Sectarian—nonsectarian

   c Local—state

---

[1] Published annually as *Education Directory,* part III, by U.S. Office of Education, Washington, D.C., and hereinafter cited as U.S. Office of Education Directories.

2　Level of degree offered

3　Type of program offered

4　Sexual composition of student body

5　Student enrollment

6　Institutions added

7　Institutions dropped

8　Institutions merged

The tables and analyses that follow outline only the most significant trends that developed from a survey of the data. For a more complete picture of the trends from 1941 to the present, please refer to the tables in the Appendix to this chapter.

CHANGES IN PUBLIC VERSUS PRIVATE CONTROL　There is a strong parallel between numbers of public and private institutions for almost any given time period between 1941 and 1966 (see Table 1, Appendix). Both show drops during the war years (1941–1945). From 1955 to 1966, both public and private campuses show increases (see Figure 2).

The percentages of institutions in public and private control show virtually no change in proportions since 1941, when 33 percent of all institutions were classified as public and 67 percent were classified as private; in 1966, 36 percent of all institutions were public and 64 percent private. Throughout the 25-year span, proportions never varied more than four percentage points.

Although little change has occurred in the relative number of private and public *institutions,* there has been a drastic shift in

FIGURE 2
Number of institutions by control, public and private

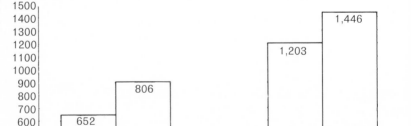

Total number of institutions

SOURCE:　U.S. Office of Education, *Education Directory,* part III, Higher Education.

TABLE 10
*Average number
of students in
public and
private sectors*

Year	*Average number of students enrolled in a public institution*	*Average number of students enrolled in a private institution*
1947	2,102	1,039
1966	4,911	1,374

SOURCE: U.S. Office of Education, *Education Directory*, part III, Higher Education.

total student *enrollments* carried by private and public sectors (see Table 1, Appendix). Perhaps a more comprehensible measure can be seen from a comparison of the average number of students enrolled in public or private institutions in 1947 and 1966.

A comparison of the proportion and number of students enrolled in private and public institutions in 1947 and 1966 shows a dramatic expansion in the public sphere (Table 11, below).

Thus it becomes apparent that the increased influence of public institutions comes not from the ability to spawn new institutions but from the capacity to expand existing campuses. In the 20-year span, the public institutions more than doubled the average number of students enrolled; each added an average of 2,809 students during the period from 1947 to 1966, while each private institution added an average of only 335 students.

CHANGES IN SECTARIAN VERSUS NON-SECTARIAN CONTROL

For the 20-year time span, sectarian and nonsectarian institutions show parallels in their growth and decline patterns. In four specific years, both sectarian and nonsectarian schools decreased in total number of institutions; in seventeen other years, both show increases. Since 1956 both have shown consistent growth (see Appendix, Table 4).

The sectarian schools had net gains similar to the nonsectarian institutions. The proportion of sectarian versus nonsectarian type of control is the same today as it was in 1941; for both 1941 and 1968, 40 percent of the institutions were sectarian and 60 percent were nonsectarian.

During the war years (specifically from 1941 to 1945), both

TABLE 11
*Proportion of
students in
public and
private sectors*

Year	*Proportion of all students enrolled in public institutions*	*Proportion of all students enrolled in private institutions*
1947	49%	51%
1966	67%	33%

SOURCE: U.S. Office of Education, *Education Directory*, part III, Higher Education.

TABLE 12
Net gains in sectarian-nonsectarian institutions, 1941–1966

	Net increases in number of institutions	Net losses in number of institutions	Total net gains 1941–66
Sectarian	239	28	211
Nonsectarian	388	103	285

SOURCE: U.S. Office of Education, *Education Directory*, part III, Higher Education.

TABLE 13
Loss rate of sectarian-nonsectarian schools

	Number of institutions in 1941	Number of institutions in 1945	Number lost	Rate of loss
Sectarian	699	688	11	1.5%
Nonsectarian	1057	997	60	5.6%

SOURCE: U.S. Office of Education, *Education Directory*, part III, Higher Education.

sectarian and nonsectarian classifications generally had losses in number of institutions; however, the loss for the sectarian schools was 60—or, for every sectarian school lost, 5 nonsectarian institutions were dropped. In relative terms, from the total number of institutions in existence in 1941, the percentage rate of loss is less than 2 percent for sectarian schools and approximately 6 percent for nonsectarian institutions.

The figures above may offer some suggestions about survival possibilities. In more prosperous times, it seems to be the nonsectarian groups which respond quickly. For example, between

TABLE 14
Shift in numbers of institutions by control and degree

	Less than B.A.			B.A.		
	1949	1966	Gain/loss	1949	1966	Gain/loss
State	54	62	+ 8	162	92	−70
Local	201	346	+145	9	3	− 6
Sectarian						
Protestant	104	82	− 22	287	290	+29
Catholic	35	75	+ 40	147	214	+67
Private						
Nonsectarian	106	117	+ 11	229	215	−14
NET TOTALS*	500	682	+182	834	814	−20

*Totals do not include "other" sectarian institutions besides Catholic and Protestant schools.

SOURCE: U.S. Office of Education, *Education Directory*, part III, Higher Education.

1948 and 1950, major increases were made in nonsectarian institutions, which increased by 149, while sectarian institutions increased by only 20.

CONTROL AND LEVEL OF DEGREE From 1949, when the U.S. Office of Education revised its criteria to include level of degree offered, certain trends have become apparent (see also Appendix Tables 11 and 12).

From Table 14, it can be seen that there are major shifts in the level of degree offered by institutions under the several types of control. First, there is clearly a major decline in the number of state-controlled institutions awarding the bachelor of arts as the top degree (a loss of 70 between 1949 and 1966) but, concurrently, an increase of 55 in state-controlled institutions which grant the Ph.D. All other categories of institutions offering the Ph.D. are fairly static for the same period, leading to the assumption that most of the state institutions moved from a minority position in 1949 (when one-third of all Ph.D.'s were granted by state institutions) to a much stronger position in 1966 (when almost half of all Ph.D.'s were granted by state institutions).

At the master-of-arts level, there are again increases for state-controlled institutions (up 80). Catholic institutions also show a gain of 50. Overall, it appears that during the 17 years, state institutions substantially upgraded their institutions by increasing the level of the degree awarded (135 more state institutions offered M.A. and Ph.D. degrees in 1966 than in 1949), while the private

M.A.			Ph.D.		
1949	1966	Gain/ loss	1949	1966	Gain/ loss
101	181	+ 80	52	107	+55
11	7	− 4	3	5	+ 2
64	93	+ 29	18	23	+ 5
32	82	+ 50	11	19	+ 8
98	116	+ 18	65	74	+ 9
306	479	+173	149	228	+79

sector showed no such effort (and possibly could not make such an effort because of financial limitations).

For institutions offering the B.A. as the highest degree, there is a steady drop for the state-controlled, while Protestant and Catholic institutions showed a total increase of 70.

In the category of two-year programs awarding less than the B.A., the large increase is due almost exclusively to the locally controlled institutions. The net gain of 145 locally controlled junior colleges is the biggest in all categories. Catholic institutions, although small in number, more than double during the same time period, while Protestants show a decline.

Overall patterns of gains and losses show the biggest single increase in institutions offering less than a bachelor's degree. Substantial growth is also found in the number of institutions (especially state-controlled) offering graduate degrees, particularly the master's. Only institutions offering the bachelor's as the highest degree have decreased in number.

SEXUAL COMPOSITION OF STUDENT BODY   One generalization which holds consistently is that coeducation is the dominant pattern of American higher education. The number of coeducational institutions show a net increase of 424 between 1950 and 1966. During the same period, men's institutions increased by 4 and women's by 16. Because of the relative stability in men's and women's institutions, we can infer that virtually all new institutions from 1950 to 1966 have been coeducational. This is supported in Table 5 of the Appendix.

A further breakdown of institutions by sexual composition of student body and level of degree offered is presented in Table 15.

Of institutions offering the Ph.D. degree, the coeducational campus grew substantially (up 88) while men's institutions dropped (a loss of 8) and women's institutions remained stable.

All three types show increases in the number of institutions offering the master's degree, but again the coeducational school carries most of the increase. For schools offering the bachelor's as the highest degree, men's institutions are the only ones to show an increase, and this is small (only 5). The less-than-bachelor's-degree category shows the coeducational school carrying the bulk of additions, with an increase of 191 institutions. Thus from Table 15, it appears as if the coeducational campus accounts for almost all change in terms of level of degree offered.

TABLE 15 Changes in number of institutions by student sex and degree level*	Men's institutions		
	1949	*1966*	*Net loss/gain*
Ph.D.	29	21	− 8
M.A.	43	58	+ 15
B.A.	106	111	+ 5
Less than B.A.	46	38	− 8
TOTALS	224	228	+ 4†
	Women's institutions		
	1949	*1966*	*Net loss/gain*
Ph.D.	3	4	+ 1
M.A.	20	46	+ 26
B.A.	165	154	− 11
Less than B.A.	77	79	+ 2
TOTALS	265	283	+ 18‡
	Coeducational institutions		
	1949	*1966*	*Net loss/gain*
Ph.D.	122	210	+ 88
M.A.	244	379	+135
B.A.	563	563	0
Less than B.A.	377	568	+191
TOTALS	1306	1720	+414§

* Category "Other" from the U.S. Office of Education Directories, is not included in these totals.

† Overall gain in number of men's institutions between 1949 and 1966 = 4.

‡ Overall gain in number of women's institutions between 1949 and 1966 = 18.

§ Overall gain in number of coeducational institutions between 1949 and 1966 = 414.

SOURCE: U.S. Office of Education, *Education Directory,* part III, Higher Education.

INSTITUTIONAL STATUS (VERTICAL EXTENSION) For the most part, there is a general pattern of moving up the ladder in terms of level of degree awarded. (I have called this "higher education—the higher the better.") Tables 16 and 17 illustrate this trend. Their figures begin with 1952, when the categories for degrees granted were standardized in U.S. Office of Education statistics (see also Appendix Tables 11 to 15).

During the period 1952–1966, 195 institutions moved into the less-than-B.A. category. Presumably these were infant institutions in their first years of life or "backsliders" unable to continue offering higher degrees. Both the less-than-B.A. and the B.A. categories

TABLE 16
Totals for institutional migration patterns, 1952–1966

Highest degree offered	Institutions moved to	Institutions moved from
Nondegree	195	285
B.A.	474	565
M.A.	413	306
Ph.D.	141	64

SOURCE: U.S. Office of Education, *Education Directory*, part III, Higher Education.

had more moves out than in—90 more schools moved from the less-than-B.A. category than moved into it and, likewise, 91 more moved from the B.A. category than into it. (Data on individual institutions, too complex for presentation here, reveal the upward direction.)

The reverse trend is seen in institutions offering graduate degrees. For both the M.A.-granting and Ph.D.-granting categories, more moves were made into them than out of them. And the M.A. level shows the largest gain, with 413 institutions moving into it. The total numbers gained by degree level for this period are seen in Table 17.

Thus, the largest single gain is in the number of institutions granting less than a bachelor's degree. (These are mainly newly established community colleges.) However, increases are also substantially large for institutions granting graduate degrees, particularly at the master's level.

There is currently great concern among educators about the existence in American higher education of a single status system dominated by the graduate schools which award the Ph.D. and which are, according to the theory, the *only* models for emulation. This concern does not yet seem to be validated at the junior college level. Each year, an average of only 6.5 junior colleges become four-year institutions. However, an average of 16 B.A.-granting

TABLE 17
Number of institutions by degree level, 1952–1966

Highest degree offered	1952	1966	Difference: gain/loss
Nondegree	529	685	+156
B.A.	806	828	+ 22
M.A.	379	483	+104
Ph.D.	159	235	+ 76

SOURCE: U.S. Office of Education, *Education Directory*, part III, Higher Education.

FIGURE 3
Type of vertical extension, 1953–1963, sample total: 319

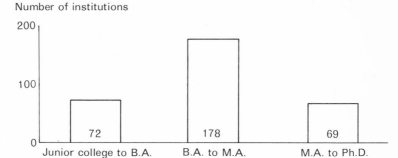

Number of institutions

SOURCE: U.S. Office of Education, *Education Directory*, part III, Higher Education.

institutions move to M.A. status each year, while 6.4 move from the M.A. to the Ph.D.[2]

It is disturbing to look at the incredibly small size of student body of institutions which undergo vertical extension—of one sample of 319 such institutions, over half had student enrollments of less than 1,000 students, while 93 (almost a third) had less than 500 students. Only 31 had student bodies of 5,000 and over, and of these, 23 were in institutions adding Ph.D. programs (see Figures 3 and 4).

FIGURE 4
Size of student body in institutions showing vertical extension, 1953-1963 (n = 319)

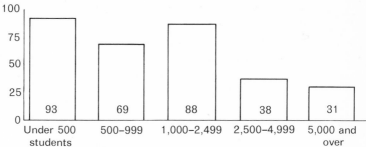

Number of institutions

SOURCE: U.S. Office of Education, *Education Directory*, part III, Higher Education.

Little is known about the reasons for these moves but there is some reason to question their educational value. Schultz and Stickler found little evidence of careful planning to ensure a valid academic program at the new degree level. Because the move to

[2] Schultz & Stickler (1965, pp. 231–241). Their data source was also the U.S. Office of Education Directory.

the M.A. level is often precipitated by a change in state requirements for public school teachers, the faculty may not take the new "educationalist" degree very seriously. It is not yet known whether other departments rush in quickly after this beachhead has been established by the department of education.

There are no studies in depth of what motivates an institution to begin awarding a higher degree, and virtually none dealing with the consequences of these and other changes on the institution. In the future other institutions going through these changes will be "flying blind" unless some useful knowledge is gathered. Our case studies attempt to deal with this issue.

Although the categories for classification were different during the war years, certain trends developed that are of interest. During this period, institutions were classified as predominantly white or predominantly Negro schools. The gains and losses in the number of these institutions between 1941 and 1944 are seen in Table 18.

For whatever reason, the war coincided with a sharp drop in the number of junior colleges (a total of 46 for both white and Negro schools) and in the number of normal schools (a total of 31). But surprisingly, the Negro institutions tended to remain open during the war and only 4 were lost compared with 67 white schools. Both white and Negro teachers colleges, as well as other colleges and universities, show slight increases. Migration patterns from category to category during the war years also are slight, as institutions "hung on" to survive.

Table 19 shows the continuous growth of professional schools, teachers colleges, and colleges and universities from 1941 to 1949. (After 1949, categories no longer were consistent.) The totals in

TABLE 18
Institutional losses and gains, 1941–1944

White institutions	1941	1944	Gain/ loss	Negro institutions
Junior colleges	466	424	−42	Junior colleges
Normal schools	49	21	−28	Normal schools
Professional schools	265	259	−6	Professional schools
Teachers colleges	176	183	+ 7	Teachers colleges
Colleges and universities	690	692	+ 2	Colleges and universities
TOTALS	1646	1579	−67	TOTALS

SOURCE: U.S. Office of Education, *Education Directory*, part III, Higher Education.

TABLE 19
Growth in number of schools by type

	1941	1949	Gain/loss
Junior colleges	489	451	−38
Normal schools	52	0	−52
Professional schools	272	277	+ 5
Teachers colleges	189	210	+21
Colleges and universities	754	790	+36

SOURCE: U.S. Office of Education, *Education Directory*, part III, Higher Education.

Table 19 combine both Negro and white institutions (see also Appendix, Table 15).

INSTITUTIONS ADDED, DROPPED, AND MERGED

The growth and decline patterns of institutions during the years 1941 to 1945 show the impact of the war on higher education. During these years, 111 institutions came into existence, while 137 closed down and 56 were reclassified (see Table 20).

The largest category of dropped institutions is junior colleges, which lost 79 schools; of these, 76 were white institutions. For all categories combined, the years when the largest numbers of colleges went out of business were 1942, 1943, and 1944, when a total of 126 stopped operating.

By 1945, the number of institutions added (11) equaled the number dropped. And by 1948, 51 were added while only 11 were dropped. This suggests that a large number of the institutions which closed during the war actually reopened very shortly after the cessation of hostilities, if not before.

Few institutions were reclassified during the war, but after its conclusion the status pattern of reclassifying toward higher degrees becomes apparent. Most reclassification involves moving from

1941	1944	Gain/ loss	Total gains/ losses
23	19	−4	−46
3	0	−3	−31
7	7	0	− 6
13	14	+1	+ 8
64	66	+2	+ 4
110	106	−4	−71

	Added	*Dropped*	*Reclassified*
Junior colleges	59	79	5
Normal schools	1	9	0
Teachers colleges	6	6	23
Professional schools	32	34	3
Colleges and universities	13	9	25
TOTALS	111	137	56

SOURCE:　U.S. Office of Education, *Education Directory,* part III, Higher Education.

the community college to the B.A. category and from the B.A. to the M.A. category. There is also a slow but steady pattern for reclassification from the M.A. to the Ph.D. category. It is clear that the new college boom which began in 1948 was led by the substantial additions of junior colleges (see also Appendix Tables 6, 8, and 9).

By far the largest growth is seen in the number of institutions offering less than a bachelor's degree and with a liberal arts and general program. Of the 898 new institutions added between 1949 and 1966, 40 percent, or 361, were in the less-than-B.A. category of liberal arts school. However, the institutions dropped during the same period follow a similar pattern.

Approximately 35 percent, or 126 of the 366 institutions dropped, were those offering less than a B.A. and with a liberal arts or general program. The losses in the B.A. category were about evenly split between the liberal arts and general institutions (53) and the professional and technical institutions (54). In institutions offering the M.A., almost all changes were in professional and technical programs, with 39 losses. The same situation applies to Ph.D.-granting institutions, although the number was small (a loss of 9).

The mortality rate is highest in the less-than-B.A. institutions (a loss of 165), with the numbers dropping steadily to the Ph.D. institutions (a loss of 12). Thus, as one "gets up in the world" educationally, the chances of surviving get progressively better.

One might speculate on why this is so. Does the offering of a higher degree mean fiscal stability? Increased reputation? Better students and faculty? Better fund raising opportunities? Theoretically, none of these should necessarily apply to an institution just because it offers a higher degree. But as we have suggested, there is a functioning status system within higher education, ensuring "success" to those institutions which offer advanced degrees. Some of the criteria for status can be seen in the data on institutions dropped, compiled by type of program offered.

The high number of institutions dropped with professional and technical programs (123) is interesting in that it occurs largely in institutions offering the B.A. and M.A. These institutions which were closed were most likely never able to get started, as professional and technical programs are typically found in more advanced degree areas.

With only minor exceptions, the chances for survival increase in *all types of programs* offered as one moves up toward the highest level of degree awarded. Only 12 institutions in the category of more than one professional school were dropped during the period, while the *same program* (liberal arts and general) *without* the professional school or schools lost 188.

There may be an analogy between those institutions which have an "up or out" policy with faculty members and the process a new institution has to go through to become a stable member of the educational fraternity. Just as the faculty member who has moved through the ranks, from instructor and assistant professor to associate professor with tenure, has assured himself of a permanent berth, the institution which offers less than a B.A. will tend to move through increasing status levels as it begins to award higher degrees. Otherwise, it will not survive. The "granting of tenure" for *institutions* clearly comes with the granting of the Ph.D.

This material, put together for the first time here, is suggestive for the interpretation of educational changes in the last two decades.

TABLE 21
Institutions added and dropped by year

Year	Added	Dropped
1941–42	47	11
1942–43	27	39
1943–44	24	62
1944–45	13	25
1945–46	11	11
1946–47	23	10
1947–48	15	12
1948–49	51	11

SOURCE: U.S. Office of Education, *Education Directory,* part III, Higher Education.

We were able to gather data both on institutions entering a category and those leaving it. If they entered, we know whence they came; if they left, we know where they went. Thus, if there are institutional migration patterns, we should be able to see them (see Appendix Tables 11 and 12).

With regard to level of degree, it is likely that there is operating in America a system of vertical mobility, that institutional change exists in a hierarchy based on the highest level of degree offered. As one would expect, the greatest amount of change occurs when programs change without being accompanied by corresponding changes in the highest level of degree offered. But when one looks at changes in degrees, it is clear that institutions move from less than B.A. to B.A., from there to M.A., and from there to Ph.D. This we can call "upward mobility," and it is clearly the conven-

TABLE 22
Number and degree levels of institutions added from 1949–1966 (total: 898)

	Terminal occupational	Liberal arts and general	Teacher preparatory	Professional and technical
Less than B.A.	88	361	38	23
B.A.		152	8	100
M.A.		23	2	41
Ph.D.		3		11
Other	2	5	1	17
TOTALS	90	544	49	192

SOURCE: U.S. Office of Education, *Education Directory,* part, III, Higher Education.

TABLE 23
Number and degree levels of institutions dropped from 1949–1966 (total: 366)

	Terminal occupational	Liberal arts and general	Teacher preparatory	Professional and technical
Less than B.A.	19	126	9	11
B.A.		53	7	54
M.A.		4	3	39
Ph.D.		2		9
Other		3	5	10
TOTALS	19	188	24	123

SOURCE: U.S. Office of Education, *Education Directory,* part III, Higher Education.

tional and most widely followed path. Relatively few institutions reverse this trend and offer a "lower" degree than previously offered and the consequences are often painful.

Without pushing the analogy, there would seem to exist a parallel between the upwardly mobile individual, as studied extensively by sociologists, and the upwardly mobile institution; increased status, wealth, power, and influence are a part of the process. Downward mobility in individuals results in high rates of schizophrenia, suicide, and alcoholism which are due to a decline in economic and social status. One wonders whether there are institutional equivalents for these personal processes.

Our data tend to support those who argue that a monolithic status system exists in American higher education and pervades virtually all colleges and universities; that there is one central

Liberal arts and general, more than one professional school	*Total*
	510
12	272
6	72
	14
5	30
23	898

Liberal arts and general, more than one professional school	*Total*
0	165
4	118
3	49
1	12
4	22
12	366

pattern, based on specialization of interest and competence in a discipline; that students and faculty are rewarded as they attain higher levels of specialization, etc. This organization, called the "versity" by one scholar, comes in three sizes — miniversity, university, and multiversity. But they are all basically the same in terms of their "upward" direction of institutional migration. This calls into question the great faith we have in the pluralistic nature of American higher education.

Appendix to *Chapter* 2

TABLE 1 *Enrollments and numbers of institutions, public and private, 1947–1968*

Year	Public Number of institutions	Public Total number of students	Public Students per institution	Private Number of institutions	Private Total number of students	Private Students per institution
1947	548	1,152,377	2,102	1,141	1,185,849	1,039
1948	568	1,190,441	2,095	1,155	1,217,808	1,054
1949	594	1,218,580	2,051	1,209	1,238,261	1,024
1950	640	1,154,456	1,803	1,212	1,142,136	942
1951	638	1,051,990	1,648	1,221	1,064,450	871
1952	643	1,113,700	1,732	1,246	1,034,584	830
1953	646	1,203,558	1,863	1,205	1,047,143	868
1954	653	1,372,937	2,102	1,204	1,095,659	910
1955	652	1,498,510	2,298	1,203	1,180,113	980
1956	661	1,681,671	2,544	1,225	1,265,314	1,032
1957	669	1,780,280	2,661	1,268	1,288,137	1,015
1958	677	1,912,232	2,824	1,280	1,346,324	1,051
1959	698	2,002,868	2,869	1,313	1,399,429	1,065
1960	703	2,135,690	3,037	1,325	1,474,317	1,112
1961	721	2,351,719	3,261	1,319	1,539,511	1,167
1962	743	2,596,904	3,495	1,357	1,609,768	1,168
1963	762	2,872,823	3,770	1,377	1,655,693	1,202
1964	784	3,205,783	4,089	1,384	1,782,084	1,287
1965	790	3,654,578	4,626	1,417	1,915,693	1,351
1966	806	3,959,000	4,911	1,446	1,988,000	1,374
1967	820	4,366,000	5,324	1,474	2,134,000	1,447
1968	1,015	5,469,472	5,388	1,476	2,102,164	1,424

SOURCE: U.S. Office of Education, *Education Directory,* part III, Higher Education, and Chandler, 1969.

Year	Public	Private	Total all U.S. institutions
1941	588	1168	1756
1942	582	1164	1746
1943	561	1141	1702
1944	546	1139	1685
1945	555	1131	1686
1946	563	1137	1700
1947	548	1141	1688
1948	568	1155	1728
1949	594	1209	1808
1950	640	1212	1857
1951	638	1221	1859
1952	643	1246	1889
1953	646	1205	1851
1954	653	1204	1857
1955	652	1203	1855
1956	661	1225	1886
1957	669	1268	1937
1958	671	1280	1957
1959	698	1313	2011
1960	703	1325	2028
1961	721	1319	2040
1962	743	1359	2100
1963	762	1377	2139
1964	784	1384	2168
1965	790	1417	2207
1966	806	1446	2252
1967	1000	1489	2489
1968	1037	1500	2537
1969	1079	1472	2551

SOURCE: U.S. Office of Education, *Education Directory,* part III, Higher Education.

TABLE 3
Type of control,
local, state,
1941–1969

Year	Local	State	Total all U.S. institutions
1941	224	364	1756
1942	217	365	1746
1943	201	360	1702
1944	192	354	1685
1945	196	359	1686
1946	199	364	1700
1947	192	356	1688
1948	206	362	1728
1949	224	370	1808
1950	263	377	1857
1951	272	366	1859
1952	274	369	1889
1953	279	367	1851
1954	283	370	1857
1955	281	371	1855
1956	282	379	1886
1957	287	382	1937
1958	291	386	1957
1959	311	387	2011
1960	314	389	2028
1961	328	393	2040
1962	343	398	2100
1963	357	405	2139
1964	359	425	2168
1965	354	436	2207
1966	361	445	2252
1967	455	545	2489
1969	364	707	2551

SOURCE: U.S. Office of Education, *Education Directory,* part III, Higher Education.

TABLE 4 *Private* *institutions by* *sectarian* *control,* *1941–1969*		

Year	*Sectarian*	*Total* *all U.S.* *institutions*
1941	679	1756
1942	692	1746
1943	688	1702
1944	688	1685
1945	687	1686
1946	692	1700
1947	690	1688
1948	694	1728
1949	708	1808
1950	710	1857
1951	717	1859
1952	733	1889
1953	719	1851
1954	721	1857
1955	723	1855
1956	744	1886
1957	763	1937
1958	771	1957
1959	793	2011
1960	805	2028
1961	807	2040
1962	842	2100
1963	870	2139
1964	877	2168
1965	893	2207
1966	910	2252
1967	877	2252
1969	804	2551

SOURCE: U.S. Office of Education, *Education Directory,* part III, Higher Education.

	Year	Male institutions	Female institutions	Coeducational institutions	Total all U.S. institutions
TABLE 5 *Sex of student bodies in higher education, 1950–1969*	1950	227	266	1364	1857
	1951	222	258	1379	1859
	1952	225	257	1407	1889
	1953	215	252	1384	1851
	1954	214	248	1395	1857
	1955	216	244	1395	1855
	1956	223	249	1414	1886
	1957	225	252	1460	1937
	1958	222	248	1487	1957
	1959	228	252	1531	2011
	1960	236	259	1533	2028
	1961	232	259	1549	2040
	1962	241	276	1583	2100
	1963	240	280	1619	2139
	1964	238	276	1654	2168
	1965	236	282	1680	2207
	1966	232	283	1737	2252
	1967	214	248	2027	2489
	1969	174	229	2148	2551

SOURCE: U.S. Office of Education, *Education Directory,* part III, Higher Education.

	Terminal-occupational	Liberal arts and general	Teacher preparatory
Less than B.A.	19	126	9
B.A.		53	7
M.A.		4	3
Ph.D.		2	
Other		3	5
TOTALS	19	188	24

SOURCE: U.S. Office of Education, *Education Directory,* part III, Higher Education.

Professional and technical	Liberal arts and general, more than one professional school	Total
11		165
54	4	118
39		46
9	1	12
10	4	22
123	9	363

TABLE 7 *Institutions merged—number of institutions leaving category due to merger, 1941–1967*

Year	Junior colleges	Normal schools	Teachers colleges	Professional schools	Colleges and universities	Total
1941–42	0	1	0	3	0	4
1942–43	3	0	0	2	1	6
1943–44	1	1	0	4	0	6
1944–45	1	0	0	2	0	3
1945–46	0	0	0	2*	1*	3
1946–47	0	0	1	1	1	3
1947–48	1	0	1	3	2	7
1948–49	1	0	0	0	2	3

	Non-degree	B.A.	M.A.	Ph.D.	Other	Total
1949–50	4†	1	0	0	0	5
1950–51	3	4	4	0	0	11
1951–52	2	1	3	2	0	8
1952–53	1	3	1	0	0	5
1953–54	0	3	0	2	0	5
1954–55	4	4	3	1	0	12
1955–56	1	0	0	0	0	1
1956–57	1	1	1	0	0	3
1957–58	0	1	0	0	0	1
1958–59	1	3	0	0	0	4
1959–60	1	1	1	0	0	3
1960–61	1	1	2	0	1	5
1961–62	0	0	0	0	0	0
1962–63	2	2	4	0	0	8
1963–64	2	1	1	2	0	4
1964–65	2	3	0	0	2	7
1965–66	5	2	0	0	0	7
1966–67	2	2	0	1	0	5
TOTALS	32	33	20	8	3	96

* One sold, one given.
† Two administered through another school.
SOURCE: U.S. Office of Education, *Education Directory,* part III, Higher Education.

TABLE 8 *Number of institutions closed, by type and degree level, 1941–1967*

Year	Junior colleges	Normal schools	Teachers colleges	Professional schools	Colleges and universities	Total
1941–42	0	0	0	0	0	0
1942–43	3[a]	0	0	0	1	4
1943–44	26[a]	1[a]	0	5[a]	0	32
1944–45	11[a]	1	3[a]	1	0	16
1945–46	3	0	0	0	1	4
1946–47	3[a]	0	1	1	1	6
1947–48	3	0	0	0	1	4
1948–49	6	0	0	1	0	7
TOTALS	55	2	4	8	4	73

	Non-degree	B.A.	M.A.	Ph.D.	Other	Total
1949–50	1	3[b]	0	0	0	4
1950–51	6	0	0	0	0	6
1951–52	13[c]	5[c]	0	0	1	19
1952–53	6	1	0	1[d]	0	8
1953–54	6[e]	5[e]	0	0	1	12
1954–55	2	2	0	0	0	4
1955–56	4	3	0	0	0	7
1956–57	0	1	0	0	0	1
1957–58	5	1	0	0	0	6
1958–59	1	0	0	0	0	1
1959–60	2	0	0	0	0	2
1960–61	0	0	0	1	0	1
1961–62	5	3	0	0	1	9
1962–63	0	1	0	0	0	1
1963–64	0	0	0	0	0	0
1964–65	5[f]	1	0	0	0	6
1965–66	+10[g]	2[g]	1	0	1[g]	14
1966–67	6[h]	4[h]	2[h]	0	1[h]	13
TOTALS	72	32	3	2	5	114

[a] Closed for duration of war.

[b] Discontinued.

[c] One closed, war emergency.

[d] Dropped, no students.

[e] One closed for reorganization, 1953–54.

[f] Two discontinued.

[g] Dropped (one nondegree), one discontinued.

[h] Dropped (one nondegree, two B.A., two M.A.).

SOURCE: U.S. Office of Education, *Education Directory,* part III, Higher Education.

TABLE 9

		Institutions closed, discontinued, or dropped, 1949–1966	
Institutions merged, 1949–1966			
2 year, less than B.A.	32	*2 year, less than B.A.*	72
B.A.	33	*B.A.*	32
M.A.	20	*M.A.*	3
Ph.D.	8	*Ph.D.*	2
Other	3	*Other*	5
TOTAL	96	TOTAL	114

SOURCE: U.S. Office of Education, *Education Directory*, part III, Higher Education.

Appendix to chapter 2 **61**

	Net increases		Net decreases	
Year	*Local*	*State*	*Local*	*State*
1941–42		1	7	
1942–43			16	5
1943–44			9	6
1944–45	4	5		
1945–46	3	5		
1946–47			7	8
1947–48	14	6		
1948–49	18	8		
1949–50	39	7		
1950–51	9			11
1951–52	2	3		
1952–53	5			2
1953–54	4	3		
1954–55		1	2	
1955–56	1	8		
1956–57	5	3		
1957–58	4	4		
1958–59	20	1		
1959–60	3	2		
1960–61	14	4		
1961–62	17	5		
1962–63	12	7		
1963–64	2	20		
1964–65		11	5	
1965–66	7	9		
TOTALS	183	113	46	32

TABLE 10
Growth patterns of institutions by local versus state control, 1941–1966

SOURCE: U.S. Office of Education, *Education Directory,* part III, Higher Education.

		I. 2–4 year, nondegree			II. Bachelor/1st professional degree		
Year	Total number of institutions	Total #I	Moved to I	Moved from I	Total #II	Moved to II	Move from
1949–50	1808	500	*	*	834	*	*
1950–51	1857	541	*	*	828	*	*
1951–52	1859	527	*	*	800	*	*
1952–53	1889	529	5	16	806	32	40
1953–54	1851	517	7	11	768	35	55
1954–55	1857	518	9	10	747	24	53
1955–56	1855	510	3	7	732	42	57
1956–57	1886	525	12	11	714	20	43
1957–58	1937	548	13	18	723	26	39
1958–59	1957	557	13	15	720	31	34
1959–60	2011	585	14	23	718	29	39
1960–61	2028	593	9	14	739	37	26
1961–62	2040	593	14	27	741	36	33
1962–63	2100	628	14	18	766	35	29
1963–64	2139	644	32	41	792	45	33
1964–65	2168	656	14	25	801	26	18
1965–66	2207	664	20	28	823	34	29
1966–67	2252	685	16	21	828	22	37

TABLE 11
Number of institutions moving from or to different degree levels, 1949–1967

* Data not available for this year.

SOURCE: U.S. Office of Education, *Education Directory,* part III, Higher Education.

III. Masters/2nd professional degree			IV. Ph.D./ equivalent degree			V. Other		
Total #III	Moved to III	Moved from III	Total #IV	Moved to IV	Moved from IV	Total #V	Moved to V	Moved from V
307	*	*	154	*	*	13	*	*
324	*	*	147	*	*	17	*	*
360	*	*	155	*	*	17	*	*
379	24	9	159	7	2	16	2	3
390	38	23	163	10	3	13	2	0
406	37	17	171	10	5	15	3	1
415	27	18	180	13	4	18	1	1
426	21	18	191	9	1	30	7	1
442	19	7	193	4	1	31	6	3
449	22	19	197	10	5	34	1	3
462	30	22	205	12	4	41	4	1
455	16	19	210	8	4	31	0	7
455	24	23	219	16	6	32	2	3
458	28	25	223	8	2	25	1	12
455	32	32	213	12	14	25	2	3
464	22	19	224	3	2	23	0	1
472	25	21	227	7	6	21	0	2
483	48	34	235	12	5	21	0	1

TABLE 12
Number of institutions by migration into categories by degree and program, 1952–1966

		1^a	2^b	3^c	4^d	5^e	Total
$I\text{-}I^f$		3	166	0	15	0	184
$I\text{-}II^g$		0	77	4	18	5	104
$I\text{-}III^h$		1	0	0	0	0	1
$I\text{-}IV^i$		0	0	0	1	0	1
$I\text{-}V^j$		0	3	0	5	2	10
	TOTAL	4	246	4	39	7	300
II–I		1	9	0	1	0	11
II–II		0	99	13	27	49	188
II–III		0	134	26	35	40	235
II–IV		0	3	0	10	4	17
II–V		0	2	0	10	2	14
	TOTAL	1	247	39	83	95	465
III–I		0	1	0	1	0	2
III–II		0	26	1	16	12	55
III–III		0	81	3	15	61	160
III–IV		0	10	1	20	56	87
III–V		0	0	0	3	0	3
	TOTAL	0	118	5	55	129	307
IV–I		0	0	0	0	0	0
IV–II		0	1	0	2	1	4
IV–III		0	3	0	11	6	20
IV–IV		0	3	0	12	25	40
IV–V		0	0	0	0	0	0
	TOTAL	0	7	0	25	32	64
V–I		0	3	0	0	1	4
V–II		0	4	0	15	9	28
V–III		0	0	0	4	0	4
V–IV		0	0	0	0	0	0
V–V		0	2	0	3	1	6
	TOTAL	0	9	0	22	11	42
	GRAND TOTAL	5	627	48	151	274	1,178

[a] Terminal-occupational.

[b] Liberal arts and general, liberal arts and general and terminal-occupational, liberal arts and general and teacher preparatory, and liberal arts and general teacher preparatory and terminal-occupational.

[c] Teacher preparatory.

[d] Professional or technical, professional and teacher preparatory, and professional and terminal-occupational.

[e] Liberal arts and general with one or two professional schools and liberal arts and general with three or more professional schools.

TABLE 13   *Institutions added, 1949–1966, by function and degree level*

	Terminal-occupational	Liberal arts and general	Teacher preparatory	Professional and technical	Liberal arts and general, more than one professional school	Total
Less than B.A.	88	361	38	23		510
B.A.		152	8	100	12	272
M.A.		23	2	41	6	72
Ph.D.		3		11		14
Other	2	5	1	17	5	30
TOTALS	90	544	49	192	23	898

SOURCE: U.S. Office of Education, *Education Directory,* part III, Higher Education.

TABLE 14
Institutional migration—1952–1966—summaries

Institutional movement from *and* to:

I	*Less than B.A.*	300
II	*B.A.*	465
III	*M.A.*	307
IV	*Ph.D.*	64
V	*Other*	42
	TOTAL	1,178

Institutional movement into:

1. *Terminal-occupational*	5
2. *Liberal arts and general*	627
3. *Teacher preparatory*	48
4. *Professional and technical*	151
5. *Liberal arts and general, more than one professional school*	274
TOTAL	1,178

SOURCE: U.S. Office of Education, *Education Directory,* part III, Higher Education.

(Table 12 footnotes continued)
[f] Two–four year, nondegree.
[g] Bachelor's/first professional degree.
[h] Master's/second professional degree.
[i] Ph.D. and equivalent degrees.
[j] Other.

SOURCE: U.S. Office of Education, *Education Directory,* part III, Higher Education.

TABLE 15 *Number of institutions by function and degree level, 1941–1967*

Year	Junior college	Normal schools	Teachers colleges	Professional schools	Colleges and universities	Total
1941–42	489	52	189	272	754	1756
1942–43	474	36	204	277	755	1746
1943–44	455	20	207	268	752	1702
1944–45	453	21	197	266	758	1685
1945–46	438	*	218	260	770	1686
1946–47	436	*	216	266	783	1700
1947–48	429	*	212	265	782	1688
1948–49	451	*	210	277	790	1728
	Less than B.A.	B.A.	M.A.	Ph.D.	Other	Total
1949–50	500	834	307	154	13	1808
1950–51	541	828	324	147	17	1857
1951–52	527	800	360	155	17	1859
1952–53	529	806	379	159	16	1889
1953–54	517	768	390	163	13	1851
1954–55	518	747	406	171	15	1857
1955–56	510	732	415	180	18	1855
1956–57	525	714	426	191	30	1886
1957–58	548	723	442	193	31	1937
1958–59	557	720	449	197	34	1957
1959–60	585	718	462	205	41	2011
1960–61	593	739	455	210	31	2028
1961–62	593	741	455	219	32	2040
1962–63	628	766	458	223	25	2100
1963–64	644	792	455	213	25	2139
1964–65	656	801	464	224	23	2168
1965–66	664	823	472	227	21	2207
1966–67	685	828	483	235	21	2252

*Normal school category discontinued. The change in categories was necessitated by the shift in reporting in the U.S. Office of Education's *Education Directory* in 1949.

SOURCE: U.S. Office of Education, *Education Directory,* part III, Higher Education.

3. Changes in Institutional Characteristics — Questionnaire Data

We can now turn to some of the change data revealed in our questionnaire study of 1,230 institutions of higher education. This material will be presented in terms of the following dimensions: (1) changes in type of control (public, sectarian, nonsectarian); (2) institutional size; (3) geographic area; (4) comprehensiveness; and (5) highest degree awarded. Then we will look at the data from institutions that have actually made some of the more important "from-to" changes to see how the change has affected them on a number of dimensions. The changes we will examine are (a) from private to public control; (b) from sectarian to nonsectarian control; (c) from teacher preparatory to expanded program; (d) from small to large size; (e) from two-year to four-year status; (f) from B.A. or M.A. to Ph.D.; (g) from four-year to state college; and (h) from single sex to coeducational. These brief sections are followed by a general summary which relates what types of change have taken place in what types of institutions.

All these data are contained on the master Charts 1 and 2 for the study which appear on pages 26–33. The reader is invited to make use of the charts while reading this section of the report.

1. BY TYPE OF CONTROL The sampling included an analysis of institutions by control, consisting of 535 public; 392 sectarian; and 240 private, nonsectarian colleges and universities. In general, one is impressed with the lack of significant differences in change patterns between public and private institutions in the sample. There are some differences, but they are not as impressive as their commonality, which suggests that private institutions may be becoming more like public ones than our heralded theme of diversity of institutional types would suggest.

Students The diversity of students seems to have increased across all three types of institutions, with very few differences. One striking difference is that the sectarian institutions have become more open to students of varying religious backgrounds. (This finding has special implications for the so-called unique approach of the sectarian institution which stresses a given denominational commitment.) It is probably true that the other categories of institutions have always had greater religious diversity of student background, but 48 percent of the sectarian institutions indicate an increased diversity of student religious background, which seems a very high figure indeed. Compared with 22 percent for public institutions and 37 for private nonsectarian, the national norm for increased diversity of religious background of students is 34 percent. Again, in all three kinds of schools increased diversity of students by socioeconomic background is significantly less than increased diversity by ethnic composition. The student body has become more diverse racially than is true for social class.

The increase in diversity of students by age is largely a phenomenon of public institutions (29 percent report increased diversity by age), while only 6 percent of the nonsectarian and 17 percent of the sectarian institutions report increased student heterogeneity by age. Fewer public institutions reported increased numbers of out-of-state students than did the private and sectarian schools. This is due primarily to the large number of community colleges which are considered public in control and have a local mission rather than a state or national draw. The public institutions, because of the increased heterogeneity of student age, also have a higher percentage of married students than either the sectarian or nonsectarian institutions. Interestingly enough, on-campus student protest tended to run almost the same for all three institutional types—30 percent of the public institutions reported an increase in protest, 23 percent of the sectarian institutions, and 33 percent of the nonsectarian, compared with a 27 percent increase nationwide.

More of the sectarian and nonsectarian categories reported some increase in the quality of student participation in high school than did the public sector, again perhaps due to the number of community colleges that are often required to accept any high school graduate. In most of the other categories of student types, there are remarkably few differences by institutional control. Interesting is the difference in school spirit across the three categories—16 percent of the public institutions reported a net increase in school spirit among students, while 6 percent of the sectarian institutions reported an increase; but 3 percent of the nonsectarian institutions reported a decrease. One can only speculate about the meaning of this, but it is quite clear that the nonsectarian institution, characteristically devoid of the privatism and vocational emphasis of the public institution and the religious or humane commitment of many of the sectarian institutions, may need some kind of an equivalent to increase the morale of its students. It is also clear that underground publications and films are present in more public and nonsectarian institutions, but to a lesser degree in the sectarian sector. However, even there, 11 percent of the institutions report an increase in underground publications and films, compared with 18 percent for public and 20 percent for nonsectarian. It would appear, then, that even a commitment to a denominational position will not keep an institution free from an increase in the underground publication and film movement.

Administration and Finance

Although the overall picture again is of similarity, there are some major discrepancies between public institutions and the two private categories. In percentage of total budget based on federal support, all three kinds of institutions clearly are relying more and more heavily on federal funding. In fact, 60 percent of the public institutions reported an increase in federal proportion of the budget; 50 percent of the sectarian institutions; and 58 percent of the private, nonsectarian. Public institutions, however, having no clearly defined constituency, suffer with regard to alumni support. Thirty-one percent of the sectarian institutions and 37 percent of the nonsectarian reported an increase in percent of budget based on alumni support, while only 7 percent of the public institutions reported such an increase. On the other hand, this means that public institutions are free from the sort of control and influence that can accompany heavy alumni support: 13 percent of the sectarian institutions reported an increased influence of alumni on institutional policy making and 11 percent of the nonsectarian reported an increase, but only 2 percent of the public institutions reported such an increase. Public institutions, which are apparently becoming more fiscally and institutionally dependent on state departments of education, have far more of a problem in this area than do the other two categories. For instance, 23 percent of the public institutions reported increased influence of the state department of education on policy making within the institution, while only 14 percent of the sectarian and 14 percent of the nonsectarian institutions reported an increase. The reader is left to decide whether he prefers his influence to come from alumni or from state departments of education.

The authority of central campus administration seems to be declining at approximately equal rates in the three kinds of institutions. And they stand equally strong in the number of institutions reporting increased efforts to attract students from disadvantaged homes, in administrative attempts to increase communication, and in number of working relations with other colleges and universities. However, the public sector has almost twice the number of institutions that report increased cooperative programs with local industries. This is due undoubtedly to the number of community colleges in the public sector, which necessitate strong cooperative programs with industry in order to support their vocational curricula. All three categories are to some extent similar in their declining ability to control student behavior—29 percent of the public institutions reported a decrease in institutional control, while 45 percent of the sectarian and 41 percent of the nonsectarian reported such a decrease. Again, a large number of commuter campuses within the public sector may help to explain why the decline is less there than in the other two, which are often almost completely residential.

It is interesting to note that more public institutions seem to be increasing the number of institutionwide and departmental requirements for the undergraduate degree than are the sectarian or nonsectarian institutions. Whether this is a search for status or simply an increased sophistication with regard to vocational programs and their prerequisites for graduation is not ascertainable from our data.

It also may be that a reported decline in presidential longevity is most characteristic of the nonsectarian institutions. Under length of service of major administrative officers, 18 percent of the public institutions reported an increase, as did 20 percent of the sectarian, while only 9 percent of the nonsectarian institutions reported an increase. The national figure is 17 percent reporting an increase in length of service of administrative officers. It is conceivable that it is easier to dismiss a president from a nonsectarian institution as there is often no clearly defined constituency that would take a position in his favor. In both public and sectarian institutions the board often is responsible to some larger constituency which, if it favors the current president, could make life very difficult for the board. This, however, is sheer speculation, and the real answer will have to await another analysis.

As one looks at the data on change by type of control, one is struck with the similarities in most situations. It appears, however, that the public sector of our sample (heavily laden with community colleges) contributes a vocational, pragmatic, and utilitarian complexion which is not matched in sectarian or nonsectarian institutions. All three types of institutions seem far more open than formerly to direct student participation in the management of the institution and in their own affairs. They also seem to have made significant moves toward greater faculty autonomy and toward increased emphasis on research. In fact with all the talk about the heralded pluralism of American higher education and the necessity of continuing a diversity of institutional types, one is struck by the similar direction of trends across public, sectarian, and nonsectarian lines. One can make a strong case from these data that there is a blurring of individual institutional uniqueness and an increased centralization, so that all institutions tend to respond to social stimuli from the culture in approximately equal amounts. Whether this is good or not is for the reader to decide, but it is very clear from our data that the diversity by type of control is decreasing in American higher education. This also would lead one to question the doctrine of "institutional uniqueness," which is one of the major factors that eliminate change in American education. The idea that each institution has a unique background and a unique history and therefore responds to incentives and pressures from the society in a unique way is certainly not borne out by these data. All institutions are becoming far more alike by institutional control than they are different. Thus higher education in America is becoming more homogenized than was true in the past.

2. BY INSTITUTIONAL SIZE—A CRUCIAL FACTOR

One of the most interesting analyses in the study indicated that enrollment is probably a far more pervasive factor in sorting out differences in institutions than is "control" or even "highest degree awarded." We divided our institutions into five categories: small (under 1,000 students), medium (1,000–5,000), large (5,000–15,000), giant (15,000–25,000), and super (25,000 and over). There are 520 small institutions in the sample, 475 medium, 128 large, 31 giant, and 9 super. This again is quite close to the total national distribution of institutions by size. One thing that interested us was the question of whether a "critical mass" existed beyond which increased student enrollments drastically affected institutional activities and policies. This study did not locate such a critical mass. One sees instead a continuous influence of increased student bodies on a number of institutional activities and policies rather than a sharp, exponential increase at some stage on the graph.

Students   It was quite clear from the analysis of students that it is the large institutions where diversity has increased the most. Although most institutions reported increased heterogeneity of student body, the number reporting increases got larger as the student enrollment increased. It was also true of all five size categories that ethnicity increased in more institutions than did socioeconomic background. Institutions of all sizes are thus more open to members of various races than they are to members of various classes (89 percent of the super institutions reported an increase in diversity of student ethnic composition, while only 44 percent of the supers reported an increase in heterogeneity of the student socioeconomic background. Nationally, 53 percent of the institutions reported increased diversity by student ethnic background, while only 40 percent reported an increase by socioeconomic background). With only one exception, as the institutions get larger, the diversity by political affiliation, age, percentage of out-of-state students, percentage of foreign students, and percentage of married students increases.

One of the most striking findings of the study was the percentage of institutions reporting an increase in on-campus student protest. It was quite clear from these data that size has more impact than the highest degree awarded. For example, 12 percent of small institutions reported an increase in student protest, 32 percent of medium, 59 percent of large, 75 percent of giant, and 89 percent of super. It must be said that the giant and super categories are small in terms of the number of institutions represented, but the enrollments on each campus are so enormous that they have greater impact for that reason. It also must be pointed out that all five size categories reported a steady and consistent increase in the percent of student protest as one went up the size continuum. Again, there seemed no critical mass in this area, but rather a steady increase of approximately 15 to 20 percentage points by each size category.

It is also interesting to look at the item of quality of student preparation in high school. Fifty-nine percent of the small institutions reported an increase in the quality of student preparation, the items going steadily upward from there to the super institutions, which reported in eighty-nine percent of the cases an increase in the quality of student preparation. This suggests that the larger institutions are getting the best-prepared students. Reinforcing this is the fact that the percentage of freshmen completing degree requirements is much higher for the super institutions than for any of the others, and also the fact that academic dismissals are down strikingly in the super institutions compared with the other four categories. While the other four reported either very minor increases or some losses in the percentage of dismissals for academic reasons, the super institutions are unique in that 33 percent of them reported a decrease in dismissals for academic reasons. Interestingly enough, with all the student protest and activity, all five categories of size reported a decrease in the number of dismissals for non-academic reasons. This is perhaps due to the finding reported earlier that most institutions have diminished in ability to control student behavior. On the variables describing student control in various activities of the institution, it is quite clear that size was not a major factor in all the categories. Very high percentages in all size levels reported increased student control in academic and social matters on the campus. However, even there the super institutions stood out as having made the major gains in student control (it is also to be observed that student control in the *establishment* of regulations governing students is far more pervasive than student control in the *enforcement* of regulations governing students). Another consistent finding which makes size important is the percentage of graduating class planning on continuing education: 70 percent of the small institutions reported an increase of students planning on continuing education, 76 percent of the medium institutions, 85 percent of the large, 90 percent of the giant, and 100 percent of the super. This suggests once again that not only are large institutions getting a better quality of students, who are better prepared in high school, but large institutions retain their students for a longer period and their students' aspirations include advanced education.

However, size has its negative aspects. One which is quite significant involves school spirit, for which I think "institutional loyalty" is an acceptable synonym. Here 14 percent of the small institutions reported an increase in school spirit; as the size of the student body increased, school spirit dropped steadily. Declines were reported as 7 percent of the medium, 5 percent of the large, 6 percent of the giant, and 11 percent of the super. There is ample evidence in the student protest section of this report showing why size produces this decline in institutional loyalty. It is also clear that the larger institutions with less control over what students are doing are centers for underground publications and films. Only 7 percent of the small institutions reported an increase in student underground publications and films, while 18 percent of the medium, 36 percent of the large, 48 percent of the giant, and 56 percent of the super reported increases. This suggests again that size makes it possible for small subgroups within the student body to acquire and maintain autonomy and influence on the campus without the administration either knowing or being able to do much about it. We also found that as size increased, the percentage of students participating in community volunteer programs increased. This is an item highly correlated with the existence of student protests on campus, perhaps due to such students bringing back to campus the perceptions of urban life which they learned about in their volunteer work. Sixty-one percent of the small institutions reported an increase in student participation in community volunteer programs, eighty-nine percent of the super institutions reported such an increase, and the percentages are spread out uniformly in the middle ranges.

The percentage of transfer students entering the institutions is another item which correlates with student protest. Here again 46 percent of the small institutions reported an increase, while 78 percent of the supers did, with percentages gradually rising according to size of the institution. It also seems likely that in the larger institutions graduate programs are being carried on at the expense of undergraduates who unwillingly and unwittingly may be subsidizing highly expensive graduate education. Among institutions which have graduate programs, the percentage of graduates to undergraduates is rising with the size of the institution. A certain percentage of the small institutions reported an increased ratio of graduates to undergraduates; 22 percent of the medium-sized reported such an increase, 60 percent of the large, 81 percent of the giant, and 89 percent of the super. It is also clear that as the size of the institution grows, so does the percentage of graduate students who actually complete degree requirements. There is a 7 percent increase in small institutions and a 78 percent increase in super institutions with regard to the percentage of graduate students who actually complete their degree requirements. In the categories of large, giant, and super, one gets the impression of an institution geared particularly toward graduate training, which has perhaps sacrificed some aspects of the undergraduate life to an increased emphasis on the graduate student. In many states, funding from the state to the institution is supplied on a formula which gives the institution considerably more money per graduate enrollment than per undergraduate. This policy may be a contributing factor to the rampant growth of graduate programs. Although these data would indicate that there is no particular critical mass beyond which things change more drastically, the greatest degree of change occurs between the medium-sized institutions and large ones. But change increases at approximately the same rate across the other categories as well. Thus the critical mass theory is refuted by the data. It would seem that as the size of enrollment increases, so do the diversity of students and virtually every aspect of student involvement in the institution, from setting policy to getting the degree.

Faculty In this area again we proposed the critical mass hypothesis and found that we had to reject it. Changes seemed to be continuous across institutional size, beginning at some specific point. Some of the data here are truly interesting with regard to the explanation of certain factors. It would appear that the amount of faculty turnover is a definite function of institutional size. This is also true of the average age for award of tenure, commitment toward teaching, and commitment toward the institution. As the size of the institution grows, so does the amount of faculty turnover, and rather startlingly (again, one of the largest jumps is between the medium and large institutions). Four percent of the small institutions reported an increase in faculty turnover, while forty-four percent of the super did so. This is perhaps due partially to the large institution's ability to attract the more highly mobile Ph.D. professor who is involved in research and consultation, and travels around the country a good deal. It is highly likely that this access to other institutions makes him more aware of desirable positions elsewhere.

One of the most spectacular findings by size concerns the average age at which tenure is awarded. Whereas 12 percent of the small institutions reported that the faculty were younger when they received tenure, 89 percent of the super institutions reported tenure coming at an earlier and earlier age. This is quite clearly a size function and relates again to the reward system which the large institutions must have in order to attract and hold able young faculty. Commitment toward teaching also seems to be inversely related to size; the small institutions reported an increased commitment in 29 percent of the institutions, while 19 percent of the giant institutions reported a decreased commitment. For some reason, the super institutions broke the trend by reporting an *increase* in a commitment toward teaching in 33 percent of the institutions. Whether this is due to the graduate teaching that goes on there, which faculty members enjoy, or to some other factor is not clear from the data. Commitment toward research also increases with the size of the institution, except that the super category again represents a smaller increase than the large and giant categories. Commitment toward the institution increased in 15 percent of the small institutions, while 13 percent of the medium institutions reported an actual decrease, as did 20 percent of the large, 52 percent of the giant, and 44 percent of the super. Hours spent teaching also declined with the size of the institution, suggesting that the larger institutions were able to decrease the teaching loads by increasing the amount of faculty responsibility for research. One finds a parallel between the decline in hours spent in teaching and the increase in hours spent in research.

It is also interesting to note that although the four smaller categories reported a decrease in external pressure limiting the freedom of the faculty, 11 percent of the super institutions reported a significant increase. This may be a significant dimension of the future problems which the super institutions will face. It is also interesting to note that as the size of the institution grows, so does the percentage reporting greater faculty support of students who oppose administrative practices. Only 19 percent of the small institutions reported an increase in faculty support of such students, while in the giant category 61 percent did. (It then drops mysteriously to 44 percent in the super institutions.) One finds to supplement this a generally increasing pattern of faculty who advocate positions on issues of national policy as the size of the institution increases. It is also interesting to note that faculty involvement in determining institutionwide policies, which is almost always very high, drops off sharply at the super category. This suggests that such institutions are *so* big that the faculty have never been able to organize themselves effectively to participate as a body in making institutionwide policy. Seventy-two percent of the small institutions reported an increase in faculty involvement in this sort of determination, eighty-two percent of the medium, eighty percent of the large, seventy-eight percent of the giant, and only thirty-three percent of the super. The case study material tends to support this: if there is a critical mass, it is not in terms of the size of the student body but in terms of the faculty. The super institutions have faculties which are so large that they appear to be nongovernable. An institution of 30,000 students with a faculty of 1,500 will find it extremely difficult to organize those 1,500 in any way to participate in making meaningful decisions at the institutional level. This does not mean, however, that at the departmental level they are in any difficulty. We have no data to support that. However, there is a critical mass in the sense that the super institutions show significantly different patterns of faculty participation than do the other four. Note that these discrepancies do not show up under the student data, while they do show up under the faculty data. This suggests, as far as student participation is concerned, that there seem to be significant differences between the medium (1,000–5,000) and the large (5,000–15,000) student bodies. With faculty, however, when one reaches the giant category, there are significant differences between those institutions that have up to 25,000 students and those that are over 25,000 with regard to the *faculty's* ability to govern itself and to participate in the governance of the institution. It also suggests that in the super institutions any contact between faculty and administration will be minimal and fairly routine. The number of personal contacts that can be made across this gap must be small indeed.

Administration There are only a few items in the category of *administration* that show differences by size of institution. One of these is the percentage of total budget based on federal support. Whereas 46 percent of the small institutions reported an increase in percentage of budget based on federal support, the entire population of super institutions reported such an increase. They go up steadily from 62 percent of the medium, and 68 percent of the large, to 74 percent of the giant institutions.

There are some interesting data on the efforts to attract students from disadvantaged homes. While 53 percent of the small institutions reported an increase in such efforts, 100 percent of the supers did, with the percentages steadily increasing as the size increased. (This may well be one explanation for the large number of student protests which have occurred at the larger institutions.) The degree to which the institution controls student behavior decreased as size of the institutions increased. While 28 percent of the small institutions reported a decrease in institutional control, 67 percent of the supers did (this is a student variable, but note again that the largest increase in percentages occurs between the medium and the large institutions—38 percent of the medium institutions reporting decreased institutional control and 54 percent of the large reporting such a decrease).

These data are suggestive of the enormous influence in size of student body on institutional styles of participation. Whether it is a "critical" mass or not is relative. But it is clear that as far as student variables are concerned, the institutions which have between 1,000 and 5,000 students look very different from the institutions that have 5,000 to 15,000 students. On the other hand faculty seem to be significantly different in institutions with more than 25,000 students than in those with less than 25,000. There are costs and casualties in size, as well as advantages; the large institutions apparently are getting better students, they are getting a decline in institutional loyalty, and they are getting an increasingly autonomous and research-oriented faculty. The faculty perhaps are aided in their support of students who oppose the administration and in making advocacy statements on national issues because of their relative anonymity in extremely large institutions. The coercive effect a small town has on its membership is well-known. It is obvious that a small institution may have much the same kind of control over student and faculty activity, whereas the super institution representing a major urban area today simply cannot establish communication systems which allow any kind of control over the constituent groups. It seems obvious that when the institution gets over 25,000 students, the administration's ability to make significant contact with the faculty declines drastically. This may be a very important decision for the future of these institutions—what does one do when one has grown too large, too fast?

We also were able to divide our institutions into the regions of the country in which they existed. The breakdown consisted of eight categories, all relatively familiar in this type of research: the New England states (111 institutions), the Mideast or Middle Atlantic states (224), the Southeast (220), the Great Lakes (208), the Plains (157), the Southwest (78), the Rocky Mountain area (38), and the Far West (172). As noted earlier, the distribution of institutions by geographic area falls within 1 percent of the distribution of all institutions of higher education in the nation. This is thus a remarkably accurate sample of approximately 50 percent of the national total.

By and large the data refute the commonly held assumption that there are major differences in educational institutions in different sections of the country. Again there seems to be a remarkable commonality to institutional change patterns regardless of where in the country the institution happens to be located. Although one often hears statements about the virtues of attending a school in a given area, say, New England, there seems to be little objective evidence that those schools are much different in terms of their present trends from schools in the rest of the country.

The stereotype would suggest that institutions in the Southeast, Plains, and Southwest would be the least open and modern, but the data do not support this to any considerable degree, at least in terms of reported changes.

Students
On the variables which deal with *institutional openness,* there are virtually no differences by region, with the one interesting exception—that the Rockies and the Southwest seem to be unusually high in the increased heterogeneity of *students by age.* While the remaining areas indicate between a 15 and 20 percent increase in heterogeneity of students by age, the Southwest and the Rockies show 33 and 32 percent increase, respectively. One would assume that a similar relationship would hold with the percentage of *married students,* but this is not the case. Apparently student age is one isolated phenomenon of institutional openness which does not square with the rest of the factors we have analyzed. Most of the regions reported a strong increase in the percent of *out-of-state students,* with the exception of the Rocky Mountain states. All

categories reported a marked increase in the percentage of *foreign students,* particularly in the Great Plains institutions.

Almost all sections of the country reported an increase in the *quality of student preparation in high school,* which could be characterized as an extremely strong trend, with the exception of the Southwest where the percentage dropped to 54 percent, still very strong. The variable percentage of *on-campus student protest* is particularly interesting in that the evidence is quite clear that no region of the country is immune from student protest. Although we hear most publicity given to protests in the New England, Mideastern, and Far Western areas, the data indicate quite clearly that all sections of the country have had an increase which could be characterized as marked. (This analysis is carried further in the special discussion of student protest.) In terms of *institutional effectiveness,* the commonalities are again striking, although there is a stronger institutional effectiveness for freshmen to complete degree requirements in the Southeast, the Great Lakes, the Southwest, and the Rockies than in New England, the Mideast, the Plains, and the Far West. However, these differences are not particularly significant. The decline in dismissals for academic and social reasons is particularly marked in the New England institutions compared with the rest of the country. But even there the tendency toward a decrease in the number of dismissals could only be called slight. The percentage of the graduating class that plans on continued education is high and represents a very strong trend in all areas of the country, with no exceptions. Similarly all sections of the country (with no exceptions) reported a slightly increased percentage of graduate students to undergraduates, which could be called moderate.

In terms of the factors called modernity, again we are struck with the similarity of institutions across the country by geographic area. In amount of student control in academic decision making, there is a trend which could be called strong operating in all regions of the country. The same can be said for the amount of student control in institutionwide policy formation, which is a strong trend in all cases except the Southwest, where the percentage reporting an increase in student control drops to 46 percent. Exactly the same can be said of student control in the establishment and enforcement of social regulations, a strong trend across the country with a slight decline in the Southwest.

The percentage of students who participate in community volunteer programs seems universally high in all areas of the country, again a strong trend with the one exception of the Rockies, where perhaps there are not enough urban areas for students to enter in terms of community welfare and volunteer programs. With the one exception of a few variables which point out the Southwest as being different, one is struck with the sameness in student characteristics in all eight regions of the country. The only other exception to this statement which could perhaps be pointed out is that fraternities quite clearly are a declining force in the Far West, while an increased number of men and women are joining fraternities in the Southwest—but here again the trend is only moderate.

Faculty   In terms of the faculty responses by geographic area, a few more interesting differences can be pointed out, although there are also some commonalities. New England seems to lead the nation with 18 percent of the institutions reporting increased faculty turnover. At the low end of the scale are the Far West and the Southeast with 5 percent and 7 percent, respectively, reporting an increase in turnover. These differences are not particularly significant but may represent the expectation at many institutions, particularly in New England, that a faculty member will not finish up his teaching career at that institution but is supposed to go to other sections of the country. (Harvard has for years had an "up or out policy" in which after a certain number of years of teaching it is assumed that the faculty member will leave Harvard and go elsewhere.) However, a number of institutions are clearly emulating this policy in other sections of the country, and this may explain the fact that there is no clearly designed export-import model with regard to faculty. Faculty turnover is remarkably light considering the amount of publicity given to the highly mobile professor who never stays at one institution for more than a year or so. One gets the impression from these data that most faculty tend to stay in one institution for a fairly considerable period of time.

There is a strong trend in all sections of the country to have an increased proportion of the faculty on tenure, particularly so in the Far West. Similarly the average age at which tenure is awarded is declining in a marked trend in all sections of the country but particularly so in the Mideastern Great Lakes, and Rocky Mountain states. Commitment to teaching, which differentiates institutions nicely on a number of other dimensions, does not make any significant differentiation by geographic area. There is a moderate trend in all areas of the country toward an increased commitment to teaching. However, in all sections of the country there is a trend of approximately twice the strength in favor of increased commitment to research. Although we tend to think of research as being concentrated in the "think-tank areas" of the East and West Coasts, these data reveal that an underlying commitment to research is widely shared by institutions in all sections of the country.

With regard to the commitment to the institution, there are some differences that approach significance by regions of the country. The New England and Great Lakes areas report approximately a 10 percent decrease in commitment to the institution, while the Southeast reports a 10 percent increase and the Far West a 9 percent increase. (The national figure on this item for all institutions in the sample is 3 percent of the institutions reporting a decrease in commitment to the institution.) It is theoretically possible, of course, that the New England and Great Lakes areas were known in the past for having faculty who were extremely loyal to the institutions they served, and therefore the decline is seen in a more important and elevated way by their presidents than by presidents of institutions in other sectors of the country. In that there is no ready explanation for this discrepancy on commitment to the institutions, the reader is left to fend for himself. There is a strong trend in all areas of the country to promote student-faculty discussions without exception, although the trend is strongest in the Far Western and Mideastern areas. The trend toward increased faculty willingness to accept student course evaluation is marked, with a particularly strong showing in the Rocky Mountain states. On hours spent in teaching (which is a more specific checking out of the responses about commitment), we find considerable variation by region although all regions reported a decline in hours spent in teaching. The number of hours of teaching time was most drastically reduced in the New England and Great Lakes areas (even though these areas also reported the highest percentage of increase in faculty turnover). In the Southwest area, only 14 percent of the institutions reported decrease in hours spent in teaching, suggesting higher teaching loads in that area than in many others.

Interestingly enough there is almost no difference by region in faculty hours spent in research. This positive trend could be called marked and indicates a 30 percent increase in terms of the institutions reporting increased faculty time spent in research. External pressures limiting faculty freedom also seem to be a uniform variable in all sections of the country. A moderate trend toward reducing external pressures on faculty freedom is reported in all areas of the country with no significant exceptions. Faculty support of students who oppose administrative policies is somewhat higher in New England, the Mideast, the Great Lakes, and the Far West than is true of the other areas of the country, particularly in comparison with the Rockies, where only 16 percent of the institutions reported an increase in faculty support of students who opposed the administration. Faculty autonomy in grading indicates a slight to moderate trend in the direction of increased autonomy in all areas of the country, although the trend is stronger in the Mideast than in any other section of the country (21 percent of the institutions reporting increased autonomy for faculty), compared with the Rockies, where only 3 percent of the institutions reported an increase in faculty autonomy. On faculty autonomy in academic programs the results seem to be quite uniform although the Southwest is low with 19 percent of the institutions reporting increased faculty autonomy in academic programs, while the three high areas are the Far West with 34 percent, New England with 35 percent, and the Mideast with 36 percent.

There are some regional differences in terms of the percentage of faculty who publicly advocate positions on national policies. The Great Lakes region is high for the nation with 51 percent of the institutions reporting increased percentages of faculty taking positions of advocacy, followed closely by the Far West with 49 percent, the Mideast with 48 percent, and the New England area with 46 percent. Low on this variable is the Southwest—with only 23 percent of the institutions reporting increased percentage of faculty taking advocacy positions. On one of the most crucial variables in the faculty section—faculty involvement in determining institutionwide policies—all sections of the country report a marked increase. The trend could be called extremely strong with the one exception, perhaps, of the Southwest, where the percentage reporting increased involvement drops to 71 percent; but the consistent pattern remains in all areas of the country. The faculty clearly have a greater say in involving themselves than was true in the past. There is no region that has not reported this to be the case. Similarly the trend toward increased faculty willingness to experiment with new methods can be characterized as extremely strong in all areas. Although New England seems to take a more conservative position on this variable, with 59 percent of the institutions reporting increased willingness, the Great Lakes and Plains areas are high with 71 percent and 74 percent, respectively. In general, we can say that there is again a picture of basic uniformity within which some rather interesting differences exist. Commitment toward the institution is one. In another, one could argue that certain areas of the country have perhaps a greater number of "activist" faculty than other areas. New England, the Mideast, the Great Lakes, and the Far West tend to be the regions that rank highest in the study on the two items of faculty support of students opposing administrative policies and percentage of faculty publicly advocating positions on national policies. Although an exact head count is now difficult to come by, one could argue that New England, the Mideast, the Great Lakes, and the Far West have had more than their share of student protests and demonstrations lately. Indeed, those four regions rank highest in reporting an increase in student protest. Between the extent to which faculty contribute to student protest and the extent to which they advocate positions against both the local and the national administrations, there seems to be a fairly consistent relationship.

Administration and Finance

There is a strong trend in every region of the country for an increased percentage of the total budget to be based on federal support, although the trend is particularly marked in the Southeast, the Southwest, and the Rockies. A much less obvious shift toward an increase in percentage of total budget based on alumni support can be found in New England, the Mideast, the Southeast, and the Great Lakes, approximately 20 to 29 percent of these institutions so reporting. The low region for this is the Far West, in which only 11 percent of the institutions reported an increase. The trend toward increased alumni influence on institutional policy making seems to be very weak in virtually all areas of the country, while the influence of state departments of education on institutionwide policy making shows some interesting differences by region. The Southwest is high for the nation. In the Southwest 38 percent of the institutions reported an increase in the influence of the state department of education, while in New England only 2 percent reported an increase. Outside of the Southwest and New England, close to 20 percent of the institutions reported an increase. This finding could be reported as some kind of a "muscle index" for state departments in various sections of the country. Whether the impact of state departments of education on policy making has been good or bad, we are unable to say. There are, however, significant differences by region of the country.

There are also interesting discrepancies in terms of the authority of central campus administrations by region of the country. In the Southwest, 5 percent of the institutions actually reported an increase in authority of central campus administrations, while in the Rocky Mountain states 18 percent of the institutions reported a decrease. All other sections of the country reported a decrease in central campus administrative authority, although none as high as the Rockies. (It is interesting to observe that the Rockies also have the highest score for a decline in school spirit.) All sections of the country reported increased attempts to attract students from disadvantaged homes, and this trend could be called strong. The Mideast and Far West have the highest percentage scores on this item, with both reporting 74 percent of the institutions indicating increased attempts to attract disadvantaged students. Low for the item is the Southwest area, where only 49 percent of the institutions reported increased efforts. This item seems to be one in which there is *no* regional difference whatsoever. Also, administrative attempts to increase communication emerged as a very strong trend in all areas of the country.

There are some interesting differences with regard to the number of cooperative programs with local industry. The trend could be called strong to very strong in the Rockies, the Far West, the Southwest, and the Southeast, whereas in New England and the Mideast the percentages reporting increased number of cooperative programs dropped to about half the number for the rest of the country. This is probably due to the liberal arts mentality, which perhaps pervades the New England and Mideastern areas. The junior college movement, which perhaps came rather late to those areas, is the most likely factor in explaining this difference.

There is a reasonably significant difference by areas of the country in terms of requirements for undergraduate degrees. The Southeastern institutions emerge on the high end of the variable: 14 percent of Southeastern institutions report an increase in the number of institutionwide requirements for the undergraduate degree, while the Rockies, the Southwest, and the Plains also show considerable increase. On the other hand, the Mideast reports that 14 percent of the institutions show a decrease in the number of institutionwide requirements. In terms of departmental requirements for the degree, all areas of the country report an increase which could be called slight to moderate. The irony of the situation has been remarked on before: as institutions lower the number of institutionwide requirements for the degree, they often increase the number of departmental requirements, thereby strengthening the hand of the faculty, which controls the departmental requirements, and weakening that of the administration, which often is responsible to some extent for institutionwide requirements for the undergraduate degree. The Southeast is high in this item, with 21 percent of the institutions reporting an increase in departmental degree requirements, while the Far West is low, with only 5 percent reporting increase.

We were surprised to find that, in terms of length of service of major administrative officers, there is a uniform trend in all areas which could be described as moderate. However, the Southeastern area is significantly higher in its reportage in that 27 percent of the institutions there report an increased length of service for major administrative officers compared with 11 percent in the Mideast and 12 percent in the Great Lakes. All regions of the country report an increase in the number of working relations with other colleges and universities, and this trend could be described as very strong. There are no exceptions, and one gathers that the trend toward collaborative relationships will probably continue. There seem to be some significant differences in the degree to which institutions control the behavior of their students. All sections of the country reported a decrease in institutional control, but the Great Lakes and Mideast were high with 45 percent and 40 percent of the institutions, respectively, reporting decreased control over student behavior. At the other end of the scale is the Southwest, where only 17 percent of the institutions reported a decrease.

In summary, although the Southeast and Southwest seem to have certain tendencies that could be called conservative, the basic pattern is remarkably similar for the various regions of the country. The stronger the trend, the more uniformly it can be found in all geographic areas. One could also speculate about the existence of an "activism quotient," which would be found in a higher degree in New England, the Mideast, the Great Lakes, and the Far West, at least in terms of certain student and faculty characteristics. However, this tendency is slight and again should not be over-emphasized to the point of minimizing the commonalities that exist across the country. It would appear once again from this analysis that we are moving toward a far more homogeneous system of institutions of higher education, at least in terms of the geographic areas in which these campuses are situated.

4. BY COMPRE- HENSIVENESS

According to an earlier definition, the concept of institutional designation has two dimensions, namely *highest degree offered* and *comprehensiveness* of school. The former will be explored in the following section. Both dimensions may be equally important. It is assumed that institutions of higher education vary widely in their internal organization—a large university offering doctoral programs in academic and professional subjects is a more complex organization, a more comprehensive school, than a two-year college. The categories used are two-year colleges (315 institutions), four-year colleges (285), colleges granting the master's degree (142), universities granting the master's degree (61), and universities granting the Ph.D. degree (118).

The Student Body

a. Openness of Institution With regard to *ethnic composition, religious background, socioeconomic background,* and *political affiliation,* the trend is noticeably in one direction though not to the same degree: most schools report an increase in the hetero- geneity of the student body in terms of those four variables. The trend toward greater heterogeneity is, in general, noticeably stronger with respect to ethnic composition than with respect to the three other variables. When examined by *institutional designa- tion,* the trend toward greater heterogeneity is noticeably weaker with respect to all four variables for the two-year colleges than for the other four school types. This does not mean that two-year colleges are less "open" than the other schools; however, most two-year colleges were established as open schools right from the outset and thus did not need to increase their openness much, while the more complex schools were relatively less open at the outset (they usually date back to a period when the principle of universal higher education had not yet been formulated) and had to make greater efforts to achieve a higher degree of openness.

While there is an increase in heterogeneity of the student body with regard to *age* of students in all types of schools, the differences between them are quite small. Interestingly enough, presidents of four-year colleges report a somewhat lower rate of increase than do presidents of other types of schools. The most likely explanation for this phenomenon is that the majority of four-year colleges are under private control and therefore are less likely to cater to such less typical groups as older students than are other types of schools.

With the above exception, two-year colleges show a consistently lower rate of increase than the sample as a whole, while the more "comprehensive" types of schools show a consistently higher rate of increase.

The increase in the proportion of *out-of-state students* is much stronger for the more comprehensive types of institutions than for the two-year colleges. The result is not surprising: the large majority of two-year colleges are publicly controlled and serve a specific area; thus, their constituency is primarily local. This trend is also true with respect to the proportion of foreign students: while the increase has been quite marked in all types of schools, it has been lower for two-year colleges than for the more comprehensive schools. Again, the visibility factor offers the best explanation: if two-year colleges are barely visible outside their immediate local area, they are presumably even less visible abroad. The data reveal a positive relationship between relative increase in the proportion of foreign students and the degree of comprehensiveness of institutions: the more comprehensive an institution, the more likely the relative increase.

There has been a strong overall increase in the enrollment of *married students.* Again, the more comprehensive schools show a stronger trend toward increase than do the two-year colleges. Even more pronounced is the proportionate increase in the number of *transfer students entering the institution:* while there has been a strong increase in all types of schools, the increase is significantly higher in the more comprehensive institutions than in the two-year colleges. In the case of married students, the explanation for their proportionately lower rate of increase in two-year colleges is again based on the fact that those schools were always open to such "atypical" older and married students, whereas the other schools were aimed more toward the "majority," or "typical," student.

As for increase in the proportion of transfer students, the reason for the considerably higher rates in the more comprehensive schools is quite obvious: The majority of transfers takes place at the end of an academic year, and there is thus only one major transfer opportunity in two-year colleges, namely between freshman and sophomore year. In the case of a four-year college or the undergraduate division of a more comprehensive school (the transfer data are limited to the undergraduate level), there are three major transfer opportunities—at the end of the freshman, sophomore, and junior years.

A comparison between these data and the data for the whole sample shows again that increases for the two-year colleges are below the samplewide average, while they are above that average for the institutions. The more comprehensive schools have thus undergone considerably more far-reaching changes within the last 10 years than have the two-year colleges.

b. Effectiveness of institution   One of the more obvious indicators of a school's effectiveness is the proportion of *freshmen completing their degree requirements.* If the proportion increases, the effectiveness of an institution increases, and vice versa. The large majority of all five types of schools reported an increase; however, the increase was strongest in universities with Ph.D. programs and weakest in two-year colleges. The public two-year colleges usually accept all high school graduates, and because of their lower selectivity they are found to have a large rate of attrition. The other school types are likely to be more selective; thus, their attrition rate should be relatively lower.

The proportion of *graduate students completing their degree requirements* has been increasing in the large majority of institutions with graduate programs; the more comprehensive the school, the stronger the increase. The trend is thus very similar to the one for undergraduate retention.

It might be expected that the proportion of *dismissals for academic reasons* would be negatively related to the proportion of undergraduate and graduate students completing their degree requirements. This is only true in the case of universities with Ph.D. programs, which show a rather marked decrease. Colleges with M.A. programs show a slight decrease, and the other three types show a slight increase in the proportion of dismissals for academic reasons. But these data would still tend to confirm the trend that the most complex type of school is the most successful in retaining its students.

The presidents of most schools in the subsample reported an increase in the proportion of *students planning on continued education;* the more complex schools seemed to be more successful at convincing their students to consider further education. This result is not surprising since most two-year colleges offer predominantly vocationally oriented terminal programs. In view of this fact it does seem amazing that over half the presidents of two-year colleges in the subsample reported increases. A possible explanation might be that the two-year colleges have been strengthening their academic programs in order to become stepping stones to four-year institutions. That the schools with more advanced programs should show an extremely strong increase is not surprising; those schools have graduate and undergraduate programs with faculty members teaching at both levels. As a result, the graduate program is quite visible to the undergraduate at such a school, while this direct contact with a graduate program is largely removed from the experience of a two-year college student. Also, advanced undergraduates are usually able to register for graduate courses, a policy that deliberately aims at interesting the brighter and more advanced undergraduates to do graduate studies in their major.

In those schools which have graduate programs, the proportion of *graduate to undergraduate students* has been increasing in the majority of institutions; the more comprehensive the institution, the stronger the increase. The explanation is likely to be the same as the previous one.

The more comprehensive schools also show a comparatively stronger increase than does the sample as a whole, while the increase for the two-year colleges is below that for the sample. In those schools which have graduate programs, the proportion of graduates completing their degree requirements is much higher than that for the sample as a whole.

c. Modernity of student body   There is a strong positive relationship between comprehensiveness of school and the *amount of student control in academic decision making.* Most presidents of all types of schools reported an increase. The increase is considerably more widespread in schools offering four-year or more advanced programs than in two-year colleges. The same trend is true for the *amount of student control in institutionwide policy formation,* and in the *amount of student control in establishing and enforcing regulations governing student conduct.* The only possible exception to the trend is the increase in the amount of student control in *establishing* regulations governing student conduct: both two-year and four-year colleges show the same rate of increase, which is lower than that for the more comprehensive schools. Interestingly enough, student control in establishing regulations has increased more in all five types of schools than student control in *enforcing* regulations. One possible explanation is that while students feel that *they* should establish the rules governing their conduct, they are not likely to be eager to police themselves.

The increase in the proportion of *students participating in voluntary community* programs has been considerable on campuses of all types, but the trend toward increase has been particularly strong for the four-year colleges and above. On a predominantly vocationally oriented two-year college campus with a nonresident student population whose composition changes often, there is less likely to be a student subculture that would tend to encourage students to donate time for such projects.

The increase in the appearance of *underground newspapers and films* ranges from very slight to rather strong. The more comprehensive a school, the more likely it is to show an increase. Underground newspapers and films are likely to be an expression of student discontent with "official" student activities on campuses that have a large contingent of resident students with time to involve themselves in such activities; there is less likely to be such a subculture which could support such new means of communication and entertainment on a two-year college campus.

There is a strong positive relationship between the proportion of *on-campus student protests* and the comprehensiveness of schools: the more comprehensive an institution, the more likely it is to show an increase in the proportion of such protests. While the increase is slight for two-year colleges, it is very strong for universities with Ph.D. programs. Apart from the influence of the size-of-enrollment factor, which was discussed in a previous section, the phenomenon might be explained in terms of two other factors, namely, the average time spent by a student on a given campus and the major orientation of school. A student who spends only two years on a college campus—such as the two-year college student—will probably not have enough time to become involved in the affairs of his school, while a student who spends four years or even longer (graduate studies) on the same campus is likely to have the time. Furthermore, the two-year colleges are the least likely to have a resident student population that can develop its distinct subculture. As to the second factor, most two-year colleges tend to have a strong vocational-education objective; and vocationally oriented students are not as likely as nonvocationally oriented students to participate in or initiate on-campus student protests.

An increase in the variables of *school spirit, number of men joining fraternities,* and *number of women joining sororities* reflects an increase in student traditionalism. The data show that an increase in modernity does not necessarily preclude an increase in traditionalist traits: there has been a slight increase in some types of schools with regard to all three variables. With regard to both *increase in the number of men joining fraternities* and *increase in the number of women joining sororities,* the growth is very slight for two-year and four-year colleges and more marked for the three most comprehensive types of schools. Fraternities and sororities thus show the same growth patterns. With regard to *school spirit,* there has been a very slight decline in the case of the three most comprehensive types, while the schools with less advanced programs show an increase—very slight for four-year colleges and much more pronounced for two-year colleges (but still far from strong). This increase in school spirit in two-year colleges may be explained by the "traditionalist" norms of the vocationally oriented two-year college student. He has little time for such frills as fraternities and sororities, which are *sustained* activities, but he may have time to manifest his loyalty to his institution by attending *occasional* college-sponsored events. The data might justify the statement that traditionalism manifests itself differently in two-year colleges than in the more comprehensive schools (although the increase in traditionalism, compared with the growth in modernity, has been very slight): traditionalism is characterized by a slight increase in interest in *Greek societies* in the more comprehensive colleges and by a slight increase in *school spirit* in two-year colleges.

If one concentrates on the indicators of modernity and leaves the indicators of traditionalism momentarily aside, it can be stated that the increase in modernity has been more pronounced in the four-year and more advanced schools than in the two-year schools.

The increase in the number of men joining fraternities and the number of women joining sororities has been lower than the samplewide average for two-year and four-year colleges but higher for the three most comprehensive types of schools.

d. Dismissals for nonacademic reasons   There has been a decline over the last 10 years, ranging from very slight for the two-year colleges to somewhat stronger (but still slight) for the universities with Ph.D. programs. The more comprehensive an institution, the more pronounced the decline.

e. Quality of student preparation in high school The majority of presidents of all five types of institutions reported an increase in the quality of student preparation in high school; however, this increase is considerably stronger for the more comprehensive institutions than for the two-year colleges.

Examination of change by comprehensiveness of school clearly shows that a sharp division emerges between the two-year colleges and all the other types of schools. While the trends do not necessarily go in different directions, their magnitude almost always differs between the two-year and the more comprehensive schools. The more comprehensive institutions have, in the view of their presidents, experienced the strongest trend toward openness; furthermore, their student bodies have shown the most dramatic increase in modernity and the strongest trend toward institutional effectiveness. Finally, they are the schools in which the decline in dismissals for academic reasons and the increase in the quality of freshman applicants have been most noticeable. The more comprehensive schools have thus changed to a considerably larger extent than have the two-year colleges.

The Faculty *a. Faculty mobility* There is a positive relationship between the comprehensiveness of an institution and the *amount of faculty turnover:* the more comprehensive an institution, the more marked the increase (which ranges from a slight decrease for the two-year colleges to a rather marked increase for universities with Ph.D. programs). The rather marked increase for the most comprehensive schools is probably best explained in terms of faculty visibility: since those schools are among large and comparatively well-known universities, members of their faculties are highly visible and sought after, as a result of which they are much more mobile than their counterparts in less comprehensive schools. The slight decrease in mobility for two-year college teachers may reflect an increased security of teaching appointments at those schools.

The trend toward an increase in the *proportion of tenured faculty* is most pronounced for four-year colleges, slightly less so for two-year colleges, and considerably less so for the three most comprehensive types of schools. The two least comprehensive types of schools may be those which had to change their tenure rules most in the last 10 years to stay competitive in the academic job market, while the three most comprehensive schools, those with graduate programs, already had a relatively high proportion of tenured faculty.

The fact that tenure has become more widespread than in the past is also reflected in the general decrease in *average age when tenure is awarded.* The decrease is most dramatic for universities with Ph.D. programs, least so for the two-year colleges. This general decrease no doubt reflects the fact that tenure is no longer the prerogative of the most senior faculty. There is, as can be expected, a positive relationship between age and rank; since tenure is now awarded at a lower *rank* than it used to be, the average *age* at which tenure is awarded has also decreased.

Compared with the sample as a whole, faculty mobility has increased somewhat above average for the three most comprehensive schools and slightly below average for two-year and four-year colleges.

b. Faculty commitment As the comprehensiveness óf a school increases, *commitment toward teaching* decreases. The range goes from a rather marked increase for two-year colleges to a slight decrease for universities with a Ph.D. program. The decrease in the more comprehensive schools is less pronounced than could be expected.

On the other hand, there is very definitely a clear positive relationship between increase in *commitment toward research* and comprehensiveness of an institution: the more comprehensive the school, the more pronounced the increase in commitment toward research (there are no data for the two-year colleges for the obvious reason that those schools are pure teaching institutions which do not attract the research-oriented faculty, and neither do they provide research facilities).

The above data would tend to validate the assumption that commitment to research has replaced commitment to teaching. But while there has been a clear increase in commitment toward research, commitment toward teaching has only decreased slightly, and only in the most research-oriented institutions—the universities with Ph.D. programs.

An increase in commitment toward teaching or toward research should be reflected in an increase in hours so spent, and there is in fact a close relationship between the two: *hours spent in teaching* have declined for all five types of institutions; the more comprehensive schools show a more dramatic decline, however, than do the two-year colleges. Equally, the *hours spent in research* have increased, and there is a dramatic difference by comprehensiveness of school: the increase ranges from very slight for the two-year colleges to very strong for universities with Ph.D. programs. These findings certainly corroborate those reflecting the change away from commitment toward teaching to commitment toward research, except that the variables *hours spent in teaching* and *hours spent in research* provide a better, more focused indicator of commitment than do the variables dealing with commitment in general. The marked decline in time spent in teaching by two-year college teachers seems to indicate that the teaching load of junior college teachers has become more like that in the more comprehensive schools. As working conditions in the two-year colleges have improved, the faculty's commitment toward teaching seems to have improved.

There is no way of demonstrating whether or not there has been a shift away from commitment toward the institution to commitment toward the profession because of a lack of comparative data. However, the data on commitment toward the institution do show a decrease in the more "complex" schools, particularly in the two most complex types.

In sum, the data would tend to corroborate previous assumptions about the two major changes in commitment, from teaching to research and from the institution to the profession.

c. Faculty modernity The general increase in *faculty efforts to promote student-faculty discussions* has been very strong for all five types of schools during the last 10 years. Perhaps faculty members may not have had to make special efforts to promote student-faculty discussions a decade ago when the emphasis of graduate programs was more on teaching. However, now that the teacher is increasingly removed from students, he may very well have to make a special effort to communicate with them. The *increase* in faculty efforts to promote student-faculty discussions says, therefore, very little about the actual amount of such interaction.

Another indicator for the modernity of the faculty is *faculty willingness to accept student course evaluation;* there has been a considerable increase in all five types of institutions. This variable does not, however, distinguish between willingness to accept such course evaluations and actual implementation of the results of such evaluations.

While the above two indicators deal predominantly with student-faculty relations in the realm of academic matters, *faculty support of students opposing administrative policies* is in a different realm; it does partly reflect the willingness of faculty members to enter into a temporary or limited alliance with students against the third constituent group of a school, the administration. The increase in the more comprehensive schools has been higher than in the less comprehensive ones, particularly higher than in the two-year colleges. This probably reflects both a less pronounced antagonism between faculty and administration in two-year colleges than in the more comprehensive schools, and a much smaller proportion of students opposing administrative polices as compared with the comprehensive institutions (if student rebels are not visible to the faculty, they are not likely to attract its support).

The data show that *faculty willingness to experiment with new methods* has increased more in the less comprehensive schools (two-year colleges and four-year colleges) than in the more comprehensive ones. It thus seems that the real innovations in undergraduate teaching take place in schools that have no graduate programs, i.e., in schools which do not encourage teachers to concentrate on graduate rather than undergraduate instruction. In such schools, faculty members are able to concentrate on undergraduate education and have the opportunity to innovate.

Compared with the sample as a whole, the increase in modernity has been less than average for two-year college faculty, with the exception of faculty willingness to experiment with new methods, in which the increase for two-year college faculty has been above average.

d. Autonomy of faculty   There has been a distinct decrease in *external pressures limiting the freedom of the faculty;* this trend holds true for all five types of institutions. Two-year colleges and universities with Ph.D. programs show a significantly lower rate of decrease, however, than do the other types of schools.

A more direct measure of faculty autonomy, dealing with autonomy from the administration, is *faculty autonomy in grading.* There has been a general increase, slight for all types of schools, especially universities with Ph.D. programs. This may reflect the fact that grading has been a traditional prerogative of the faculty which was not challenged by the other two groups. This may of course change if students get increasingly more say over academic programs.

The increase in *faculty autonomy in academic programs* over the last 10 years has been rather strong, particularly in colleges and universities with M.A. programs.

The increase in faculty involvement in determining institution-wide policies has been dramatic, particularly for the two-year colleges. This might validate the tentative conclusion reached earlier that there may be less antagonism between faculty and administration in those schools than there is in the more comprehensive schools. (This may be a positive aspect of the lack of departments in the proper sense in two-year colleges: in a university, the administrative and organizational framework within which a teacher works is the department; his contacts with the institution-wide administration are largely through his department, which has a certain autonomy. Since the department in a two-year college is not as independent, the teacher may have more direct contacts with the institutionwide administration—a fact which may explain the lower degree of "alienation" from the administration.)

The trend with respect to the proportion of *faculty publicly advocating positions regarding national policies* is interesting: while there has been a rather strong increase in all five types of institutions, the trend has been less marked for two-year colleges than for the more complex schools. There is, in fact, a positive relationship between increase in the proportion of faculty advocating positions with regard to national policies and comprehensiveness; the more comprehensive the school, the stronger the increase. One possible explanation might be that large universities with Ph.D. programs have faculties of national reputation who are free from the constraints of local control. In other words, academic freedom in two-year colleges would seem to be more precarious than in a university with Ph.D. programs.

To sum up, the most dramatic general increase has happened with respect to faculty involvement in determining institutionwide policies, while, at the other extreme, there has been a general decrease in external pressures limiting the freedom of the faculty.

The Admin-istration *a. Scope of administrative authority* There has been very slight increase in *alumni influence on institutional policy making* for all types of schools; in four-year colleges the rate of increase was somewhat higher. It would seem that the slightly higher increase among those colleges is due to the fact that a very large proportion of them are under private control (larger than for any of the other types); privately controlled institutions tend to have much stronger alumni associations than do publicly controlled schools, since the former have to depend to a much larger degree than the latter on financial support from the alumni as a group.

The problem of public versus private control also seems to be the determining factor in the strong increase of *state department of education influence on institutional policy making* in two-year colleges; the proportion of publicly controlled two-year colleges is much higher than the proportion of publicly controlled schools in any one of the more complex categories. Four-year colleges and universities with M.A. programs show a moderate increase, while the increase for colleges with M.A. programs and universities with Ph.D. programs is very slight.

For those campuses which are part of multicampus institutions, there has been a general decrease in the *authority of the central campus administration.* The decrease is very slight for two-year colleges and universities with Ph.D. programs, however, while it is marked for the other three types of institutions.

With regard to the number of institutionwide requirements for *undergraduate degrees,* no particular pattern emerges: two-year colleges and universities with M.A. programs show a slight increase, while the other types of schools show a slight decrease. These three other types of schools thus seem to show a decline in the scope of administrative authority, while two-year colleges and universities with M.A. programs show an increase in scope.

The number of departmental requirements for undergraduate degrees has increased for all types of schools, ranging from very slight (two-year colleges and universities with Ph.D. programs) to more marked (four-year colleges and colleges with M.A. programs) to rather strong (universities with M.A. programs). The data seem to indicate that the scope of administrative authority is relatively large in two-year colleges and, quite possibly, in universities with Ph.D. programs. This coincides with the former finding about the scope of administrative authority in two-year colleges where the department, as such, doesn't have a strong bargaining position. The very slight increase in the number of departmental requirements in universities is not astonishing; the departments have traditionally had much say in curriculum matters (of which departmental requirements for a degree are part), so that this area was not one in which they had to fight in order to get more autonomy.

The *number of cooperative programs with local industry* has, according to most college and university presidents, increased. But an even more dramatic increase has happened in the *number of working relations with other colleges and universities.* Both increases may point to the fact that the college or university now has to look outside for support—cooperative programs with local industry create, if nothing else, good will for the institution, which may be translated into financial support. In the case of junior colleges, such relationships would probably center around vocational programs specifically aimed at the needs of local industry; in the case of its opposite on the comprehensiveness scale, the university with Ph.D. programs, it would probably result in research contracts with local industry. The increase in the number of working relations with other similar institutions shows that higher education is now a national system; the cooperation among similar institutions (because of the great diversity within higher education there still isn't a national organization that speaks for all institutions) makes them more effective in defending their rights.

b. Modernity of administration   Most presidents in all five types of schools report that they have increased *attempts to attract students from disadvantaged homes;* the increase appears particularly high in the case of universities with Ph.D. programs (these most comprehensive universities are presumably the ones which can best integrate disadvantaged students because of both the size of the student body and the variety of their facilities). Even stronger is the reported increase in *administrative attempts to increase communications* among the three groups that constitute a university or college—students, faculty, and administration. Almost every president reports that the administration of his school did increase its attempts to improve communications. Again, it should of course be kept in mind that a president's estimate of the situation does not necessarily reflect the facts—if students or the faculty were asked whether the administration did indeed attempt to increase communications, the answer might be quite different.

All types of schools *control student behavior* less than they did in previous decades; the college's and university's assigned role of acting *in loco parentis* seems to be on the wane everywhere. There are, however, important differences among the five types of schools—the more complex an institution, the more likely it is to have decreased the degree of control over student behavior, and the more likely it is to be a "modern" institution.

c. Length of service of major administrative officers In the two least complex schools there has been an increase in the length of service of these administrators; in the three more comprehensive types of schools, virtually no change seems to have taken place.

d. Financing of institution The *proportion of the total budget based on federal support* has increased in most schools of all five types. As expected, the increase is most marked for universities with Ph.D. programs, least so but still strong for two-year and four-year colleges. The nature of that part of the budget which is federally financed is not specified, but for the most part these funds would seem to be research contract grants for the more comprehensive institutions and outright grants for the less comprehensive institutions. To a very large degree, these research contracts help pay for the existence of the comprehensive institutions which, in return, sell the government services that the latter might have difficulties obtaining elsewhere. But to a certain extent these huge amounts spent on comprehensive universities represent just as much outright grants as they do for the smaller institutions which have no useful services to sell.

Although almost all colleges and universities claim that they have difficulties making ends meet, the *proportion of the total budget based on alumni support* has increased in all five types of schools, but to a far lesser extent than the proportion of the budget based on federal support. Two-year colleges show the weakest, four-year colleges the strongest increase. Again, the control variable could be used to explain this difference: the schools which have to cultivate their alumni most (and which in return get most out of them) are privately controlled. Since the majority of these schools are found among the four-year colleges, it seems natural that this group should show the highest proportion of increases in alumni contributions. The privately controlled schools have probably become more aggressive in their alumni solicitation in the last 10 years. As opposed to the four-year colleges, the overwhelming majority of junior colleges are publicly controlled, and since in these schools alumni donations are never expected to be of much significance, they spend less energy (as a group) on attracting additional alumni contributions. A second explanation is that there is neither the occasion nor the time to nurse the kind of institutional loyalty among their students which can later be translated into massive financial support (alumni loyalty here is more likely to appear as voter support for legislative actions affecting the institutions, such as bond issues). Four-year colleges, however, being predominantly residential, have both the occasion and the time to create this loyalty, which can later be translated into financial support for the institution.

. BY HIGHEST DEGREE AWARDED
The change by highest degree awarded is quite similar to our discussion of change by institutional designation. Here we have the less-than-B.A. category with 404 institutions, the B.A. institutions (351), the M.A. institutions (264), and the Ph.D. institutions (163).

With regard to the openness of the institutions, the readings vary little in this analysis from those of the one by institutional designation. Once again the less-than-B.A. institutions appeared to be less open than the other three categories, but this is due unquestionably to the fact that they were open to begin with. Again, for all four categories of highest degree awarded, students are more heterogeneous now by race than by social class. In all other student variables the data reveal no trends that were not revealed in the analysis by institutional designation. It would appear once again that the less-than-B.A. institutions are not exercising selectivity in their student admissions and therefore their students often appear lower on measures of aspiration for further higher education. However, the data are interesting in revealing some important changes with regard to the retention rates of the less-than-B.A. institutions, with some ground for cautious optimism. It should also be pointed out here, as is explained in the analysis of institutions by size, that size is a better predictor of a number of student variables than is the highest degree awarded by the institution.

Faculty
For example only 35 percent of the Ph.D.-degree-granting institutions reported an increase in underground publications and films, while institutions in the super category (25,000 students and over) reported an increase in underground publications and films in 56 percent of the institutions. While 58 percent of the Ph.D. institutions reported an increase in the percentage of on-campus student

protests, 89 percent of the super institutions reported such an increase. Thus on a number of dimensions within the student category, size is more significant than highest degree awarded in revealing these student parameters. As with students, the data for faculty show little difference between the comparisons by highest degree awarded by the institution and the institutional designation analysis. It should be pointed out again that on all variables which reveal a significant increase in favor of the more complex and comprehensive institutions, this increase is even more greatly intensified by the analysis of institutional size than is true for complexity, comprehensiveness, or highest degree awarded. On the variable of commitment of the faculty toward the institution, the analysis by highest degree gets higher. Compared with this fact, the data on institutional size show in stark detail the impact of size on loyalty to institution. On the items of commitment to teaching and to research, both size and highest degree awarded seem to contribute to the relative decline in commitment to research as institutions get larger and offer higher degrees. The two factors work in a complementary fashion. This is also true in the decrease in hours spent in teaching and the increase in hours spent in research. As with the institutional designation analysis, an increase in both the size of the institution and its highest degree awarded is accompanied by an increase in the amount of faculty support of students who oppose the administration and also in the number of faculty who publicly advocate positions on national policy. Again the data by size reveal the trend to a slightly more intense degree than the data by highest degree awarded.

Administration   The data on administrative characteristics by highest degree again resemble closely the data by institutional designation. Once again, however, the trends noted are revealed in a more intensive fashion in the analysis by size than they are by either highest degree awarded or institutional designation. For example, there is clearly a decline in the degree to which the institution governs student behavior, which increases as the highest degree awarded increases. But this phenomenon is seen more intensively in the analysis by size than by highest degree awarded or by institutional designation. Although size and highest degree awarded generally have a strong relationship (the higher the degree awarded, the larger the institution), there is one notable and important exception to this trend. In the public sector the less-than-B.A. institutions have a mean size of 2,372 students, while the B.A. institutions in the public sector have a student body averaging 1,703 students. Publicly controlled M.A.-awarding institutions have a mean student size of 5,056, while the Ph.D.-awarding institutions have a mean size in the public sector of 12,422 students. Thus in the public sector the community colleges and other less-than-B.A.-granting institutions are larger than the B.A.-awarding institutions. In all other sectors, private sectarian and private nonsectarian, the arrangement is continuous. That is, the less-than-B.A. institutions are the smallest; the B.A., M.A., and Ph.D. institutions get steadily larger (this information is reported in greater detail in the section of this report on institutions and student protest). In conclusion there seem to be very few differences, if any, in the analysis by highest degree awarded and the analysis by institutional designation; the former has four categories for analysis, the latter five. The trends revealed in both these data sources are intensified in a consistent way by analyzing the data by size of institution.

4. Change by Institutional Movement

FROM PRIVATE
TO PUBLIC
CONTROL
Change is reported in faculty, students, and administration. Although only eight institutions in our sample made the move from private to public, they are of greater significance than one would normally assume because this is a move many other private institutions seem to be contemplating. Thus the "handwriting on the wall" may be useful to institutions engaged in reassessing their control.

Students It is quite clear that when the move from private to public takes place, an increase in the diversity of the student body follows. In ethnic and religious composition, the institutions that have made the private to public move are higher in the heterogeneity dimension than the national sample. (Nationally 53 percent of the institutions report the net gain of heterogeneity and ethnic composition, while 63 percent of the institutions that have moved from private to public indicate a more homogeneous student-ethnic background.) Interestingly enough, the process of change from private to public seems to engender an increased school spirit. In the national sample, the net gain for increase in school spirit is 9 percent of the institutions, whereas in the institutions that have gone from private to public status the net gain involves 25 percent of the institutions.

Faculty Changes One of the most spectacular findings suggests that when an institution makes the move from private to public status, it increases its retention of faculty. Nationally, a net of 9 percent of the institutions report an increase in faculty turnover, whereas in this sample 38 percent of the institutions report a decrease in faculty turnover. This may be due partially to increased funding and higher faculty salary levels, but it is also based perhaps on a new reward

105

structure. Tenure is awarded at an earlier age in a net of 50 percent of the institutions that have made the private to public shift; in the national sample 23 percent report a decrease in age and tenure. This suggests that the institution that becomes public is able to award tenure to bright young faculty as another blandishment to keep them on the payroll. Surprisingly enough, this group is not the group of institutions where teaching and commitment to students are in a decline. In fact, at these institutions faculty commitment toward teaching is much higher than the national sample: a net of 38 percent of the institutions that have made the move from private to public report an increase in commitment toward teaching compared with 19 percent of the national sample.

Also commitment toward the institution, which nationally declines to a decreased commitment in 3 percent of the sample, shows an increased commitment toward the institution from 38 percent of the institutions that have moved from private to public (perhaps people are loyal to institutions when they suddenly are paid significantly more than they used to be paid). Support for this interpretation comes from the fact that nationally 41 percent of the institutions report a decrease in hours spent in teaching, while in the institutions that have moved from private to public only 13 percent report such a decrease. Similarly, hours spent in research increases nationally in 32 percent of the institutions, while the increase here is only 13 percent of the institutions. Also, a few members of the faculty seem to support students who oppose the administration—this increases in only 13 percent of the private to public institutions, while the national sample shows 29 percent of the faculty supporting students who oppose the administration.

Similarly, only 13 percent of the institutions moving from private to public report an increase in the percentage of faculty publicly advocating positions on national policies, whereas in the national sample 41 percent of the institutions report increased faculty advocacy of national policy positions. There then would seem to be something of a "honeymoon period" during which faculty are quite taken with new salary schedules, new responsibilities, and a new expansion of their horizons. During this period they show considerable institutional loyalty and do not seem to encourage the students to oppose the administration.

Administration Clearly, federal money is not the major source of new funding for institutions that move from private to public status. Nationally

55 percent of the institutions indicate an increase in percent of total budget based on federal support. In the private to public institutions, only 13 percent report such an increase. The money also does not come from alumni—nationally 21 percent of the institutions report an increase in the percentage of budget based on alumni support, whereas in these institutions a net of 13 percent report a decrease in percentage of budget based on alumni support. Quite clearly it is the state department of education which is the new source of policy and money. Nationally 18 percent of the institutions report an increase in the influence of the state department of education on the institution, while in the private to public institutions 38 percent report an increase in such influence. There is also some evidence of a rise in departmentalism at the stage in the move from private to public. Twenty-five percent of the private to public institutions report an increase in the number of departmental requirements for the undergraduate degree, while nationally only twelve percent of the institutions report such increase. In conclusion, the shift from private to public, although the sample is small, would indicate increased money, energy, and dedication to a larger task than previously seen for the institution. This spirit tends to infuse both faculty and students and suggests a greater willingness to "pull together" than one would expect in most institutions. The central administration does not seem to appear to be as threatened as in many other cases, and the possibility of getting genuine support from faculty and students seems quite high. However, the question our data cannot answer is, What happens when state-level funding begins to taper off after an institution has gotten used to the increased funding awards which are made possible by the shift from private to public control?

FROM SECTAR-IAN TO NON-SECTARIAN CONTROL Twenty schools moved from sectarian to nonsectarian control. Although this is a small subsample, it is nevertheless worthwhile to examine the data pertaining to student body, faculty, and administration changes in order to see whether any kind of interesting trend emerges. The change from sectarian to nonsectarian control is a form of change that has been quite typical over the years: colleges and universities (but primarily the former) established by a particular church and aimed at training members of that denomination discover that they need to broaden their selection of students for both financial and academic purposes. The second step is, later on, for the college to get more lay teachers and often a lay board (this has happened not only to Protestant but to Catholic colleges as well).

The Student Body *a. Openness of an institution* There has been a very strong trend during the last 10 years toward an increase in the heterogeneity of the student body, in particular with respect to *ethnic composition* and *religious background.* Contrary to the data for other typologies of schools, colleges which moved from sectarian to nonsectarian control show a stronger increase in the heterogeneity of *religious background* than in ethnic composition. This is perhaps one of the best indicators of change—nonsectarian schools are under no obligations to accept students of one faith. But the increase in heterogeneity is also strong with regard to *socioeconomic background* and *political affiliation. Age* heterogeneity has increased less, but the increase in the proportion of *out-of-state students* has been very strong. This again might be characteristic of the transition from sectarian to nonsectarian control: the changeover to nonsectarian control enables a school to seek its students outside a strictly local constituency. The increase in the proportion of *foreign students* has been moderate, but the increase in the proportion of *married students* has been quite strong. Finally, there has been a very strong increase in the proportion of *transfer students.* The data thus show that a change in the control of an institution is accompanied by a rather strong increase in the heterogeneity of the student body.

When compared with the trend for the whole sample, schools which moved from sectarian to nonsectarian control show a significantly higher increase in heterogeneity of the student body for all variables, with the exceptions of proportion of foreign students and proportion of married students.

b. Effectiveness of institution The increase in the proportion of *freshmen completing their degree requirements* is strong. Of those schools which have graduate programs, only very few report that there had been an increase in the proportion of *graduates completing their degree requirements.* The increase in the proportion of *dismissals for academic reasons* is very slight.

A very dramatic increase in the proportion of the *graduating class planning on continued education* has taken place; this may reflect upgraded programs with better teachers who are more likely to encourage their students to do graduate education than did their predecessors under sectarian control; in other words, the college may now see its role as preparing students for more advanced education rather than being a terminal and at least partly vocational school. In those schools which have graduate programs, the proportion of *graduate to undergraduate students* has been increasing slightly.

Schools which changed from sectarian to nonsectarian control thus seem to have become more efficient institutions.

c. Modernity of student body   The *amount of student control in academic decision making* increased very strongly, but the *amount of student control in institutionwide decision making* increased even more strongly, very dramatically so. With regard to the increase in the *amount of student control in establishing regulations governing student conduct* as compared with control over *enforcing* those regulations, the pattern which has emerged so far holds true: the increase has been strong in both cases, but more so with regard to the establishment than with regard to the enforcement of regulations.

There is a very strong increase in the proportion of students participating in *voluntary community programs.* When it comes to such indicators of student modernity as increase in *underground publications and films* and increase in the proportion of *on-campus student protests,* however, the rate of increase has been moderate (thus, while students in these institutions have made great inroads in the sphere of control, a parallel increase in "deviant" students' subcultural traits has not emerged).

There has been a very slight decrease in *school spirit.* On those campuses on which *fraternities and sororities* exist, there has been a moderate increase in men and women joining.

It thus seems that on these campuses changes toward modernity are primarily changes in student power, not in the general character of the student subculture.

d. Dismissals for nonacademic reasons   No trend in either direction is apparent.

e. Quality of student preparation in high school   This is the single most remarkable finding: There is an extremely strong increase generally in the quality of high school preparation of those students who enter the college. Of the 20 colleges in the sample, 19 report an increase. This certainly reflects a greater diversity of the student body: schools are more selective and broaden their constituency; this is reflected in the better quality of future freshmen.

The Faculty *a. Faculty mobility* There has been moderate decline in the *amount of faculty turnover.* In this particular case, this decline can be interpreted as an increase in social mobility rather than a decrease in geographic mobility: it is likely that the faculty at the now secular college are better paid and enjoy more favorable working conditions than their predecessors under sectarian rule, a fact which would tend to encourage faculty members to stay on. This is at least to a certain degree borne out by the fact that there has been a moderate increase in the *proportion of tenured faculty* and that there has been a slight decrease in the *average age when tenure is awarded.* Change in control does not bring about dramatic changes in faculty mobility as might be expected, especially when compared with the samplewide trend.

b. Faculty commitment *Commitment toward teaching* shows a moderate increase, *commitment toward research* a stronger increase. There has been a marked decrease in the *number of hours spent in teaching,* which no doubt reflects better working conditions than existed under sectarian rule. The increase in the *number of hours spent in research* is quite strong; it seems that there has been a rough transfer of time from teaching to research.

Very interesting is the rather strong decrease in the *commitment toward institution.* This no doubt reflects a higher degree of "professionalism" on the part of today's teachers at these formerly sectarian schools.

Faculty commitment has thus clearly shifted from teaching to research, and quite possibly from loyalty to the institution to loyalty to the profession. Compared with the samplewide trend, the decrease in commitment toward institutions has been very strong indeed.

c. Faculty modernity The increase in *faculty efforts to promote student-faculty discussions* is very strong. *Faculty willingness to accept student course evaluation* is not nearly as strong, but this is understandable since the latter is a sensitive area, while the former is not (a teacher is certainly more willing to talk to students than to accept student course evaluation, which violates the principle that only the teacher's peers are permitted to judge his performance). *Faculty support of students opposing administration policies* is quite strong; one can certainly infer that the faculty in a nonsectarian college would tend to be more independent from the administration than in a sectarian college. Finally, *faculty willingness to experiment with new methods* increased very substantially.

It thus seems that the faculty in colleges which went from sectarian to nonsectarian control within the past two decades have definitely become more progressive in their relations with students.

d. Autonomy of faculty *External pressures limiting the freedom of the faculty* have decreased strongly. As the data concern private colleges and universities in which there would be little public interference in faculty affairs, the pressures which must have existed during the base year (1958) must have come from the church. Academic freedom does seem to have improved along with a shift of control from sectarian to nonsectarian. Faculty autonomy in *grading* has increased moderately, and so has *faculty autonomy in academic programs* (the latter has increased more strongly). The increase in *faculty involvement in determining institutionwide policies* is, despite the small size of the sample, short of phenomenal: every school reports an increase. A smaller, but still strong, increase has happened with respect to proportion of *faculty publicly advocating positions regarding national policies.*

Faculty autonomy in schools which went from sectarian to nonsectarian control has thus increased strongly. The data do not permit the inference that the change in control did result in this increase, but this is certainly the most likely explanation.

The Administration

a. Scope of administrative authority The shift in control from sectarian to nonsectarian does not seem to have brought about a radical change in *alumni influence on institutional policy making;* the increase is only slight, as is *state department of education influence on institutional policy making.* However, while relatively moderate, the latter influence has to be explained — while colleges and universities are, in general, self-policing, with regard to minimal quality standards, through their trade associations which accredit or fail to accredit a particular institution, state departments of education can act as regulatory agencies too by permitting or prohibiting a certain institution from granting degrees. It is most probably to this fact that state department of education influence on institutional policy making refers. Recent examples have indeed shown that these departments do take their watchdog role seriously. Where the schools are part of multicampus institutions, the *authority of the central campus administration* has slightly declined. A slight decline is also apparent for the number of *institutionwide requirements for undergraduate degrees.* While one would expect that decline would be followed by an increase of the same magnitude in the number of *departmental requirements for undergraduate degrees,* this is not so — no trend toward either increase or decline is visible. There has been a rather strong increase in the number of *cooperative programs with local industry* and a nearly phenomenal increase (including all but one institution) in the number of *working relations with other colleges and universities.* Colleges that went from sectarian to nonsectarian control obviously lost their main support (the support may or may not have been financial) and had to find support elsewhere — which they must have done by establishing closer ties with other colleges and local groups. Also, the lack of parochial church support may finally have made it possible for some colleges to establish professional relations that were not necessary or possible before.

b. Modernity of administration The increase in *administrative attempts to attract students from disadvantaged homes* has been very strong indeed, as have *administrative attempts to increase communication* with the other two constituent groups on campus — all institutions in the sample report an increase in the latter. On the other hand, the decrease in the *degree to which the institution controls student behavior* has also been very strong.

Thus, if one is to believe the presidents of colleges that have gone from sectarian to nonsectarian control, the increase in modernity has been very strong in the last 10 years, possibly because the breakaway from church domination gave the institutions an opportunity to experiment with innovations.

c. Length of service of major administrative officers The increase has been slight only.

d. Financing of institution The schools which went from sectarian to nonsectarian control show a very strong increase in the *proportion of the total budget based on federal support.* While the data give no information about the form of these appropriations and about their extent, it can be assumed that they are a vital source of income for the colleges. Breaking away from the church may have helped them to get funds they wouldn't have been given before, or at least not as easily. The *percentage of total budget based on alumni support* has increased too, but not nearly as much as federal support. However, it is a remarkable rate of increase in comparison with other schools in the sample — in a good many of these schools, the more recent alumni (those who graduated after the change in control) may contribute more than did the old alumni, i.e., those who graduated from the sectarian college.

FROM TEACHER PRE-PARATORY TO EXPANDED PROGRAM
Of the 1,230 institutions represented in the study, 57 have made the transition from teacher preparatory to expanded programs. This is a large enough group so that some fairly interesting conclusions can be drawn about what the change seems to bring. The changes are quite pervasive and indicate that as an institution moves from teacher prep to expanded programs it takes on the aura of the "big time."

Students
Certainly as institutions make this transition they tend to become more open in terms of the heterogeneity of student body. In ethnic composition, religious background, socioeconomic status, political affiliation, and age, the institutions that have made this transition show an increase in heterogeneity above the national percentages (even here, however, it should be pointed out that ethnicity is more of a factor in this diversity than is social class. Sixty-six percent of the institutions that have moved from teacher prep to expanded programs report an increase in heterogeneity of students by race, whereas only forty-nine percent of them report a similar increase in student heterogeneity by social class). They also are above the national figures for percentage of out-of-state students, percentage of foreign students, and percentage of married students, which indicates again a marked increase in the diversity of student body in these institutions. The quality of students in these institutions that have made the transition has shown a remarkable jump. In the national sample 67 percent of the institutions report an increase in quality of student preparation in high school, whereas of the institutions that have moved from teacher preparation to expanded programs, 89 percent of the institutions report an increase in the quality of high school preparation. They clearly are now attract-

ing students who are more hungry for higher education. Nationally, 73 percent of the institutions report an increase in the percentage of graduating class planning on continuing education, whereas in institutions that have moved from teacher prep to expanded programs, 95 percent report an increase in the percent of graduating class going on for further education. While 50 percent of the national sample report an increase in the proportion of transfers entering the institution, in the teacher preparatory to expanded program institutions 82 percent report an increase in transfers.

The student body then could be perhaps classified as "on the make." They want more of higher education, they are more carefully selected, and they plan to continue their education for a longer period of time. Unfortunately there are certain costs and casualties which seem to go with this kind of transition in regard to the student body. While nationally 27 percent of the institutions report an increase in the amount of on-campus student protests, in the transitional institutions moving from teacher prep to expanded programs 35 percent of the institutions report such an increase. At the same time 21 percent of these transitional institutions report an increase in underground publications and films as against 16 percent on the national sample. While school spirit has increased in 9 percent of the institutions nationally, it has increased 5 percent in the transitional institutions. This would also suggest that the students who are currently enrolled in these institutions are brighter, are more interested in higher education, plan to stay in longer, and are less malleable and more independent than previously. They also clearly are picking up a number of the folkways and mores of students at the major universities.

There is also a significant increase in the percentage of graduate students to undergraduates in these institutions. Nationally 21 percent of the institutions show a ratio favoring graduate students to undergraduates, whereas in these transitional institutions 49 percent show an increase in the number of graduates to undergraduates. They too are interested in completing their programs. Nationally, 20 percent of the institutions report an increase in the percentage of graduates who complete the degree requirements, whereas in the transitional institutions, from teacher prep to expanded programs, 51 percent report an increase in the percentage of completion of graduate degrees. Although this all suggests a move toward the avant-garde or "new" university, it also should be pointed out that they have had the largest increase in the number of men and women who join fraternities and sororities of any break-down of our institutions. Nationally only 8 percent report an increase in the number of men and women joining fraternities and sororities, whereas in this case 32 percent of the institutions report an increase in the number of men joining fraternities, and 36 percent report an increase in the number of women joining sororities. This suggests that although these institutions are moving *intellectually* toward the model of the great universities in terms of the social life on campus, they still perhaps represent the more cohesive, fraternal model of an earlier time.

Faculty The faculty study shows some truly astonishing divergences from the national data for those faculty in institutions that have moved from teacher preparation to expanded programs. Just as we suggested earlier that they are beginning to attract "big-time" students, it also could be said that they are attracting "big-time" faculty. In any such operation a change of this sort generally produces a significant alteration in the faculty culture and reward system, and some sort of housecleaning is necessary. As the structure changes and research becomes more significant in the reward structure, one would naturally suspect a high degree of faculty turnover. The data indeed support this conclusion. Nationally 9 percent of the institutions report an increased faculty turnover, whereas of the 57 in our transitional group 38 percent report an increase in faculty turnover. This would suggest that some of the individuals who fit well into a teacher preparation model were simply unprepared for the new demands of research skills and sophistications and left the institution.

In their desire to expand their horizons, these institutions have also expanded the number of faculty positions available and tried to fill them with "bright young men." Nationally 42 percent of the institutions report an increase in the percentage of tenured faculty, while within the institutional group that has moved from teacher preparation to expanded programs, only 5 percent report an increase in the percentage of tenured faculty. Also nationally 23 percent of the institutions report that tenure is awarded at an earlier and earlier age, while in this transitional collection of institutions 34 percent report a decreased age at tenure, suggesting once again the importance of luring younger faculty to the institution and then trying to set a reward structure that will keep them there.

As further evidence of "big-time" orientation, the commitment toward teaching has declined significantly at these institutions, and the commitment toward research has shown a sharp increase. Perhaps the strongest evidence of all is the commitment toward the institution, which has declined in 34 percent of the institutions that have moved from teacher prep to expanded programs, while nationally it has only declined in 3 percent of the institutions. On the commitment toward research, 20 percent more of the transitional institutions report an increase than is true of the national sample. With regard to hours spent in teaching and research, faculty are spending far fewer hours in teaching than the national average and spending many more hours in research than the national average institution. Also external pressures limiting the freedom of faculty have declined twice that of the national sample of institutions.

In this almost classic picture of the "on the make" faculty, we would suspect that faculty support of students who oppose administrative policies and the percentage of faculty publicly advocating positions on national policies would also be high. The data indeed bear this out. While nationally 29 percent of the institutions report increased faculty support of students who oppose the administration, in the transitional group of institutions that have moved from teacher prep to expanded programs 49 percent of the institutions report increased faculty support of students who oppose the administration. Nationally 41 percent of the institutions report an increase in the percentage of faculty who advocate positions on national policy matters, while within the transitional institutions 58 percent of the institutions so report. Also the institutions in this group are interesting in that the faculty are less willing to accept student course evaluation than nationally and they are also significantly less willing to experiment with new methods and devices.

All of this suggests a faculty culture which has done a sharp about-face in the last few years. The teacher preparation program naturally showed a commitment toward pedagogy and the analysis of pedagogy, whereas the institution is hell-bent for research. This commitment can be seen in terms of the kind of young teacher the institution is trying to attract, the reward system it has established for faculty, the increased number of faculty who leave because they cannot measure up to the new requirements, the large decline of faculty interest and time spent in teaching and an increasing pickup of time in research activities, and the loss of commitment toward the institution and the increasing faculty autonomy and willingness to support students who defy the administration. At the same time one sees political liberalism emerging, one also sees, unfortunately, academic and intellectual conservatism in faculty attitudes toward the institution.

Administration One statistic emerges from this collection of data as the most interesting difference between the sample of institutions here and our national sample. That is in the area of the number of departmental requirements for undergraduate degrees. Nationally, 12 percent of the institutions report an increase in departmental requirements, whereas in this group of transitional institutions 47 percent report an increase in departmental requirements for the degree. This then is an institution in which the department now reigns supreme and "standards" are being established which may differ significantly from previous ideas of student reward and assessment systems.

At the same time that the faculty power has obviously been increasing through more clearly defined structures and rules, the central administration has clearly lost ground in terms of the power relationship with other campus factions. Fifty-two percent of the institutions in the transitional group report a loss in the institution's ability to control student behavior compared with 35 percent of the national sample which so reports. It also would appear that administrative officers do not last as long in these institutions as they do nationally. In these institutions there seems to be little evidence of counter forces that could perhaps force the institution to reassess its position from time to time. Alumni support is low, alumni have relatively little influence on policy making at the institution, and the state department of education has very little influence on institutional policy. A number of these institutions have probably expanded the student body and faculty very quickly and have been assured additional funding from the state to implement their graduate programs.

All this suggests a condition which could be called the "euphoria of rapid growth." During this transitional period, faculty typically forget the institution at which they work and concentrate on departmental and personal achievement. Undergraduates are characteristically neglected and attention is focused instead on the graduate student. As legislators begin to level off the funding available from the state sources for higher education and as the same applies on the federal level, these institutions may well be caught in an agony of rising expectations in which the faculty, having always gotten everything they asked for, will be unable or unwilling to adapt to a more stringent budgetary arrangement where money will have to be spent for either one project or another but not both. The undergraduate students who are now admitted to these institutions are superior to the students in the past and will not be willing to be led around by the nose. This means that more attention will have to be paid to them and their perceptions about the inadequacies of the undergraduate curriculum. The central campus administration clearly has a major responsibility here in terms of educating or re-educating the faculty to a new or a renewed commitment to the undergraduate sector of the institution.

FROM SMALL TO LARGE The total enrollment in American higher education increased dramatically within the last 20 years, part of the higher enrollment being absorbed by new institutions; but most of it had to be absorbed by existing ones. Large schools grew to giant size, small schools to medium size, etc. The most interesting changes occurred, however, in those which grew from small (1,000 students or fewer) to large size (between 5,000 and 15,000). As the size of these institutions grew more dramatically within a relatively short time, it had been expected that student body, faculty, and administration per se, as well as the relationships among these groups, would have changed considerably.

The Student Body *a. Openness of institution* It is remarkable that while the heterogeneity of the student body increased, it did so to a lesser extent than for the sample as a whole, with the exception of *socioeconomic background,* which increased strongly and significantly more so than for the sample as a whole; also the proportion of *married students* increased very strongly, again significantly more than samplewide. The increase in the proportion of *transfer students entering institutions* was strong for both the subsample and the sample as a whole.

With regard to all other factors affecting the openness of these schools, the growth rate was less than that for the whole sample; but *ethnic composition* increased strongly—that is to say, a great many schools reported some increase—while *religious background* increased only slightly, as did *political affiliation. Age, heterogeneity,* and the proportion of *foreign students* increased moderately; the proportion of *out-of-state students* markedly. Thus, while these rapidly growing schools showed a significant increase in the heterogeneity of the student body, the increase was not as large as expected.

b. Effectiveness of institution   The increase in the proportion of *freshmen completing their degree requirements* was high, somewhat more so than for the total sample, while the increase in the proportion of *graduate students completing their degree requirements* (on those campuses which had graduate programs) was only moderate, but still considerably more so than for the sample as a whole. The proportion of *dismissals for academic reasons* grew slightly. Interestingly enough, while the proportion of the *graduating class planning on continued education* grew strongly, it did so to a far lesser extent than the one visible in the total sample. The proportion of *graduate to undergraduate students* increased moderately, more so than in the sample as a whole.

Thus, while these growing institutions are no doubt now more effective than they were 20 years ago, their overall degree of effectiveness is not higher than that for the sample as a whole.

c. Modernity of the student body   A very strong increase, more so than in the total sample, has taken place with respect to the amount of *student control in academic decision making,* the amount of *student control in institutionwide policy formation,* the amount of *student control in establishing regulations governing the conduct of the student body,* and the amount of *student control in enforcing these regulations.* The increasing size of the student body must clearly have given students a greater bargaining power than they had when they only constituted a relatively small group.

The proportion of *students participating in voluntary community projects* increased very strongly too, again more so than in the total sample, while the proportion of *on-campus student protests* increased to a far lesser extent, but still more so than for the sample as a whole.

A very clear decrease of *school spirit* occurred, although it shows a slight increase for the total sample. As the institution grew rapidly, the cohesiveness of the student body must have been affected so that no really high level of loyalty to the institution could develop. There may, however, be a more convincing reason: It is most likely that an institution which grows within 20 years from an enrollment of 1,000 to at least 5 times its size does at least partly cease to be a residential school, with the result that the nonresidents will participate less than the residents in activities that reflect school spirit. The *number of men joining fraternities* and the *number of women joining sororities* on campuses having Greek societies increased slightly, in both cases more so than for the total sample.

The data suggest that the modernity of the student body increased very strongly with regard to student participation in the governance of the school, but that there was a simultaneous, though far weaker, increase in traditionalism, a phenomenon also seen elsewhere.

d. Dismissals for nonacademic reasons   While there was a very slight decrease for the sample as a whole, no such trend was apparent for the subsample of rapidly growing schools. The net trend indicates that for the subsample as a whole the level of dismissals for nonacademic reasons was unchanged over the last decade.

e. Quality of student preparation in high school   Though the increase was quite strong, it was considerably weaker than for the sample as a whole. This may very well indicate that while the quality of high school education increased nationally, the rapidly expanding institutions became relatively less selective than they were as small colleges.

The Faculty   *a. Faculty mobility*   As could be expected, the amount of *faculty turnover* increased considerably more in the rapidly expanding schools than in the sample as a whole. It is likely that the heavy influx of new, relatively better educated faculty must have driven out at least part of the "leftover" faculty from the good old days of the school as a small college. The proportion of *tenured faculty* increased markedly, but less so than for the sample in general. The *average age when tenure is awarded* decreased markedly, considerably more so than for the sample as a whole. The data thus suggest that the rapidly growing school is one which rewards the young faculty it really wants to keep by giving them tenure early, but that it is not a place where tenure in general is easier to get than in other schools; the opposite may be true.

b. Faculty commitment   While *commitment toward teaching* increased for the sample as a whole, it decreased in the rapidly expanding schools, a clear sign that the formerly instruction-oriented colleges are on the way to becoming research-oriented universities. *Commitment toward research* showed a rather marked increase, as it did for the whole sample. *Hours spent in teaching* decreased strongly, while *hours spent in research* increased markedly—in both cases the trend was stronger than the samplewide trend. This would seem to bear out the proposition that the increase in size also meant a move from "college" to "university." The most interesting finding, however, concerns *commitment toward the institution:* for the sample as a whole, there was a decline, but a very slight one indeed. The newly expanding institutions, however, showed a strong decrease in faculty commitment toward the institution. This seemed to corroborate an earlier finding that this type of institution is not likely to offer most of its new faculty the kinds of amenities that instill a certain amount of institutional loyalty, and this in turn would seem to strengthen a teacher's commitment to his profession.

c. Faculty modernity *Faculty efforts to promote student-faculty discussions* increased strongly, but not nearly so much as in the sample as a whole. As opposed to the general trend in colleges and universities, which show a marked increase in *faculty willingness to accept student course evaluations,* the increase was only slight in the rapidly expanding institutions. This may partly be because of the somewhat insecure position of many faculty at these schools—they are likely to want to hold on to such prerogatives as autonomy in planning their courses. However, where the faculty's direct interests were not threatened, they seemed more willing than their colleagues at other schools to side with students against the administration by *supporting students opposing administration policies.* The increase was strong as opposed to a moderate increase for the sample as a whole. Faculty at these rapidly expanding institutions also showed a considerably stronger increase in their *public advocacy of positions regarding national policies* than their colleagues elsewhere. *Faculty willingness to experiment with new methods* grew very strongly in such schools, but not quite as strongly as in the sample as a whole.

d. Faculty autonomy *External pressures limiting freedom of the faculty* decreased slightly, as they did for the sample as a whole—as the school expands, the faculty seem to be able to discourage such pressures more effectively. *Faculty autonomy in grading* increased only slightly because this was, at least until recently, one of the undisputed prerogatives of the faculty. *Faculty autonomy in academic programs* increased moderately, possibly indicating that in the course of the last decade or so the faculty were able to gain more control from the administration over academic programs such as curriculum planning. There was a very strong increase in faculty involvement in determining institutionwide policies, a trend which held true to roughly the same extent for the sample as a whole. The proportion of *faculty publicly advocating positions regarding national politics* grew very strongly, much more so than for the sample as a whole. This may indicate that the tensions between faculty and administration in these rapidly expanding schools are particularly acute.

On the whole, faculty autonomy grew considerably as it has in the sample as a whole.

The Administration

a. Alumni influence on institutional policy making increased very slightly, while the *influence of the state department of education on institutional policy making* increased more strongly—two trends which were true to about the same extent for all schools in the sample. On those campuses which are part of multicampus institutions, there was a slight increase in the *authority of the central campus administration,* but a decrease for the sample as a whole. No change was apparent with regard to the *number of institution-wide requirements for undergraduate degrees,* while there was a very slight increase in the *number of departmental requirements for undergraduate degrees.* The *number of cooperative programs with local industry* increased very strongly, almost twice as strongly as within the sample as a whole. Most of the increase was probably due to research contracts with local industry, and also to a more comprehensive educational program that may fit the needs of local industry better than the more restricted academic program of the former small school. In line with the general trend, the *number of working relations with other colleges and universities* increased very strongly.

The scope of administrative authority thus increased rather strongly, although not as strongly as one might expect. Since it is primarily the administration which plans and implements the changes affecting the school as a whole, the dramatic expansion of the size of these schools might have suggested an equally dramatic increase in the scope of administrative authority.

b. Modernity of administration *Attempts to attract students from disadvantaged homes* increased extremely, much more so than in the sample as a whole. This suggests that the increase in size of the institution also resulted in a considerably more open admissions policy than was the case when the school had college status only. *Administrative attempts to increase communication* within the institution, as in other types of schools, also increased very strongly. The *degree to which the institution controls student behavior* decreased strongly, more so than in the sample as a whole. These data suggest that, compared with college and university administrations in general, schools which have rapidly and dramatically increased in size are more likely to exhibit modern characteristics.

c. Length of service of major administrative officers While there was a slight increase in the sample as a whole, no particular trend emerged for those institutions which moved from small to large in size.

d. The financing of the institution The proportion of the *total budget based on federal support* increased greatly, much more so than for the sample as a whole, while the proportion of the *total budget based on alumni support* increased very slightly and significantly less so than for colleges and universities in the sample in general. This seems to suggest that a majority of the institutions in the present subsample are publicly controlled; it is almost impossible to imagine any significant number of private institutions that would be able to expand fivefold or more within a period of two decades.

FROM TWO-YEAR TO FOUR-YEAR STATUS Eighty-nine two-year colleges became four-year colleges in the period between 1948 and 1968. While this only represents about 8 percent of the total sample, it is nevertheless a move which has occurred with a certain frequency, and one which has important consequences for the school. This is true in many respects; a school that wants to become a four-year institution has to hire new faculty with considerably better academic qualifications (while the professional qualifications of many two-year college faculties are hardly different from those of high school teachers, four-year colleges strive as much as possible to emulate the larger universities in terms of the academic respectability of its faculty—almost every catalog of a four-year college will mention the ratio of Ph.D's on its faculty, while a two-year college doesn't usually brag about its doctoral holders). However, much more than a changing faculty is involved—student selection is likely to become stricter, the range of programs is likely to be expanded significantly, library resources are likely to be improved considerably, etc. The change from two-year to four-year status is likely to bring about even more radical changes in the institution than the change from college to university.

The Student Body
a. Openness of Institution As in the sample as a whole, there has been a strong increase in the heterogeneity of *ethnic composition* of the student body. Though less marked, the increase in heterogeneity in *socioeconomic background* has been strong (more so than for the sample as a whole), while the increases in heterogeneity for *religious background, political affiliation, and age* have been considerably weaker.

The proportion of *out-of-state students* has increased strongly, much more so than for the sample as a whole—while two-year colleges tend to have a local constituency, a four-year college would likely have to broaden its constituency and attract students from beyond the community or the local area. While only a certain proportion of four-year colleges has a national constituency, the others would in most cases tend to have at least a regional appeal. As in the sample as a whole, the proportion of *foreign students* has increased markedly and that of *married students* strongly. The increase in the proportion of transfer students has been very strong, significantly stronger than for the sample as a whole. This is most probably due to the increase in points of transfer, a term we have discussed earlier.

Thus, two-year colleges that became four-year colleges have become considerably more open within the last 10 years (this is seemingly in contradiction with findings that show a greater openness for a two-year colleges than for four-year colleges; however, it may very well be that at least for the first few years after its conversion to a four-year college, the institution maintains a relatively higher degree of openness than the other more established four-year colleges).

b. Effectiveness of institution Just as in the sample as a whole, the proportion of *freshmen completing their degree requirements* has increased strongly in the "new" four-year colleges. The proportion of *dismissals for academic reasons* has increased very slightly, possibly because the new four-year college does not aim as much as the two-year college to retain all students it accepted.

The increase in the proportion of the *graduating class planning on continued education* is extremely strong, significantly more so than in the sample as a whole. One might expect that a school which only recently attained four-year college status would still to a large measure be vocationally oriented and/or terminal.

c. Modernity of student body As in the sample as a whole, the increase in the amount of *student control in academic decision making* has been strong; however, the increase in the amount of *student control in institutionwide policy formation* has been even stronger. Amount of *student control in establishing regulations governing student conduct* and amount of *student control in enforcing those regulations* have increased very strongly (more so than for the sample as a whole); again, as in the previous sections, the increase in *establishing* the regulations has been stronger than the increase in *enforcing* them. There has also been a very strong increase in the proportion of students *participating in voluntary community programs.* The increase in *underground publications and films* has been very slight on the new four-year college campuses, much slighter than in the sample as a whole. This would seem to suggest that some "subcultural" aspects of modern student life are missing on these campuses, a situation which is borne out by the fact that the proportion of *on-campus student protests* has increased only slightly, an increase which is significantly weaker than that for the sample as a whole.

School spirit has increased rather markedly, contrary to the general trend in the total sample. It may very well be that the increase is due to a larger number of resident students on campus who have the time and the interest to engage in school activities (as opposed to the vocationally oriented two-year college where students commute and have less time for "collegiate activities). As in the sample as a whole, the *number of men joining fraternities* and *number of women joining sororities* have increased only very slightly.

The strongest increase has thus occurred in student participation in the governance of their institution, a trend which was not duplicated by an equally strong trend toward a modern student subculture per se.

d. Dismissals for nonacademic reasons   As in the case of all schools in the sample, dismissals for nonacademic reasons have decreased very slightly.

e. Quality of student preparation in high school   The quality of student preparation in high school has increased very strongly, somewhat more so than for the sample as a whole. When the two-year colleges became four-year institutions, they probably became somewhat more selective in their admissions policies (although the actual degree of selectivity is probably still low compared with many long-established colleges and universities).

The Faculty   *a. Faculty mobility*   In line with the general trend, the increase in the *amount of faculty turnover* has been very slight; however, the *proportion of tenured faculty* has increased very strongly, significantly more so than for the sample as a whole. The *average age when tenure is awarded* has decreased slightly, but not quite as much as is the case for the sample as a whole. These three trends together seem to indicate that no revolutionary changes have happened in the composition of the faculty; it may very well be that faculty "quality" was increased to a certain extent by promoting and granting tenure to teachers who went through the transition from two-year to four-year college.

b. Faculty commitment   *Commitment toward teaching* has increased markedly, considerably more so than is the case for the whole sample. *Commitment toward research* has increased more strongly, and again more so than for the whole sample. Curiously enough, *hours spent in teaching* have increased markedly, while they decreased strongly for the sample as a whole. *Hours spent in research* have increased only moderately, somewhat less so than for the total sample. While the *commitment toward the institution* has decreased very slightly in general, there has been an increase for the new four-year colleges.

It seems that the new four-year colleges have thus become institutions in which teachers are very committed to teaching and to their institution. While in some previous sections the increase in commitment toward teaching could possibly be attributed to lighter teaching loads, this does not seem to be the case in the new four-year institutions, where an increase in commitment toward research has been accompanied by an increase of the same magnitude in hours spent teaching. The explanation must be that other things not measured by the questionnaire have improved—higher status, higher salaries, and a more generalized policy of awarding tenure may account for increases in commitment toward teaching and toward the institution.

c. Faculty modernity *Efforts to promote student-faculty discussions* have increased very strongly, as is the case for all institutions in general. But as for the sample as a whole, *faculty willingness to accept student course evaluation* has increased considerably less. *Faculty support of students opposing administration policies* has increased only moderately, significantly less than for colleges and universities in general. *Faculty willingness to experiment with new methods* has increased very strongly, as in all institutions in the sample.

It thus seems that teachers in the new four-year colleges have indeed become more modern, but not significantly more than in other schools.

d. Faculty autonomy *External pressures limiting the freedom of faculty* decreased moderately on the new four-year college campuses. *Faculty autonomy in grading* shows a moderate increase, *faculty autonomy in academic programs* shows a rather marked increase, and *faculty autonomy in institutionwide policies* shows an extremely strong increase. In all these cases, the trend for the new colleges follows that for the sample in general but is more pronounced, indicating that faculty in the new colleges have taken larger steps toward academic freedom than their colleagues in the sample as a whole.

The *proportion of the faculty publicly advocating positions with respect to national policies* has increased rather markedly, but somewhat less so than is the case for the sample as a whole. This would indicate that the faculty on "new" college campuses are probably more concerned with consolidating their positions than are their colleagues on more established campuses.

a. Scope of administrative authority *Alumni influence on institutional policy making* has increased very slightly, while the increase in *state department of education influence on institutional policy making* has been more marked. In cases where the new college is part of a multicampus institution, the *authority of the central campus administration* has decreased very slightly. In all three cases, the trend is of the same magnitude for both the new colleges and the sample as a whole.

The *number of institutionwide requirements for undergraduate degrees* has increased slightly, more so than for the total sample, while the *number of departmental requirements* for the same degree has increased moderately, again significantly more than for other institutions in the sample. The relatively stronger increase in departmental requirements reflects the increasing autonomy of the departments.

The *number of cooperative programs with local industry* has increased markedly, but not quite as much as for the sample as a whole, while the *number of working relations with other colleges and universities* has increased very strongly, as it did for the total sample.

There is thus no doubt that the scope of administrative authority in the new colleges has grown, but not to the point of encroaching on the faculty's newly acquired rights.

b. Modernity of administration While the sample as a whole shows a very strong increase in the *administrative attempts to attract students from disadvantaged homes,* the trend is less marked for the new colleges—which possibly reflects the fact that at least for the first few years the new college follows an open-door policy similar to that of a two-year college. The increase in *administrative attempts to increase communication* within the college is very strong. There has been a moderate decrease in the *degree to which the institution* controls student behavior, very much in line with the general trend.

c. Length of service of major administrative officers The length of service of major administrative officers has increased rather markedly, considerably more so than is the case for the sample as a whole, indicating that administrative "housecleaning" does not accompany this change from two- to four-year programs.

d. The financing of the institution The *percentage of the total budget based on federal support* has increased strongly, but slightly less than for the sample as a whole, while the *percentage of the total budget based on alumni support* has increased moderately only, but more so than for the sample as a whole.

FROM B.A. OR M.A. TO PH.D. Of the total 1,230 schools in the sample, 61 moved from B.A.- or M.A.-granting institutions to Ph.D.-granting universities. For the purpose of this section, B.A.- and M.A.-granting institutions are combined, although the two types together include a wide range of different schools. It would of course be unrealistic to expect all schools having moved up to Ph.D.-granting status to be a homogeneous group—just as the B.A.- and M.A.-granting status includes a wide range of schools, the Ph.D.-granting status is equally wide. Some of these schools may have become full or comprehensive schools offering a large number of doctoral programs, while many of them may in fact be semiuniversities offering doctoral programs in only a few select fields. It is not at all unlikely that this one trend actually incorporates two different ones: the first trend would be from a B.A.-granting institution (i.e., from a school which may or may not have had a range of M.A. programs) to a semiuniversity; the second trend is likely to be from an M.A.-granting institution (which probably offered a wide range of M.A. programs) to a comprehensive university, through the semiuniversity stage. While there are no data on the particular step taken by any given institution, these two probable trends will have to be kept in mind in the analysis.

The Student Body *a. Openness of institution* Both the *ethnic composition* and the *socioeconomic background* of the student body show a strong increase in heterogeneity (the increase in the latter is considerably above the increase for the whole sample). Increases in heterogeneity by *religious background, political affiliation,* and *age* are weaker (but in the case of the latter still much stronger than the average for the whole sample). The data show clearly that while the schools in the subsample have, as a group, become substantially more open to hitherto underrepresented groups, it is really the ethnic minorities and the lower social classes who have primarily profited from this openness.

While the proportion of *out-of-state students* has increased strongly, the proportion of *foreign students, married students,* and *transfer students* has increased considerably more. Compared with the samplewide rate of increase, the increase in foreign students has been dramatic. This seems to be the result of increased visibility of these institutions: as full universities or semiuniversities they are likely to be better known than as colleges. Also, a large proportion of foreign students (especially from overseas) come to the United States for graduate studies on the doctoral level and would thus hardly fit into the pattern of a college, even if it offered M.A. programs.

It thus seems that the institutions in the subsample have become more open in both geographic and social terms, but primarily in the latter.

b. Effectiveness of institution   The proportion of *freshmen completing their degree requirements* has increased strongly in line with the samplewide trend, but the increase has been much stronger with regard to the proportion of *graduate students completing their degree requirements.* The latter trend is especially interesting when compared with the samplewide increase which is only moderate: schools which move toward university status obviously carry out vast changes with respect to their graduate programs; and since these changes obviously make graduate studies much more attractive than before to students, the school's retention rate becomes higher. Although the evidence is lacking, this finding might suggest that such a new Ph.D.-granting school is able to attract a better type of graduate student than it did before as a primarily undergraduate institution.

The high propensity to retain graduate students in these new Ph.D.-granting universities is also reflected in the fact that the proportion of *dismissals for academic reasons* has hardly grown at all. These schools with recent university status also seem to have made great progress in encouraging their *graduating classes to plan on continued education*—the overwhelming majority of the new Ph.D.-granting universities report such an increase. Again, this can best be explained in terms of the visibility of graduate programs: small, first-year graduate programs at small colleges are less likely to be nationally or regionally visible to the undergraduate than larger, Ph.D.-level graduate programs. Also, since the faculty in the latter schools are in general more visibly interested in graduate students, undergraduates must feel that there are advantages to being a graduate student at such a school, in terms of what a student can expect from the faculty.

Not surprisingly, the establishment of doctoral programs also meant a very strong increase in the proportion of *graduate to undergraduate students*—even in "complex" colleges the main emphasis is on undergraduate instruction, which is reflected in a relatively lower proportion of graduate students as compared with universities which emphasize graduate rather than undergraduate instruction. The samplewide increase in the proportion of graduate to undergraduate students is only moderate; it is thus the school growing in comprehensiveness which is most likely to show a sharp increase in the proportion of graduate students.

c. Modernity of student body The amount of *student control in academic decision making* has strongly increased, but the amount of *student control in institutionwide policy formation* has increased even more markedly, which follows the trend for the whole sample. This may reflect the interesting fact that once students became involved in governance, their interest did not stop with the issue of academic decision making but went further to the governance of the school as a whole (the transition from an almost total lack of interest—the traditional student government concept has nothing whatsoever to do with real governance—to a very pronounced interest of some students in the running of schools has happened in an amazingly short time).

The amount of *student control in establishing regulations governing student conduct* has increased very strongly, considerably more so than the amount of *student control in enforcing regulations governing student conduct*. The trend follows that reflected in the whole sample, and as for the latter the explanation may be that the enforcement of regulations obviously comes after the establishment of such regulations and that the enforcement procedure takes time to become operational, also, it can be assumed that students are more hesitant to apply the rules and to actually police their peers than to create such rules.

A very strong increase is noticeable with respect to the proportion of *students participating in voluntary community projects,* the same trend that can be observed overall in the sample. The increase in *underground publications and films* has been moderate but still considerably stronger than for the whole sample. The increase in the proportion of *on-campus student protests* has been strong, almost twice as pronounced as in the total sample. This again may mean that the new university attracts a different type of student than did the college.

It so far appears that, in comparison with the total sample, new universities experienced an especially strong increase in student modernity. However, as we have pointed out before, a certain minor increase in traditionalism is the corollary to a strong increase in modernity. This trend is again evident for the schools which became Ph.D.-granting institutions within the past two decades: while the increase in *school spirit* has been slight and approximately equal to that in the total sample, there has been a stronger increase with regard to *number of men joining fraternities* and *number of women joining sororities* in those new universities that have Greek letter societies on campus—the increase has been considerably stronger than that for the whole sample. This relatively more marked increase may very well be the result of an increase in status of those societies which parallels with an increase in status of the institution; it may well be that new, more prestigious, nationally affiliated fraternities and sororities spring up on a new university campus and that these societies are able to attract students who would not have joined one of the earlier societies.

d. Dismissals for nonacademic reasons These dismissals have decreased slightly, as they have for the whole sample, which may indicate both changes in student behavior and changes in faculty and administration attitudes.

e. Quality of student preparation in high school The quality of student preparation in high school has increased very strongly indeed, considerably more so than is the case within the whole sample. However, this result is not surprising: an institution that moves from a primarily undergraduate school to a university with a strong graduate program is likely to become more selective in this admission practice for *both* graduate and undergraduate students. While it is undoubtedly true that the academic level of high school education in general has increased over the last 20 years, the new university will also attempt to attract better freshmen than it was able to do as a college.

The Faculty *a. Faculty mobility* Faculty *commitment toward teaching* has decreased slightly, while *commitment toward research* has increased very strongly indeed. This general change in commitment is reflected in hours spent in teaching and in research: *hours spent in teaching* have decreased strongly, while *hours spent in research* have increased very strongly. In all four cases, these results differ very significantly from those for the whole sample in which there has actually been a moderate increase in commitment toward teaching and a somewhat stronger increase in commitment toward research, as well as a far less marked increase in hours spent in research. In terms of a transition from a college to a university the change in commitment from teaching to research is particularly typical; it can safely be assumed that the new impetus of research is due to the hiring of better, research-oriented faculty who chose to come to a "new" university because of research facilities and— a corollary—doctoral programs.

The ascent of this new breed of research-oriented faculty on the new university campus also explains the moderate decrease in *commitment toward institutions:* the new teacher finds the rewards for his work outside his campus, among his peers; the teacher remaining from the college days, however, is likely to become even more committed to his institution as a result of the college's move to university status because he knows that he cannot compete with his younger peers in terms of academic production. As one of the case studies to be reported in a later publication shows, old faculty are likely to become even more "inner-directed" and to band together as a result of institutional changes.

b. Faculty modernity While *faculty efforts to promote student-faculty discussions* have increased very strongly, *faculty willingness to accept student course evaluations* has increased considerably less, a situation which holds true for the sample as a whole. Faculty members are now much more willing to hold discussions with students than they were 10 years ago, probably because the new faculty members are younger and were themselves at least partly brought up in the "postcollegiate" area, and also because they simply have to discuss things with students since there is student pressure toward an increase in such discussions. Faculty willingness to accept student course evaluations is something else, however; student-faculty discussions per se have no influence on the prerogatives of the faculty, while student course evaluation obviously does. The fact that there has been an increase in faculty willingness to accept such evaluations by students can probably be attributed to the young teachers, rather than to the old ones who feel threatened by both their younger colleagues and their students. It is certainly due to those same young teachers that *faculty support of students opposing administrative policies* has increased — as a recent study shows, the junior faculty are much more likely to side with the students in case of a universitywide conflict than are the senior faculty (who would comprise the "old-timers"). In new universities, the degree of support is noticeably stronger than it is for the sample as a whole, and the young faculty contingent is probably larger.

Faculty willingness to experiment with new methods has increased very strongly, but not quite as strongly as for the sample as a whole. This slight difference may partly be explained in terms of the new faculty's research orientation — the research-oriented faculty are not likely to spend much energy on such a chore as teaching; it can be assumed that the innovations are brought about by those younger faculty members who have consciously opted in favor of teaching.

The new universities thus show a strong trend toward greater faculty modernity.

c. Faculty autonomy While there has been a certain sample-wide increase in *external pressures limiting the freedom of faculty,* the new universities show a moderate decrease — such external pressures are stronger on the faculty of less comprehensive schools than on those of universities; also, faculty members at less comprehensive institutions are less likely to have the means to protect themselves against such pressures than do faculty at universities where strong American Association of University Professors (AAUP) or American Federation of Teachers (AFT) chapters exist. This may again be linked to the inner-directedness of the faculty member at a less comprehensive institution who is more likely to have his peers inside the school and who therefore cannot mobilize his colleagues in other institutions. *Faculty autonomy in grading* shows a slight increase only, both in the new universities and for the sample as a whole: even in schools where faculty autonomy is very limited, the faculty are likely to have at least the prerogative of deciding on grades without interference from the administration. *Faculty autonomy in academic programs* has increased moderately, in this particular case probably as a result of the upgrading of graduate programs, a matter in which the faculty may have greater competence than the administration. A very strong increase has taken place with regard to *faculty involvement in determining institutionwide policies;* the increase is very slightly stronger for new universities than for the sample as a whole. Since the new breed of research-oriented faculty in new universities is the single most important asset that permitted a school to leave behind the "college" status, the faculty carry great potential power which they can actuate by demanding a share in the governance of their institution to a larger extent than did their predecessors in the old college days. The proportion of *faculty advocating positions regarding national policies* has also increased strongly, considerably more so than for the sample as a whole. Again, this trend must be due to the new faculty who are likely to be politically more radical than their colleagues from the old college days. Altogether, it can be said that faculty autonomy in the new universities has increased strongly.

The Administration   *a. Scope of administrative authority*   As in the sample as a whole, *alumni influence on institutional policy making* has increased only very slightly, a trend which can probably be explained by the decrease in the proportion of the total operating budget of many schools contributed by alumni. *State department of education influence on institutional policy making* has slightly increased in the new universities, as it has for all other institutions, a trend which probably reflects an increase in state appropriations for these institutions, of which many are publicly controlled. In those new universities which are part of multicampus institutions, there has been only a slight decrease in the *authority of the central campus administration,* probably because the new university was given a greater amount of autonomy for the specific purpose of upgrading its graduate programs. There has been a slight decrease in the *number of institutionwide requirements for undergraduate degrees,* coupled with a very slight decrease in the *number of departmental requirements for undergraduate degrees.* The first trend is as expected—the move from college to university is followed by a strengthening of the power of departments in the area of academic programs and a parallel decrease in the power of the central administration in the same area. But this assumption may be wrong insofar as the departments are concerned—the move from college to university may very well involve a great increase in enrollment, with a subsequent increase in the central administration's scope. For the sample as a whole, there has been a very slight increase in the number of institutionwide requirements and a somewhat larger increase in the number of departmental requirements. The increase in the *number of cooperative programs with local industry* is strong for both the new universities and for the sample as a whole, and for both groups the *number of working relations with other colleges and universities* has increased very strongly.

b. Modernity of administration The new universities, like the other institutions in the sample, show a strong increase in *administrative attempts to attract students from disadvantaged homes,* a trend which has resulted, as demonstrated before, in a strong increase in the heterogeneity of the student body in terms of socioeconomic characteristics. The increase in *administrative attempts to increase communication* among the three constituent groups of a school is extremely strong, slightly more so than for the sample as a whole. The *degree to which the institution controls student behavior* has decreased strongly for the new universities, somewhat more so than for the sample as a whole. This may best be explained in terms of a proportionate increase in graduate to undergraduate students in these universities; institutions of higher education in the United States have traditionally controlled the behavior of graduate students far less than that of undergraduate students. However, it is not only the proportional increase of graduate students but also the increasing unwillingness of schools to act *in loco parentis* for all students which has presumably led to this significant decrease.

Today's administration is much more modern than it was a decade ago, primarily so in the case of new universities.

c. Length of service of major administrative officers In both the new universities and the sample as a whole, the length of service of major administrative officers has increased slightly (this may not be true, though, for the top officer, the president—it would seem from the analysis of our presidents that the speed of the "circulation of the presidential elite" has increased very substantially within the last few years).

d. Financing of institution The *proportion of the total budget based on federal support* has increased very strongly for the new universities, noticeably more so than for the sample as a whole. This is certainly due to the influx of federal funds for the strengthening of the graduate program (the federally funded "centers of excellence" are a case in point), but also to the introduction of federal research contracts which the institution would not have obtained during its college stage.

The *proportion of the total budget based on alumni support* seems to have increased moderately. There is no ready explanation for this phenomenon, for it would seem that alumni might be reluctant to give much to an institution which may not conform to their image of the old alma mater any longer; in fact, some of these new universities have changed to such a degree that the only link between the old and the new institution may be the location, and even this may have changed. On the other hand, alumni, like anyone, like to "bet on a sure thing," and thus giving money to a university may have more related prestige than giving money to a mere college.

FROM FOUR-YEAR TO STATE COLLEGE The term "four-year college" is used to denote both private four-year colleges and those public four-year colleges which are not under state jurisdiction but rather under local jurisdiction. A "state college" is, in this case, a state-controlled institution which offers at least four-year programs and possibly graduate programs up to the M.A. level as well. In many take-over cases, the privately or municipally controlled institution is ailing both financially and academically, and the take-over by the state usually results in improving both finances and academic standards. As a state college, the institution is likely to add graduate programs. Forty-seven institutions in our sample have made this transition.

The Student Body *a. Openness of institution* As in the sample as a whole, there has been a strong increase in the heterogeneity of *ethnic composition,* followed by a slightly less marked one for *socioeconomic background.* The increase in heterogeneity of *religious background* is only moderate, considerably weaker than in the total sample.

A moderate increase has also taken place with respect to the heterogeneity of *political affiliation.* The increase in age heterogeneity has been strong, in fact twice as strong as the samplewide average.

Both the increases in the proportions of *out-of-state students* and *foreign students* are rather marked and conform approximately to the rate of increase for the sample as a whole. The increase in the proportion of *married students* and *transfer students* is strong, more so than for the total sample in both cases.

While the samplewide increases and the ones for the "new" state colleges do not exactly follow the same trend, the overall increase in the openness of the institution seems to be approximately the same for both the sample as a whole and for the new state colleges.

b. Effectiveness of institution The proportion of *freshmen completing their degree requirements* has increased strongly, somewhat more than average, while the proportion of *graduate students completing their degree requirements* has increased only slightly in those schools which have graduate programs. As in the total sample, there is hardly any change with regard to the proportion of *dismissals for academic reasons.* Interestingly enough, the proportion of the *graduating class planning on continued education,* though it has increased strongly, isn't nearly as high as that in the sample as a whole. This might possibly indicate that the new state colleges are for a time vocationally oriented, which seems to contradict the tendency of state colleges to expand their academic programs, build up graduate programs, and eventually turn into a state university. The proportion of *graduate to undergraduate students* on those new state college campuses which do have graduate programs has increased very slightly only, much less so than is the case for the total sample. This finding and that concerning the proportion of the graduating class planning on continued education may indicate that the new state colleges still have many of the attributes of their former status and still haven't reached the stage of the contemporary comprehensive state college.

c. Modernity of the student body Both the amount of *student control in institutionwide policy formation* and the amount of *student control in establishing regulations governing student conduct* have increased very strongly, significantly more so than in the sample as a whole. On the other hand, the amount of *student control in academic decision making* and the amount of *student control in enforcing the regulations governing student conduct* have increased somewhat less and conform to the samplewide average.

While the proportion of *students participating in voluntary community projects* has increased very strongly, the increase conforms approximately to the one for the whole sample. The increase in *underground publications and films* is slight only for the new state colleges and the total sample.

There has been a slight increase in *school spirit* in the sample as a whole, but the new state colleges show a very slight decline. This would tend to support the assumption that the new state colleges are still very much in transition. Both with regard to the *number of men joining fraternities* and the *number of women joining sororities* on those campuses where the Greek societies exist, the increase is very slight, as it is for the sample as a whole.

The modernity of the student body is thus primarily expressed in the increased scope of student participation in college affairs more in the area of social life than in academic affairs.

d. Dismissals for nonacademic reasons While there has been a very slight decline in the proportion of dismissals for nonacademic reasons samplewide, the new state colleges actually show a very slight increase.

e. Quality of student preparation in high school As in the total sample, the quality of student preparation in high school has increased very strongly.

The Faculty *a. Faculty mobility* Though slightly higher than average, the *amount of faculty turnover* has increased only slightly. The *proportion of tenured faculty* has increased strongly, but not significantly more than for the sample as a whole. As in the total sample, *average age when tenure is awarded* has decreased moderately. If there is any "standard" American college with respect to faculty mobility, the new state college comes nearest to it. There is no movement to unseat the former faculty group, and no immediate increase in "young Turk" factions. "Greatness" is still several steps away.

b. Faculty commitment *Commitment toward teaching* has increased markedly, more so than average, while *commitment toward research* has increased only slightly, considerably less than average.

While the total sample shows a strong decrease in *hours spent in teaching,* the new state colleges show a marked increase instead, but this is accompanied by a moderate (though weaker than average) increase in *hours spent in research.* It seems that the contradictions are more apparent than real—when the new state colleges were either private colleges or municipally controlled institutions, they may have had a somewhat lethargic faculty. It is likely that in the course of transformation new faculty were brought in who were *both* more interested in teaching and more interested in research (the two are not necessarily mutually exclusive for the average individual faculty member). While the *commitment toward the institution* has increased slightly only, there is nevertheless an increase compared to the very slight decrease in the sample as a whole. This again may indicate that the new state college hasn't reached a comprehensive stage yet at which commitment toward the institution will be replaced by commitment toward the profession. On the whole, the faculty at the new state colleges do therefore still seem to be committed to teaching and to the institution.

c. Faculty modernity With regard to the indicators for faculty modernity, the faculty at the new state colleges again seem to be very average in that their rates of increase are approximately those for the sample as a whole: *faculty efforts to promote student-faculty discussions* have increased very strongly, while *faculty willingness to accept student course evaluation* has increased far less—again a sign that the gap between noncommittal discussions and actual renunciation of some old prerogative, such as permitting students to judge a teacher's performance, is wide. The increase in faculty support of *students opposing administrative policies* is moderate. As in the whole sample, the increase in *faculty willingness to experiment with new methods* has been very strong, most probably because the faculty who teach at the new state college are not strongly threatening to the faculty who taught at the old college.

d. Faculty autonomy The *external pressures limiting the freedom of the faculty* have increased slightly; the same is true to the same degree for *faculty autonomy in grading.* Again, as in the total sample, *faculty autonomy in academic programs* has increased moderately. A significant difference exists between the sample as a whole and the faculty at the new state colleges with regard to *faculty involvement in determining institutionwide policies:*

the increase has been very strong in general but extremely strong in the case of faculty teaching in new state colleges. This may help to explain why there has been, contrary to the general trend, an increase in commitment toward the institution: faculty at the new state colleges have no major reasons for grudges against the institution. This would seem to be borne out by the fact that the proportion of *faculty publicly advocating positions regarding national policies* increased less strongly than average (advocating positions with regard to national policies may be one way of actually attacking the college administration indirectly). Faculty autonomy in these new state colleges has increased strongly, and very much so in such crucial areas of faculty involvement in institutionwide matters.

The Administration   *a. Scope of administrative authority* No change appears in *alumni influence on institutional policy making.* As could be expected, *state department of education influence on institutional policy making* has grown rather strongly (as opposed to a slight increase for the whole sample). For those institutions that are part of multicampus institutions, there has been a very slight decrease in the *authority of the central campus administration.*

A significant difference exists between the sample as a whole and the data on faculty in new state colleges regarding the increase in the *number of institutionwide requirements for undergraduate degrees:* while the increase is extremely slight for the total sample, it is rather marked for the new state colleges. But this does not necessarily mean that some power was taken away from the faculty; there is a moderate increase (as opposed to a slight one for the total sample) in the *number of departmental requirements for undergraduate degrees.* The *number of cooperative programs with local industry* has increased very strongly, almost twice as much as in the sample as a whole. As is true for all schools, the *number of working relations with other colleges and universities* has increased very strongly.

While not markedly, as for other types of schools, the administration of the new state colleges nevertheless has been able to increase the scope of its authority, although the increase occurred primarily in its relations with groups outside the campus.

b. Modernity of the administration Attempts to attract students *from disadvantaged homes* have increased very strongly, considerably more so than for the sample as a whole. *Administrative attempts to increase communication* have increased very strongly, considerably above average. An interesting difference between the sample as a whole and the new state colleges exists with respect to the *degree to which institutions control student behavior:* the decrease has been rather marked in general but only slight for the new state colleges. This probably suggests that even as an old privately or municipally controlled institution, the institution was a streetcar college which did not see part of its role as acting *in loco parentis;* consequently, not much can have changed in this respect because of the move to state college status—and since these state colleges are even less likely to act *in loco parentis* than were their predecessors, all that can happen is a slight decrease in the degree to which these institutions control student behavior.

The administration of the new state college can certainly be labeled "modern."

c. Length of service of major administrative officers As in the sample as a whole, the length of service of major administrative officers increased slightly.

d. The financing of the institution The proportion of the *total budget based on federal support* follows the standard pattern of a strong increase as in the total sample; however, a marked difference exists with respect to the proportion of the *total budget based on alumni support:* while there has been a moderate increase samplewide, the new state colleges show an extremely slight increase only. It can be assumed that they never had alumni who gave their institution strong financial support and that the alumni of the new state college are not likely to do better, until the Ph.D. is attained as the institution's highest degree, and the quest for "greatness" really begins.

FROM SINGLE-SEX TO COEDUCATIONAL The trend toward coeducational enrollment among colleges that were hitherto open to one sex only has been accelerating, particularly in the last few years. While this phenomenon is particularly visible on the undergraduate level, it is also happening in graduate institutions. Two kinds of examples for the latter change would be (1) single-sex undergraduate institutions adding coeducational graduate programs (as Vassar College plans to do in the near future and Bryn Mawr College did many years ago), and (2) Catholic universities opening hitherto male-only graduate programs to women.

The present subsample includes data on both undergraduate and graduate institutions which have moved from single-sex to coed; there are 90 cases for the former and 15 for the latter. As the number of graduate schools in the subsample is very small, the following analysis will deal primarily with the larger group of undergraduate institutions.

The Student Body   *a. Openness of institution*   The strongest increase on the undergraduate level took place in greater heterogeneity in *ethnic composition,* as is the case for the sample as a whole, but increases in heterogeneity in *religious background* and *socioeconomic background* are also strong, more so than for other schools in general. Changes in greater heterogeneity with respect to *political affiliation* and *age* are less marked, but again more so than in the sample as a whole. On the graduate level, the strongest increases in heterogeneity have taken place with respect to both ethnic composition and socioeconomic background.

The proportion of *out-of-state students* and of *married and transfer students* has increased strongly on the undergraduate level, much more so than in the total sample, while the proportion of *foreign students* has increased far less, at a somewhat lower rate than for the sample as a whole.

It is thus obvious that with the move from single-sex to coeducational enrollment a very strong increase in the heterogeneity of the student body has taken place in undergraduate programs. The rate of increase on the graduate level has been somewhat less marked, with the exception of an increase in the proportion of married students, which slightly exceeds the rate of increase on the undergraduate level.

b. Effectiveness of institution   The increase in the proportion of *freshmen finishing their degree requirements* has been strong, and there has been a slight decrease in the proportion of *dismissals for academic reasons.* The proportion of *graduating class planning on continued education* has increased very strongly. In all these three cases concerning undergraduate institutions, the changes have been in the same direction but more pronounced than for the whole sample. Very much the same phenomenon has happened in the graduate schools which decided to move from single-sex to coeducational enrollment. In these schools, furthermore, the proportion of *graduate students completing their degree requirements* increased markedly, considerably more so than for the sample as a whole. It can thus be stated that both the undergraduate and the graduate institutions which moved from single-sex to coeducational enrollment have experienced a stronger-than-average increase in their effectiveness—which is one of the reasons that single-sex schools want to go coeducational in the first place.

c. Modernity of student body The amount of *student control in academic decision making* on the undergraduate level has increased very strongly, as has the amount of *student control in institution-wide policy formation and in the establishment and enforcement of regulations governing student conduct.* In all four cases, the increase has been stronger than for the sample as a whole.

On the graduate level, the increase has been stronger than for the national average only with regard to the establishment and enforcement of regulations governing student conduct.

In the undergraduate schools that became coeducational, there has been a very strong increase in the proportion of *students participating in voluntary community projects,* stronger than for the sample as a whole. *Underground publications and films* have increased only slightly, less so than the samplewide average. On the graduate level this situation differs only with regard to underground publications and films where the rate of increase exceeds that of the sample as a whole. The increase in *on-campus student protests* has been moderate on the undergraduate level (approximately the same as in the total sample) but more pronounced on the graduate level.

On both levels the increase in *school spirit* has been very slight, differing little from the trend in the whole sample. The same is true with regard to the *number of men joining fraternities* and the *number of women joining sororities* on those campuses where Greek societies exist.

Altogether, the increase in modernity of the student body has been remarkably strong, possibly more so on the graduate than on the undergraduate level. It is not assumed that there is necessarily a causal relationship between the move from single-sex enrollment to coeducational enrollment and a marked increase in student body modernity; rather, the two together are the effect of some other institutional variables which encourage these changes and increases.

d. Dismissals for nonacademic reasons For both graduate and undergraduate schools in this subsample, the rate of decrease, though relatively slight, has been considerably more marked than for the sample as a whole.

e. Quality of student preparation in high school Although this is of less direct importance for those schools which have moved from single-sex to coeducational enrollment in their graduate programs, these schools obviously have undergraduate programs as well. In the case of both graduate and undergraduate schools that report changes by sex in enrollment, the increase in the quality of student preparation in high school has been very strong.

The Faculty *a. Faculty mobility* For both graduate and undergraduate schools in the subsample, the increase in the amount of *faculty turnover* has been slight and yet considerably stronger than for the sample as a whole. In both cases, there has been a strong increase in the *proportion of tenured faculty* exceeding that for the total sample. *Average age when tenure is awarded* has decreased moderately (as in the whole sample) for undergraduate schools but very strongly for graduate schools. It is justified to state that faculty mobility in schools which have moved to coeducational enrollment has increased strongly in general, but slightly more so on the graduate than on the undergraduate level.

b. Faculty commitment *Commitment toward teaching* has increased moderately on the undergraduate level, and so has *commitment toward research*. *Hours spent in teaching* have declined strongly, while *hours spent in research* have increased markedly. As in the sample as a whole, *commitment toward the institution* has decreased very slightly. On the graduate level, commitment toward teaching has increased somewhat less than on the undergraduate level (it coincides with the samplewide trend), while commitment toward research has increased more. Hours spent in teaching have decreased strongly too, but hours spent in research have increased moderately only (possibly because the research tradition in those programs has been well established for a long time). It is in the *commitment toward institution* that the graduate schools which went coeducational differ most from both the sample-wide average and the undergraduate schools which followed this trend: the decrease, though only moderate, is much more marked.

It is interesting that even in the graduate schools which went coeducational, faculty commitment toward teaching increased. But apart from this anomaly, it can be said that both types of schools show that commitment has been towards research and, possibly, toward the profession (and away from the institution). It may be that the faculties (made up of a male majority usually) find the presence of women in the classroom a welcome change.

c. Faculty modernity   *Faculty efforts to promote student-faculty discussion* have increased very strongly for the undergraduate schools but somewhat less (at the same rate as the sample as a whole) on the graduate level. *Faculty willingness to accept student course evaluation* has increased considerably more than for the total sample in undergraduate schools but considerably less in the graduate schools, which may indicate a somewhat stronger conservative bent of the faculty on the graduate level. For both graduate and undergraduate schools, the rate of increase in *faculty support of students opposing administration policies* is rather marked and stronger than for the sample as a whole. In both cases, *faculty willingness to experiment with new methods* has increased very strongly, though very slightly less so than in the total sample, especially for the graduate schools.

The graduate schools in the subsample thus show a somewhat below-average increase in faculty modernity, while the undergraduate schools show an above-average increase.

d. Autonomy of faculty   Contrary to a slight increase in *external pressures limiting the freedom of the faculty* in the sample as a whole, there has been a marked decrease in both the graduate and the undergraduate schools in the subsample. In both cases, *faculty autonomy in grading* has increased more strongly than in the total sample, as has *faculty autonomy in academic programs*. Both graduate and undergraduate schools show an extremely strong (somewhat stronger than in the sample as a whole) increase in *faculty involvement in determining institutionwide policies*. In both cases, the proportion of the *faculty advocating positions with regard to national policies* increased strongly, somewhat more so than in the total sample. It thus seems that both the graduate and the undergraduate schools which moved from single-sex to coeducational enrollment have granted their faculties considerably more autonomy than other universities and colleges have.

The Administration

a. Scope of administrative authority As in all institutions in the sample, both the graduate and undergraduate schools that moved toward coeducational enrollment show only a very slight increase in *alumni influence on institutional policy making.* Both show a moderate, about-average increase in the *influence of the state department of education on institutional policy making.* The *authority of the central campus administration* in those schools which are part of multicampus institutions declined, but much more so in the graduate than in the undergraduate schools (the latter show an average decrease).

While there was a very slight increase in the *number of institutionwide requirements for undergraduate degrees,* there was a moderate decrease for the undergraduate schools and a very strong decrease for the graduate schools. This again confirms the original assumption that faculty who teach in graduate programs have a wider range of prerogatives. The *number of departmental requirements for undergraduate degrees* has slightly increased in the sample as a whole, but no real change is evident for the graduate and the undergraduate institutions in the subsample. The *number of cooperative programs with local industry* has increased rather markedly for graduate and undergraduate institutions, but in both cases the rate of increase is well below the sample average. The *number of working relations with other colleges and universities,* finally, has increased very strongly and is in line with the general rate of increase.

While there has indeed been an increase in the scope of administrative authority for schools at both levels, the increase is somewhat lower overall than that for the sample as a whole.

b. Modernity of administration The very strong increase in *administrative attempts to attract students from disadvantaged homes* at both levels is similar to that for the whole sample, as are the *administrative attempts to increase communication* on campus. Where the two types of schools really differ from the average is in the *degree to which they control student behavior:* the decrease is rather marked for the sample as a whole but strong for the undergraduate schools and very strong for the graduate schools.

The administration of the schools (both graduate and undergraduate) that went coeducational is thus more modern than average only with respect to the degree to which it controls student behavior. The results would thus seem to show that for an institution to go coeducational means that it relaxes student controls in general at the same time.

c. Length of service of major administrative officers   As in the sample as a whole, the length of service of major administrative officers has increased slightly in undergraduate institutions that went coeducational. However, the graduate institutions which went coeducational show a slight decrease in the length of service of these officers.

d. The financing of the institution   In line with the general strong increase in the *proportion of the total budget based on federal support,* undergraduate schools having gone coeducational show this trend too; however, the trend is somewhat less marked for the graduate institutions. Sharper differences between the sample as a whole and the institutions in the subsample appear with regard to the *proportion of the total budget based on alumni support:* in both cases, but especially for the graduate schools, the increase is considerably stronger than for the sample as a whole, which seems to point out that many of the schools having gone coeducational must be under private control. Also, the data prove that a step which changes the image of a school as much as a move from single-sex to coeducational enrollment does not necessarily lead to a decrease in alumni support; quite the opposite is the case here.

SUMMARY OF CHANGES BY TYPE OF INSTITUTION   Finally, the questionnaire data were examined to find out which types of institutions were most likely to have undergone different kinds of changes within the last decade, and to draw some inferences from these trends.

Some of the institutional types turned out to show recurrent trends; some showed no trends at all. For this reason the typologies dealing with institutional control and geographic area are here almost completely omitted. This is somewhat unexpected with regard to institutional control since the "public-private" dichotomy is usually thought to be a rather powerful explanatory tool.

Changes Affecting the Student Body

a. Openness of institution Colleges and universities in the United States have increased their openness considerably within the last 10 years; the most important increases occurred in ethnic heterogeneity, proportion of transfer students admitted, proportion of married students, proportion of out-of-state students, and socioeconomic heterogeneity of the student body. It is interesting to note that a rather strong gap exists between the increases in ethnic and socioeconomic heterogeneity of the student body; this difference suggests a substantial lag in admissions policies between admitting members of *ethnic minorities* and admitting *poor* members of ethnic minorities. The generally strong increase in the proportion of transfer students and out-of-state students suggests a decrease in the parochialism of institutions of higher education.

A consistent pattern emerges with regard to changes in the above five areas: the increases in institutional openness have been particularly marked in schools with enrollments of over 1,000 students, in institutions with four-year or more advanced programs, and in colleges and universities with programs in a full range of subjects. In other words, changes have been more marked—in terms of greater institutional openness—in universities than in colleges. An examination of data on schools having undergone important changes in some institutional aspects within the last 20 years reveals that these schools show an almost consistently higher increase in openness than do schools which have not undergone radical changes: colleges and universities which have moved from sectarian to nonsectarian control, from teachers college to general liberal arts college, from college to university, from two-year college to four-year college, from medium to giant enrollment, and from single-sex to coeducational enrollment show a very strong increase in institutional openness. This might indicate that liberalization of institutional control, upgrading of academic programs, relatively rapid increases in enrollment, and moves toward coeducational enrollment all provide the basis for a substantial increase in the heterogeneity of the student body.

b. Effectiveness of institution The proportion of a *graduating class planning on continued education* and the proportion of *fresh-*

men completing their degree requirements emerge as the most important indicators of institutional effectiveness. The effectiveness of colleges and universities has increased rather strongly in general, but particularly so in schools with enrollments over 1,000 students, in institutions offering four-year or more advanced programs, and in schools offering general programs. A number of important increases in effectiveness are also visible in schools which have undergone important institutional changes within the last 20 years. Thus, institutions which enlarged and upgraded their academic programs (from B.A. or M.A. programs to doctoral programs and from two-year to four-year programs) and which decided to abandon the idea of a single-sex student body in favor of coeducational enrollment show a very high increase in effectiveness. These schools have become much more effective in retaining their students and in providing them with incentives to continue their education. The large university seems to be the single most effective type of institution; as was pointed out earlier, the incentive for undergraduates to go on to graduate studies seems to be the visibility of graduate programs on campus. The very strong increase in the proportion of freshmen completing their degree requirements on such large university campuses might be explained by academically more rigorous admissions requirements which reduce the relative number of potential dropouts. (In the case of large state universities which traditionally had open admissions policies, the explanation seems to be the same: due to the emergence of alternative forms of higher education in two-year colleges and state colleges, state universities can be more selective in their admissions policies without violating the principle of "higher education for all high school graduates.")

c. Modernity of student body   The modern aspects of student behavior have increased generally, but so have the traditional aspects, although to a much weaker degree. The modern aspects of student behavior are reflected in the very strong increase in student participation in college and university governance and in the proportion of students participating in voluntary community work. While such antiestablishment aspects of modern student behavior as on-campus student protests and underground newspapers and films are very visible, thanks to extensive newspaper coverage, their increase has been much less marked than that of student participation in governance. The very strong increase in the latter is the true revolutionary aspect of student modernity since it changes the traditional governance configuration considerably.

The highest increase in student modernity is evident for larger institutions (particularly those with enrollments over 5,000 students) as well as for the schools which offer graduate programs and have general curricula. As to those institutions which have undergone far-reaching changes within the last 20 years, the increase in student modernity is particularly strong for schools which have moved from sectarian to nonsectarian control, from teachers college to liberal arts college, from college to university, from two-year college to four-year college, from small to large size, from single-sex to coeducational enrollment (on the undergraduate level), and from four-year college to state college.

Student traditionalism as evidenced by *school spirit* has clearly declined in the larger schools and in those institutions offering graduate programs, while the same schools show a slight increase in the proportion of *men joining fraternities* and the proportion of *women joining sororities*. The latter trend obviously contradicts the common assumption that the Greek societies are declining — they have probably declined in influence and visibility, but not necessarily in numbers.

d. Dismissals for nonacademic reasons A general decrease in such dismissals is evident, but the trend is most marked for private institutions, schools with over 5,000 students, and institutions with graduate programs. Schools which moved from medium to giant size show the single strongest rate of increase, a trend which seems to show that colleges which increase rapidly in size are likely to be willing to shed their *in loco parentis* obligations.

e. Quality of student preparation in high school While most schools show a very strong increase, the trend is strongest for private institutions, schools with an enrollment of 1,000 students or more, and schools offering graduate programs and general curricula. Teachers colleges which became liberal arts colleges show an extremely strong increase; the inference is clear that by expanding its academic program a former teachers college can attract a much more varied student body and increase its entrance requirements.

The Faculty *a. Faculty mobility* Schools with enrollments of 5,000 or more students and schools with graduate programs show a higher rate of increase in *amount of faculty turnover* and a higher rate of decrease in *average age when tenure is awarded* than do smaller schools and undergraduate colleges; however, they show a less pronounced increase in the *proportion of tenured faculty* than do the latter. The most likely explanation is that large schools offering graduate programs—i.e., universities—have traditionally had a high proportion of tenured faculty and were under less pressure than smaller undergraduate colleges to improve working conditions by improving tenure conditions.

b. Faculty commitment The move from *commitment to teaching* to *commitment to research* is quite evident; the trend is borne out by data on *hours spent in teaching* and *hours spent in research:* the strongest decrease in commitment to and hours spent in teaching is noticeable for the larger schools and the institutions offering graduate programs; the same types of schools also show the strongest increase in commitment to and hours spent in research. Large schools and institutions with graduate programs are also the types which display a decrease in *commitment toward the institution* (while small schools and undergraduate colleges actually show a slight increase in this commitment). The hypothesis advanced earlier in this chapter—that two shifts in commitment have occurred—must be modified to read that the two shifts in commitment have occurred primarily on large university campuses.

c. Faculty modernity *Faculty support of students opposing administration policies* has increased most in the larger schools and in the institutions offering graduate instruction. The opposite trend is true for *faculty willingness to experiment with new teaching methods:* small schools and undergraduate colleges are the institutions which show the highest increase. This reflects partly the change in faculty commitment: it is obvious that the research-oriented university teacher is less likely to spend his energy on improving his teaching than is the somewhat more teaching-oriented college teacher. On the other hand, since a strong antagonism between faculty and administration is more likely to be found on a complex campus, teachers there are more likely to support students opposing administration policies than they are on a smaller, less complex campus on which better means of communication between faculty and administration are likely to exist. A particularly strong increase in faculty willingness to side with students is noticeable in schools which have grown in size at a fast rate; a possible explanation might be that while the enrollment grows, means of communication between faculty and administration become inadequate and friction increases between all campus groups.

d. Faculty autonomy The most distinct trend appears with regard to the proportion of *faculty advocating positions with respect to national policies* and *faculty involvement in institutionwide policies.* There has been a strong increase in the proportion of faculty advocating positions with respect to national policies, but the increase has been particularly strong in the case of the large schools and the institutions awarding higher degrees. Faculty involvement in institutionwide policies has been strongest in medium- to giant-sized institutions and somewhat stronger in institutions below the Ph.D. level than in the full universities. It thus seems that the institutions which have experienced the strongest increases in faculty autonomy are to a large degree (but not as much as with regard to faculty mobility, commitment, or modernity) larger institutions and schools with graduate programs.

The Administration *a. Scope of administrative authority* With the exception of *state department of education influence on institutional policy making,* changes in the scope of administrative authority *inside* the college or university have been minor. The most marked increase has taken place in public institutions, in schools with enrollments under 5,000 students, in two-year colleges, in schools which moved from private to public control, and in four-year colleges which became state colleges. While this trend is not unexpected, it shows that large and complex universities (among which are many state universities) seem to have a greater degree of autonomy than do publicly controlled two-year colleges.

The autonomy of college and university administrations has increased substantially with regard to matters that are outside the institution. The *number of cooperative programs with local industry* has increased strongly, particularly in public institutions, schools with enrollments over 1,000 students, four-year colleges, institutions with general curricula, teachers colleges which became liberal arts colleges, and schools which moved from private to public control. A clearer trend emerges with regard to the *number of working relations with other schools:* The larger institutions and the schools with advanced academic programs show the highest rate of increase. Very high increases can also be found for institutions which moved from sectarian to nonsectarian control, from medium to giant size, and from four-year to state college. A move away from church control thus seems to make it easier for college and university administrators to establish contacts with the outside.

b. Modernity of administration While the overwhelming majority of college and university presidents report an increase in *administrative attempts to increase communication within the school,* the larger institutions and the schools with advanced programs show an even stronger increase, as do multipurpose institutions, schools which moved from sectarian to nonsectarian control, colleges which became universities, small schools which grew to large size, and four-year colleges which became state colleges.

Attempts to attract students from disadvantaged homes increased most markedly in the larger schools and, not unexpectedly, in schools which moved from sectarian to nonsectarian control and from private to public control, as well as in schools which increased greatly in size during the last 20 years.

All types of schools show a decrease in the *degree to which the institution controls student behavior.* As could be expected from previously discussed trends, the increase is most marked for the larger schools and the institutions which offer advanced degrees. Schools which moved from sectarian to nonsectarian control and from single-sex to coeducational enrollment also show a very high increase; the very fact of moving from single-sex to coeducational enrollment means a decrease in control of student behavior by the administration, and with regard to the newly nonsectarian college it seems clear that the administration of such a college would be less moralistic toward students than the administration of a church-related school.

c. Length of service of major administrative officers The increase has been most marked in the small institutions and in two-year colleges, as well as in two-year colleges which became four-year institutions, and medium-sized institutions which grew to giant-size.

d. Financing of institution Every type of school shows a strong increase in the proportion of the *total budget based on federal support.* Again, it is the large institutions and the schools with the most advanced programs which show the highest increase, as do schools which moved from teachers college to liberal arts college and institutions which increased rapidly in size during the last 20 years. The pattern for the proportion of the *total budget based on alumni support* is different. Privately controlled schools, small institutions, four-year colleges, schools which moved from sectarian to nonsectarian control, and schools which moved from single-sex to coeducational enrollment show the highest increases. The strong increases for the schools which underwent basic institutional changes within the last two decades are especially interesting since it would be reasonable to expect that alumni might not be too willing to contribute to an institution which no longer looks like their alma mater. They apparently are willing to support institutions which are changing in the "right" direction—toward the multiversity.

CONCLUSION Of all institutional types, it is clearly the large university which has undergone the most far-reaching changes. These are the institutions with the most important changes with regard to institutional openness, institutional effectiveness, modernity of student body, faculty mobility, faculty modernity, autonomy of the faculty, and modernity of the administration. Size, speed of growth, and highest degree offered-institutional designation are thus the three most useful variables for the description and possible explanation of the major changes that have taken place in American higher education within the last 10 years.

Part Two

Institutional Case Studies

5. Five Case Studies

The analysis and questionnaire data in our project revealed a number of trends which we felt should be looked at in greater detail by teams of observers who actually would go to institutions undergoing change to discover firsthand what was going on. We selected five institutions which we felt represented major changes which other institutions might be going through in the future and which represented significant shifts in the institution's orientation to itself, its mission, and the outside world. Five institutions were approached and all agreed to be participants in the study. Thus in the spring of 1969 interviewing teams were dispatched to the institutions. Selected were the State University of New York at Buffalo (its change has been from private to public control, with a drastically expanded mission as a state institution), Southern Colorado State College at Pueblo (a two-year community college which has become a four-year institution as part of a state system), Oberlin College (an institution with very high standards which feels a commitment to assist members of minority groups in getting an education), Chicago State College (an urban teacher education institution which is in the process of becoming an urban university), and Northern Illinois University (an institution which has gone through extremely rapid growth in size and complexity of mission). The author of this study visited each of the five campuses in the company of trained interviewers with long experience in higher education. Three or four team members went on each of the interviewing visits. Each member of the team was responsible for writing his summary, which was then edited and returned to the institution for suggested modifications before approval by the institution. It is hoped that these case studies will reveal in a much more realistic way the hazards and opportunities which face an institution in the process of major change in its role, size, constituencies, and objectives. In each of the cases studied, the interviewers concentrated on the following:

- Where did the idea of the change originate?
- Through what processes did the idea become "policy"?
- How was the policy implemented (roles of people and structures)?
- What were the consequences of the change for the people on the campus?
- What did the change do to the institution's future potential?

In that each of the cases deals with common questions, the *series* of cases represents to some extent an integrated whole, allowing some generalizations to be made across all five institutions. It is hoped that this style of codified case studies will eliminate their chief drawback. Case studies have always been built around the "unique" qualities of the individual institution studied, and thus comparisons across institutions have been almost impossible. The method used here provides some basis for generalization across institutions. Many things have changed between the present and the time of the visits. "Present time" in the cases studied is the spring of 1969, and they should be read with that in mind.

SUNY— BUFFALO The State University of New York at Buffalo was included in this study because it has made and survived the crucial transition from a private to a public institution. At the same time it has experienced enormous growth and greatly increased fiscal resources over a relatively short period of time.

1 *Where did the idea for the change come from?*
The University of Buffalo at the time of the merger had been in existence for 116 years as a private institution. It was nonprofit and educationally incorporated under the control of a board of trustees, who were in part self-perpetuating and in part elected by the alumni. It consisted of a dozen degree-granting schools or colleges and granted associate degrees, bachelor's degrees, master's, and doctorates. It enrolled approximately 7,500 students full time and served an additional 5,000 students in evening and noncredit courses. It was in existence largely to meet the educational needs of the Buffalo metropolitan area and to some extent of the region of western New York. The State University of New York into which it merged was created by an act of the Legislature in 1948. Con-

stituent elements at the time of creation were the eleven state teachers colleges, six long-established agricultural and technical institutes which offered a two-year program, three contract colleges at Cornell University, a contract college at Alfred University, a school of forestry at Syracuse, and a maritime academy on Long Island Sound. These institutions prior to their union in the State University of New York came under the general public and legal purview of the Board of Regents and had been operated by appropriate officials of the New York State Department of Education. The State University of New York is under the immediate control of a board of trustees appointed by the Governor. The state university is, however, essentially an arm of state government, subject to all the rules, regulations, and controls of the state. It is served by the various state bureaus, including the Bureau of the Budget, the Civil Service Commission, and the Bureau of Purchases and Standards, and is subject to all the rules of the Bureau of Audit and Control administered by the state comptroller. The education law which established the State University of New York contained a clause which authorized the state university to merge with any other institution of higher learning upon the vote of the board of trustees of the state university and the other merging institution. In answering the question of why the merger, it must be said that there were advantages for the University of Buffalo and advantages for the State University of New York. In addition to the advantages of a merger, there were of course innumerable difficulties—the term "merger" itself implying one of the most obvious difficulties. The state university officials felt, of course, that a *merger* consists of the joining of two equal institutions, and they felt that this in no sense was a merger—that Buffalo was one institution simply joining the much larger entity. These contradictions and status problems seem to be endemic to this sort of transition. There are those who say that except for the accident of time and geography the University of Buffalo would have been public from its beginning. It was founded as a medical school in 1846 to prepare young men to be physicians for the then relatively young community of Buffalo. The founding fathers were a group of physicians and civic leaders headed by Millard Fillmore. The charter which was granted the university by the Legislature in 1846 was exceedingly broad. It authorized the university to offer programs and grant degrees in all fields in which degrees were granted by any university in the country. In the next 65 years the university established three additional professional schools in pharmacy, dentistry, and law. The motivation for establishing these was identical with that which led to the establishment of the university as a school of medicine, namely, to train persons to be of service to the community. It was not until 1920, however, that a college of liberal arts was started; and then mainly because the Flexner report was highly critical of Buffalo's school of medicine and stated that it should be closed. (One condition for maintaining a medical school was to have undergirding it, according to the Flexner report, a liberal arts program within the sponsoring university.)

During the period of approximately 1913 to 1930, funds were sought to enable the university to establish an endowment; but these fund-raising efforts were not very successful, and in the thirties, support for the institution's program was meager. The institution continued to be local, serving lower-middle-class students from the Buffalo area. No residence halls were built; no significant national reputation was achieved. The university was known as a "streetcar" college.

In 1950 Dr. T. R. McConnell became chancellor of the university. On his assumption of the chancellorship, several fundamental decisions concerning the future of the university were made. First, a residence hall construction program was begun. Second, basic science facilities for the professional school were removed from off-campus and brought onto the campus location. Also, evening and extension activities were brought onto the central campus. A $3 million goal for a fund-raising campaign was established and met. In 1954 Dr. Clifford Furnas became chancellor of the university and initiated another financial campaign—this one with the goal of $9 million. The programs initiated under McConnell's tenure were carried forward and extended, but it became clear in this period between 1950 and 1962 that the financial resources essential for the establishment of a major institution would not be forthcoming in Buffalo. It should be added here, however, that one reason for this discrepancy between dollars and program was an increased pattern of aspiration on the part of the university— perhaps the response to two rather vigorous presidencies.

Studies made in the late 1950s indicated that the university should expect an enrollment of 20,000 or more students by 1970, and that at that time it should have an operating budget of $40 to $50 million. It was clear that successive increases in tuition would not produce anywhere near the needed income, and it was doubted that other sources of revenue were at hand. Equally significant to the merger was the fact that the developing state university was well aware of the ever-expanding needs for higher education in western New York State. The state university stimulated conversations in the region for the further development of community colleges and frequently stressed the fact that it was uncertain that the existing institutions in western New York could meet the educational demands that would obviously emerge in the decade of the sixties.

Probably the single most important factor in the merger was the result of the report of the Heald Committee—a select committee appointed by the Regents and the Governor. This report, issued in November 1960, indicated that there was a definite need for a complex university to be established by the state of New York in the upstate western region. It proposed that the state university meet this need either by expanding one of its colleges in the area or by taking over one of the upstate universities and developing it into a major university center. It was clear that the University of Buffalo was one of the institutions which the Heald Committee had in mind as a potential member of the state university system. However it was by no means a certainty that it would be the institution selected. There was considerable fear at the University of Buffalo that the State College at Buffalo (which was primarily a teacher-training institution) might be selected to be the major university. It was also possible that some of the other private universities in the state could be chosen. It should perhaps be added here that the Heald Committee recommended the establishment of two university centers to be located in extreme ends of the state. The board of trustees, however, saw the need for expanding the state university system on a slightly larger scale and was concerned that the state university system reach maximum influence in a fairly short time. Thus the board decided that four university centers would be better. The report of the board of trustees of the state university did two things: First, the report made it clear that teachers colleges were to become multipurpose colleges with a strong liberal arts orientation. Second, it recognized the need for four university centers and indicated that one of these should be located in Buffalo. This meant then that the only real options were either to develop a new university from scratch, to make a university out of State College at Buffalo, or to choose the University of Buffalo as the new agent of the state system. The experience at SUNY, Stonybrook, indicated that it would be most difficult to begin a university from nothing and that the first few years would be extremely painful. It seemed to many to be equally hard to make a university out of a teachers college. Thus much of the evidence pointed to the University of Buffalo as the institution which would best fit the educational plan for the state of New York.

2 *How was the change implemented?*

Almost within hours of the release of the Heald Committee report, administrative officers of the University of Buffalo addressed a letter to state officials indicating that the university would be interested in discussing with appropriate officials the suggestion that an upstate university be incorporated into the state university system, and in addition that the University of Buffalo be that institution. Through informal processes it was learned that responsible leaders of the state university board of trustees would be interested in discussing such a proposition. Thus meetings were arranged between officials of the university and the State University of New York to discuss how the merger ought to proceed. Both the University of Buffalo and the State University of New York retained legal counsel and accounting experts who conducted most of the specifics of the negotiation. The actual negotiations for the merger took 20 months and covered an incredibly complex array of problems.

When the negotiations began, the University of Buffalo representatives had hoped they could make an accommodation with the state of New York which would preserve a considerable portion of their autonomy as a private university, as they sought and secured state support for the institution. However, in the very early meetings of the council of the university, it was stated by one member who had had an informal and unofficial conversation with an important representative of the state university board of trustees that the only basis under which the university could receive assistance was, in the words of this anonymous representative, to become "lock, stock, and barrel" a constituent member of the state university. While there were nostalgic discussions following this meeting, in which there were expressions of hope that the university could preserve considerable status as an autonomous institution, the realities were that as serious discussion got underway the university never expected to be anything other than a constituent member of the State University of New York. Although there was a universe of specific questions to be ironed out, some of the major issues which accounted for the lengthy negotiations can be stated as follows: (1) the disposition of a fairly substantial endowment fund which the University of Buffalo had acquired; (2) the rights of certain individuals in the university with regard to tenure, fringe benefits, and security; and (3) the problem of the development of the university in the future, and how its own vision of its future would fit into the vision of the state system.

1   At the time of merger the University of Buffalo had an endowment which had a market value of about $30 million. A fair proportion of this endowment was restricted in that the income from it was used for specific purposes. However, the income of another considerable proportion could be used at the discretion of the council. Practically all this endowment money had accrued from gifts and bequests of persons who lived in the Buffalo area. It seemed to the University of Buffalo that the interests of the university even after merger would best be served if it could be clearly specified that this endowment had an entity of its own and did *not* pass "lock, stock and barrel" into the coffers of the state of New York. Representatives of the state university on the other hand were quite conscious of the fact that if there was any semblance of misuse of the endowment funds or diversion from the purpose for which they were intended, appropriate legal processes could be invoked by which the funds might be lost altogether to the state university. State officials felt that if the State University of New York assumed all the obligations of the University of Buffalo and met the responsibilities of support which would occur, the endowment fund should be as a consequence treated as all other property of the university and should accrue to the state of New York. This item continued to be a significant issue in the merger negotiation up until the final weeks of settlement.

2   The rights of tenured faculty are particularly important in the academic world. An important question was whether or not tenure rights which had come to members of the faculty because of their position in the University of Buffalo would be acknowledged by the State University of New York. While this was an important issue, it was not a persistent one because it readily became apparent that tenure rights of the faculty could be preserved. The rights of nontenured faculty were contractual in character and for a shorter period of time. It was decided that the merger agreement would provide that the State University of New York would honor all contractual obligations of the university; hence there were no problems in honoring the obligations of the university to its nontenured faculty— no change was made. A like situation pertained to other university staff, particularly clerical and stenographic personnel, maintenance personnel,

and those administrative officers who did not have faculty positions.

More significant was the maintenance of certain fringe benefits to which the University of Buffalo staff had become accustomed and which were not in all respects comparable to the fringe benefits enjoyed by the State University of New York faculty and staff. Most important of these fringe benefits was the retirement program. The University of Buffalo's retirement program was with Teachers Insurance and Annuity Association (TIAA) and its companion organization, College Retirement Equities Fund (CREF)—a program which assures immediate conversion of *all* payments into the form of retirement benefits for the respective persons at the time of payment of the pension premium to the fund, rather than later conversion.

Members of the faculty of other state university units, however, were members of either the New York State Employment Retirement Fund or the New York State Teachers Retirement Fund. Other employees of the state university who were not faculty were members of the New York State Employees Retirement Fund. These are delayed vesting systems—allocation, or vesting, would not occur until a considerable number of years had elapsed after the time of entering state employment. All university personnel will recognize the significance to faculty members of the vesting privilege. Consequently a long process of negotiation was necessary—negotiation which ultimately resulted in legislation which permitted the State University of Buffalo tenured faculty who wished to retain the privilege of having their pension allocation continued with TIAA-CREF to do so.

3   Although these negotiations were carried on by the respective legal counsels, the interests of students, faculty, and alumni of Buffalo were very acute. These persons frequently expressed a series of concerns, which, while not openly discussed by the negotiators, were frequently reviewed by the respective administrative officials. These interests included some of the following questions: What tuition would the students have to pay if and when the University of Buffalo became a unit of the state university? To what degree would the State University of New York maintain the athletic program which had been developed at the University of Buffalo? The State University of New York did not permit nationally affiliated fraternities and sororities on its respective campuses; would this policy be enforced at the University of Buffalo if it should merge?

Among other matters which had to be settled but which did not arouse quite so much interest on the part of students and faculty were the support and management of nonacademic activities such as housing, the bookstore, parking lots, and expenditures for athletics; the disposition of the Western New York Nuclear Research Institute, which was an educational corporation independent of the university but wholly owned and controlled by it; the disposition of plans to construct several new buildings on the campus;

the disposition of a golf course, located some three miles northeast of the campus, which the university had acquired a few years before the merger; and finally the way the university would manage under an expected loss of income from gifts and grants during the negotiation period.

From a number of sources it is quite clear that the negotiators on the side of the State University of New York dealt not only with accounting and legal specialists and with educators from the state university system, but also with people whose interests were purely political. There was a habit during the negotiations of saying that "they" would not agree with a given move but "they" were never specified. In several instances of tracking down these reports, it became quite clear that "they" were for the most part wealthy and affluent New York citizens who had gotten into political matters as much as a hobby as anything else, that they, because of their wealth, had established connections at the highest level of political affairs in the state. It should be said that during all these negotiations the president of the University of Buffalo, Clifford Furnas, exercised admirable restraint and kept negotiations going when a more quick-tempered person might have succeeded in ruining the negotiations.

One of the small yet pointed issues, for example, involved the question of football. The University of Buffalo had maintained a creditable record in football, and it was quite clear that the state of New York had no aspiration for the future State University of New York at Buffalo to become a football power. Thus the negotiations with the alumni and with some faculty were tricky at best, but for those on the inside of the planning, giving in on the football issues was a small price to pay for the enormous gains the institution would receive financially. Another tricky aspect of the negotiations was that not only was agreement being reached on a merger of the present University of Buffalo into the state system—plans were also being developed at the same time for the future of the institution as it could key into the future for the State University of New York.

It may well be that during this very hectic period with great personal strain and tension there was a tendency on the part of University of Buffalo officials to blame all the problems on Albany and the state university. It was clear that the University of Buffalo did not have its own coherent plan for merging with the state system and for its future role within the system, and thus mutual confusion compounded itself. Nevertheless agreement was reached on the possibilities for maximum student size of the university and additional site acquisition for future buildings. A decision was reached after the merger that the university would have to move to a new site, which meant making do for a few years on the existing site with trailers rented for classroom use, some Butler buildings, and so on. But this transitory look, which the campus still possesses, is not a result of the merger procedures per se.

3 *What were the consequences of the merger for curriculum and programs?*

In 1962 the University of Buffalo was a modest university by most criteria. That year it granted 37 doctoral degrees, as opposed to 170 in 1968–69. The figures for graduate school enrollments were 2,300 in 1962 and 5,500 in 1968–69. The library holdings in 1962 were 400,000, compared with 1.3 million in 1968–69. Periodicals were 3,000 in 1962 and rose to 20,000 in 1968–69. As one looks at these figures, it is quite clear that the university has been through tremendous changes, but it is also clear that it was a very modest university in 1962 and really arrived in 1968–69 at the status of "comprehensive university," as that term is commonly used in the United States. It had really, then, increased its status gradually during the period. However in the first *year* of state operation, the budget shot up from $9 million to $15 million (the annual budget now runs around $55 million). It is clear that the faculty were not used to this new largesse, but they soon became accustomed to it.

During the period 1962 to 1966 or 1967, the faculty began to feel that anything they wished could be supplied—that state funds would go on forever. By the time President Martin Meyerson arrived, in 1966–67, some fiscal leveling off had already taken place and the prognosis indicated a return to a more stable state rather than the exponential budgetary explosion of the recent past.

One of the interesting things about this period of enormous growth following the merger was the decision regarding quality and numbers. It would seem that the increased financial support for the university would have come inevitably, and why it expanded its student body as quickly as it did is difficult to understand. The university could just as well have spent three or four years building up quality of instructional program before increasing the student body as quickly as was done. In part the increase was caused by several large increases in freshman enrollments which took place before the merger, expanding the entire student body as each class picked up the expansion. The attitude of many administrators and faculty was aptly summed up by the comment that the institution now resembles "a pauper who marries a rich widow and then complains because she is not as rich as he thought she was." The financial largesse resulting from the merger produced a rather short-range view of the institution's future. Academic departments thought almost entirely of how much they had this year compared with the previous year. Almost everyone at the university had to become accustomed to working in a huge bureaucracy. Too many new people were hired too fast, and the cohesive communication system of the private Buffalo began to erode. Justifications of various expenditures which had never been required previously were now required to give the citizens of the state some indication that they were getting a return in educational terms on their investment. Some new programs were added through this period of "high growth" thinking that might be questioned today.

During this period the State University of New York apparently developed the conception that each of the four major university centers would have its own area of specialization. The university at Binghamton would become the center for the arts and humanities, Albany would become the social science and teacher education center, Stonybrook would become the science center, and Buffalo would become the health and professional services center. It soon became clear however that the aspirations of each of the four universities dealt with far more comprehensive programs than this, the feeling being that one cannot build a great university around just one area, and that the multiversity concept was the valid one in terms of *each* of the institutions involved. Each is clearly moving in the direction of comprehensiveness at the present time.

During this period it also must be said that the intensive support of graduate programs had occurred at the expense of undergraduate education, which did not show any corresponding increase in quality during the period 1962–1966. This particular problem may now be increasing as the Buffalo undergraduate realizes that his education is subsidizing that of the graduate student. The quality of freshman entrants did increase during this period, but the quality of education offered them probably did not by any measurable index, indicating that brighter students were getting an education which was not changing to meet their needs. Additional problems were created by the increased selectivity of admissions: a number of Buffalo families who had assumed that the university was for them found their children rejected, and brighter students from all over the state and the nation came pouring in. Perhaps the best description of this period comes from a report of one of the councils of State University of New York at Buffalo in which they said, "The difficulties encountered have been not with people but with the system—a system which has merit in dealing with many aspects of state government but which produces a number of problems when applied to the operation of a complex university." It would seem that the criteria, values, and ways of doing things are significantly different enough to create endemic problems between a politically based state university system and an institution with a long history of private, autonomous operation. The resolution of these two conflicting factors in the Buffalo case seems to have been unusually successful, considering the hazards that could have developed.

4 *What of the future?*

An interview with Bill Austin, the current and very capable student body president, indicates that very few students have any idea of what Buffalo was like before or immediately after the merger, although this was only in 1962. With the arrival of President Meyerson, a feeling of "great expectations" seemed to develop in the student body. According to Austin there is a Big Ten syndrome now operating on the campus. Quality (which to the students now means Columbia or Berkeley) is vaguely but energetically pursued. Mr. Austin is of the opinion that 10 years from now the institution will double in size but will still be on the existing campus. This is due partly to labor and construction problems on the new campus.

Many students want all labor to be equally apportioned among the races, and this does not at the moment seem to be possible. For most students, Buffalo still has a mission to the urban center of the city of Buffalo, and if the college leaves its present location and moves to the new site, this will be interpreted as equivalent to the white man's leaving the central city and moving to the safety of the suburbs. The new campus does not seem to be a particularly popular issue with the students. Many of them seem to feel that the institution should stay where it is and build permanent buildings rather than the temporary structures which now dot the landscape. (However, students seldom favor any physical change of a campus.)

There seems to be a genuine and pervasive liking for President Meyerson among many of the students. This is expressed in the statement Austin made about the possibility of Meyerson's leaving[1] His comment was, "We will sit in his office until he decides to stay." The energetic work of the vice-president for student affairs, Richard Siggelkow, has contributed to the positive view of students toward the administration.

The university thus appears to be ending its period of enormous and exponential growth (growth rates multiply by themselves) and may be entering an era of relative stability and retrenchment caused partially by a leveling off of state and federal funds for program purposes. During this next phase the faculty's attitude with regard to unlimited funding will clearly be a source of major conflicts on the order of the case mentioned of the pauper who discovers that the rich widow he married is not infinitely wealthy. The research tradition, which has never been particularly strong at Buffalo, seems to be strengthening, and some of the new programs for experimental colleges are indeed exciting. Thus it would seem that even though the level of fiscal support may be stabilized, Buffalo will continue to be an exciting and dynamic place. This excitement and dynamism however, did not come only with the arrival of Dr. Meyerson in 1966, but is a direct outcome of the enormous amount of energy released during the merger, both in a fiscal and intellectual sense, as the level of aspiration of the institution began its mercurial rise. It seems unfortunate that so many people currently at the institution have no awareness of the impact the merger has had upon their lives and their university.

OBERLIN COLLEGE Oberlin College, in Oberlin, Ohio, is a small (enrollment approximately 2,600), coeducational, independent liberal arts college. It was selected for inclusion in this study because of the high quality of its liberal arts program and its exceedingly good reputation in academic circles. Oberlin has for decades felt a commitment to members of minority groups, and thus the normal extremely high criteria for admission are lowered to provide admission for a number of students from minority groups. We were interested in studying the impact of such a program on an institution with avowedly high standards, particularly because many other institutions are engaged in or are considering admitting larger numbers of minority

---

[1] Since the case was written, Dr. Meyerson has left Buffalo to become president of the University of Pennsylvania.

students, many of whom might not qualify by their normal admissions criteria.

1 *Where did the idea of change originate?*

Any discussion of the issue of minority students at Oberlin must begin with the college traditions, which are still powerful in the self-definition of the entire community. Oberlin was the first college in the nation to declare its program open to all races, as well as to women, and its role in the early underground railroad and its commitment to social service throughout its history (for example, the memorial arch on campus bears the names of those who died in the Boxer Rebellion in China) proved to be powerful influences on the college. Along with the realities of a conventional curriculum, Oberlin clearly operates from a liberal base with a strong concern for both high standards and social justice. Even the black students mentioned that one of the factors drawing them here was the reputation of the school as being liberal. It must be added, however, that many of them discover the word has different meanings, that there are social classes as well as races, and "liberal" may vary between them.

In the mid-twenties, according to President Carr,[2] the college began to emphasize quality education, and this meant that many disadvantaged students fell by the wayside or did not even apply—since quality was naturally enough at that time defined by conventional rank in class and test scores. By the late 1950s, but not by design, only a handful of black students—perhaps 20 or 25—were to be found on campus. When this fact was realized, the Oberlin heritage of liberalism in action was one of the motivating forces which generated the present program. Another cultural force within the college, perhaps somewhat at variance with this tradition of social conscience, is that of a traditional approach to a liberal arts education, emphasizing grades in structured classes. Oberlin is not known as a leader in educational experimentation—its faculty have few propensities in this direction and students do not come to Oberlin for that reason. A high degree of intellectual structure is thus part of the college inheritance, as is a tradition of social liberalism. It is a "university college" whose graduates usually go on to graduate study. There is also an important tradition at the college of strong scholarship and work-loan programs,

[2] Since this case was written, Dr. Carr has left the institution. He is now visiting scholar with the American Council on Education.

enabling many students to work their way through. To the credit of the institution, the initiative for manifesting the college's responsibility to black students came before it was a "popular" notion in American higher education. It was also clear that the president himself was the major initiating force in this reappraisal. By 1964, the president had begun meetings with faculty leaders to discuss the responsibility of Oberlin in this area (it could be added parenthetically that this was years before the assassination of Dr. Martin Luther King, Jr., when few institutions had done any serious work in, or thinking about, programs for minority groups).

After sounding out a number of faculty members on their positions, President Carr appointed an ad hoc committee to develop a careful proposal with regard to the college's commitment to disadvantaged students. This ad hoc presidential committee has now become, by action of the faculties of the College of Arts and Sciences and of the Conservatory, a committee of the general faculty. As the Committee on Afro-American Studies, it has been the principal body to determine policy regarding the academic programs for black students at Oberlin. It has made administrative decisions about these programs, along with the Special Education Opportunity Program Committee (SEOP), which has worked with the Rockefeller programs since 1963.

Oberlin was able to move effectively in this area partially because the president of the Rockefeller Foundation in 1964 was a member of the Oberlin College Board of Trustees. The foundation was interested in a changed status for black students in American institutions of higher learning. The assistance of the Rockefeller Foundation with grants for Oberlin programs has been a most significant factor. The Rockefeller money came to the college through two programs: the first, a summer institute (SEOP) which Oberlin has run for junior high school students, grooming them for college careers; the second, additional scholarship funds for direct enrollment of disadvantaged students—primarily blacks—in the Oberlin program. Both programs were funded for five years, from 1964 to 1969. Although the Rockefeller money is now tapering off, the college is picking up both programs with its own budget, and can, with some further assistance, see through college all such students admitted through September 1969. The college total for all-student aid is a commendable $1,250,000.

The summer SEOP institutes have involved 60 to 80 students each year, have been meticulously planned, and are by any estimation overwhelmingly successful. By 1969, Oberlin had in residence about 40 students supported by Rockefeller funds, most of them black, although some disadvantaged whites were also included. The existence of grant support from the Rockefeller Foundation was particularly important in the success of the programs in that there was little faculty resistance, since no ongoing activity had to be curtailed to make room for this additional program (it is common knowledge that change occurs more successfully when initial funding is external and does not threaten existing programs).

2 *The program implemented*

One of the ways Oberlin operates effectively is to appoint subcommittees whenever specific work needs to be done. Currently, subcommittees are functioning in two areas: one, the development of an Afro-American House, and two, the preparation of a black studies curriculum. The committees also serve as a means of communication from the students to the faculty and administration. However, it was clearly seen that additional communication links would be a necessity. This led to the hiring of William Davis as assistant dean of students, his functional role being that of dean for black students. Davis and William Parker, who is the director of the SEOP junior high school summer program, seem to be unqualified successes. Oberlin is indeed fortunate in having the services of two such men, in that they can relate effectively to both the white and the black communities.

Mr. Parker's program is worth a paragraph or two of description. Although few of the students will enter Oberlin, the program nevertheless has great significance for the future of all efforts of this sort. The precollege program takes 70 young people from the ghetto, and brings them to the Oberlin campus for six weeks' residence in the summer following their year in the seventh grade. They then return for briefer visits during the following five academic years and five summers. No test scores are used for admission; rather, reliance is placed on teachers' nominations, counselor screening, and final selection by staff (Parker has excellent contacts in the Cleveland area and seems to be particularly effective in getting good nominations from the public schools). "Poorness" is as significant as talent—60 of the last 80 selected were clearly economically deprived.

The program has the aim of preparing a child over six summers for successful college work. The important factor in this program is the follow-up after the summer session. A school team—the counselor in the schools and the teacher who was at Oberlin for the summer—work with the student and (very importantly) with his mother and father. The child is committed to be in an educational program four summers out of the five, following his first Oberlin experience. Children get a book a month free, and tutorial service is free. Parents are coached on how to get scholarships. A reunion, which is heavily attended, is held every spring. Of the 57 students in the program six years ago, 18 have graduated from high school and 16 have entered college in 1968. Another 39 of the original 57 entered college in fall 1969. There have been 327 students enrolled in the summer program, and 321 are still in it, with only 6 dropouts. This record is little short of phenomenal. Oberlin will accept some of the students who complete this program every year, but the majority of students probably will enter other colleges. It should be added that of the 52 students admitted for summer 1969, about two-thirds were males and two-thirds of them black; and of the one-third girls, about half were black.

The other half of the program involves the admission of high school seniors directly to Oberlin with massive financial support. A special caution must be entered here: The black students thus far enrolled at Oberlin under this program are still among the nation's intellectual elite. According to Mr. Davis, the mean SAT score for black students at Oberlin is 569. This puts them in about the 80th percentile nationally of all students applying for colleges. In addition, almost all are in the upper quarter of their high school graduating classes. Through no fault of its own, Oberlin has simply not had to deal with many of lesser abilities, as few apply. (It is also very unclear as to how far Oberlin wishes to extend itself down into less familiar levels of socioeconomic background, behavior, and intellectual competence.)

An interesting experiment will be tried in the 1969–70 year by Mr. Davis, who will be allowed to take 80 of the 120 applications from disadvantaged black students and pick 10 for admission who would not normally qualify on test scores or class rank, but who have nevertheless special qualities, such as a high social awareness, a hip quality, participation in social welfare, etc. Unfortunately, the 80 that Davis is drawing from do not represent much of a socioeconomic spectrum, and the 10 admittees will not be as much of a heterogenizing factor as Davis might like. Nevertheless it will be very interesting to see what effect these 10 students (who will be "really different" with regard to the normal Oberlin standards) will have on the life and styles of Oberlin college.

According to the director of admissions, the failure rate and the rate of those leaving have been about the same for the black contingent as for the total student body. This is perhaps because the black contingent differs little from the total student body in class rank, SAT scores, and socioeconomic background. It must be said that there has been a genuinely humane concern by the admissions office as well as by the faculty at large that these students not be injured by paternalistic treatment on the one hand, or by the effect of failure on the other. The overall quality of collaboration in implementing the admissions policy seems to be very high.

The chairman of the SEOP committee is also the chairman of the department of sociology and anthropology. He is white and has the academic specialty of being a student of African cultures. The program as he sees it is "in the Oberlin tradition" and will continue to be so. In more specific terms, this means that there will be a black studies program at Oberlin but not a black studies major or department. Thus, efforts will be made to develop competence in existing faculty in black approaches to their subject field, rather than to build up a cadre of specialists in black studies, who might possibly create a black studies department. The intellectual style of black studies at Oberlin will be consistent with intellectual rigor, stressing cognitive over affective dimensions (or as one white informant put it, "The black studies program here is in the white studies tradition").

3 *What have been the consequences of this program for people in the organization?*

As previously mentioned, Oberlin's minority students are still by national standards extremely high achievers; nevertheless a peculiar characteristic of Oberlin is the drive shared by faculty and students alike for rewarding and expecting greater and greater achievement. As one member of the community stated, "There is no community of *acceptance* here to match the community of *achievement.*" Consequently, people tend to measure each other here in terms of their grades and other visible achievements. Any discussion of consequences for the college or people therein revolves around this question of academic standards and achievement. This is an area of considerable sensitivity and misunderstanding.

As Mr. Davis reported, there is no apparent overt negative

faculty reaction to the program, but there are subtly expressed hostilities in the form of perennial questions such as: "Are we [Oberlin] not heading for disaster with our double standards?" "Are we not harming the black students psychologically?" "They may have *A* ambitions but because of poor preparation they are *C* students. Is this healthy?" For whatever reason then, *some* faculty (and it cannot be ascertained how many are in this camp) have tended to see the black students deficient as a group. There may only be a handful of faculty who feel this way (we interviewed three), but their impact on black students and staff has been far greater than the numbers would suggest. It was the tendency of some, according to one faculty informant, to marvel when a black student made an A in a course, instead of congratulating him. We are describing a *social* reality here, in that some of our informants said that this happened. Whether it really happened we cannot say. Several unfortunate events have added to this misunderstanding. For two successive years, for example, someone in an administrative office has sent a letter to *all* black students whether they are at Oberlin on the compensatory Rockefeller grant programs or not (and the term "Rockefeller scholarship" has developed some bad connotations), informing them that a very high level of performance was expected and that they would have to work harder than other students to stay at Oberlin. This outraged the black students, particularly those who had been admitted to Oberlin under normal admissions criteria. Several black students who were National Merit Scholarship winners were sent these letters and their feelings are understandable. This was, however, clearly an oversight on the part of the college; in no sense was it an act of ill will. It is important, however, in that it shows that some of the administration, as well as some of the faculty, seem to view black students as being deficient as a group. It is of importance to some of the black students who are obviously sensitive to such statements.

Attitudes of Black Students Toward the Program

The response of some 25 black students we interviewed at the Afro-American House is quite clear-cut. They are keenly aware of what they see as the condescension of the faculty and refuse to view themselves as deprived or disadvantaged. (It must be said that about six of the students did all the talking in our session. We cannot report the feelings of the others, as they reported none to us. Some seemed afraid to contradict the leaders.) One student said that even if special help were offered to bring him up to Oberlin

standards, he would not accept it, for to do so would be to acknowl-
edge his inferiority in the eyes of the college. Some of the black
students reject the Oberlin norms of cognitive rationality because
of their abstractness. Some feel that the Oberlin style of intellectual
analysis and acute self-criticism *un*fits them for a practical vocation
and for communication with their ghetto brothers, and they refuse
the accepted norm of the value of intellectuality. Some of them
talk about the college experience as a brainwashing in that it
attempts to wipe out what has been gained in the previous 18 years
and to fit them only for graduate work, preparing to accept an
advanced degree. They are not yet convinced that the Oberlin
style is appropriate to them. (Davis has prepared an extremely
interesting paper on this theme entitled, "The Rush Toward Black-
ness: Institutional Change and the Trick Bag.")

At our meeting with about 25 black students at the Afro-American House, the hostility of students was blatant. Some of them
called Oberlin a Santa Claus school, which would accede to almost
all requests (a completely and totally segregated Afro-American
House has, however, been denied, and a majority of black students
would probably not support such a move). Many students show
an ambivalent attitude about "making it." One young black woman
remarked, "When asked what I can do, I reply, 'I can read Shake-
speare'; that gets me nowhere." On the one hand they look with
disdain upon the traditional education of Oberlin; on the other hand
they desperately want to show that they *too* can get A's and B's.
They want to prove a point by performing well in their courses,
but they also want to question the relevance of those courses.

The SEOP report of May 1968 states on page 14:

It may strike many of us as unfortunate and puzzling that a significant
portion of the black students characterize Oberlin as neglectful and unresponsive, if not racist and hostile to their interests and their desire for
the recognition of Afro-American culture and contributions. It is obvious
that despite Oberlin's rich heritage of strong commitment and vigorous
action to enhance social justice for all, there is an absence of *shared* under-
standings between black students and the faculty and administration about
current orientations and endeavors at the College. From a history of being
engulfed in societal institutional frameworks that are either oppressively
blind or deliberately unresponsive to their claims, it should not be surprising that many black students would be inclined to generalize negative
attitudes to the College. In short, the students, in a time of growing mili-

tance, are acting exactly as they think they should be acting, given the experiences of Negroes in America.

It is in response to this attitude that the assistant dean of students, Mr. Davis, has proposed an extended workshop whereby, using the black experience as a reference point, students and community persons will try to develop a different idea of a more valid educational experience. It was not made clear to the interviewers just how the workshop related structurally to the curriculum of the college, but presumably it will be an all-black endeavor with a strong input from the community. Indeed, the workshop may turn out to be the most salient example of change and may work against a certain institutionalization of the black students by the college. It remains to be seen, however, what curricular impact, if any, the projected workshop will have, although it is stated in the proposal that "the workshop will be by method and content designed to phase into regular curricula." In addition, there are several ad hoc courses (for credit but temporarily approved until carried through regular channels) in black-ghetto-related subjects such as "images of the black men in Africa and Western Civilization," taught by a member of the sociology department.

Although the most vocal of the black students at Oberlin have serious frustrations, it is vital to note that these students do not leave Oberlin, even when they spend a semester or full year at another institution. It is quite clear that they hope to find within the college ways of developing their own interests, of satisfying their own needs, and of maintaining their own identity without too much compromise. Although enormously skilled in current black rhetoric, they nevertheless recognize that Oberlin is not unique in its attitude of "condescension," as they see it. They know that other colleges are no better and are usually significantly worse. Although one young man said, "Oberlin would love to see us huffing and puffing our way up the Mt. Everest of middle-class values," it was clear that he had no other place to go and would probably remain at Oberlin, chugging along with the rest of the white students.

Another interesting area of student involvement has been the impact of the black students on the white student body at large. The college insisted that Afro-American House be integrated, and in its first year of operation (1967–68) a closeness appeared to grow between black and white roommates who struggled through a year-long identity crisis together. This year, however, white students have been surprised at the coolness of those former roommates, who now go their own way with other black students (this conclusion comes from a study done of Oberlin roommates by O. M. Markley of the Western Behavioral Sciences Institute).

In class discussions this year a few white students have been silenced or scorned by blacks when dealing with questions relating to the black experience, which many white students resented. In the picturesque words of one Oriental faculty respondent, "The blacks have stomped on the whites this year." Many of the black students seem beyond the stage of exhibiting any interest in "educating" whites. Furthermore, the administration has been highly sensitive to the wishes of the black students and has attempted to anticipate them. This, it must be said, is not wholly appreciated by the more militant black students, who resent being deprived of confrontation. In political maneuvering the blacks have been more successful than the whites, and this has been another source of irritation. Although Afro-American House is still integrated in name, dining there is not entirely integrated, and the white students are not allowed much intimacy with some of the black students.

Any easy "liberal" attitudes on the part of white students which may have existed previously no longer seem possible, and this is frustrating and bewildering to many Oberlin students. At the same time, it is possible to overstate the solidarity of the black students' attitudes. One professor points out that there is not the unanimity among black students that the rhetoric seems to indicate. Some black students on campus are afraid to go to Afro-American House, and in a recent questionnaire study of Negro students, about half of those returning questionnaires said that they did not want to live in an all-black house, but would prefer to live with students of all races. In private discussions, there is a much broader range of attitudes among Negro students than the public language and rhetoric of the more militant black students seems to suggest. But in terms of seeking change, it is fairly clear that the vocal and aggressive element in the black student group will have to be dealt with.

4 *What has this change done to Oberlin College as an institution?*

An institution such as Oberlin, with its tradition of liberalism stretching back more than a century, could be expected to inaugurate a black students and studies program. Because it was liberal, it could invite a black student to come in; because it was educationally secure, it could make adaptation to the black student as it chose to without fear of being challenged as educationally weak, soft, or expedient. But because Oberlin tends to be educationally committed to intellectual values above all others, it has not made adaptations which deviated in any significant degree from its established program. It can adopt a black studies program, but this program must operate outside the present departmental structure rather than within the structure, where it would have an intellectual stature equal to the established disciplines. Oberlin admits black students lower in "quality" than its white students, but the black students are still very good indeed and the college can expect good performance and does. The college then has made few major compromises in its notions of standards. This is not to say that it should.

If Oberlin does change in significant ways, it will do so gradually. But the degree of commitment to assimilate minority students (and this should, by Oberlin tradition, include socioeconomic minorities as well as racial minorities) to the Oberlin style may be shaken in the future by the extent of problems which might arise. If the program to bring in more black students with high social awareness is carried through, it is possible that black students locally will become even more radicalized. If, on the other hand, a national trend toward a hard line dealing with demands of black students continues to develop, then the faculty and administration may refuse to bend further than they have.

Another major problem on the horizon is the extent of the college's financial commitment to the program. Since the Rockefeller grants are being gradually terminated, the college is assuming more responsibility for SEOP and the scholarship program. But this cannot continue indefinitely as it is a major expense. New sources of funding will be needed, and the college hopes that it can solicit new funds on the basis of its progress thus far. Although there are few black faculty and staff at Oberlin, a genuine effort is being made to attract more black faculty and staff.

One possible source of personnel is the community of Cleveland. Mr. Davis, in his interesting experimental program for the next year, plans to make extensive use of persons who live and work in the ghetto—such as cab drivers (who are often very good teachers), hustlers, etc.—in the operation of this workshop. These will be short-term adjunct personnel who will possibly have the rank of lecturer. One of the most intriguing aspects of next year's work will be the relationship between such people representing the ghetto and the regular members of the college faculty and staff, as each could learn from the other.

It is quite likely that the programs will continue in some form even if their impact on the college is minimal (even the brochure describing the Afro-American studies program is entitled *In the Oberlin Tradition*). Faculty attitudes may relax somewhat, but it is improbable that the college's academic mores will be significantly altered in the near future. If change in attitudes occurs, it will come not so much from the instigation of the more radical black students but from those interests also shared by whites, such as greater participation in college governance and an appreciation of new modes of learning, which may be less bookish and abstract and more concerned with feeling and effect as they relate to cognitive processes. A student movement in this direction is possible at Oberlin for all races, but it is unlikely.

In many ways the responses of the Oberlin community to the black students in their midst parallels rather nicely the course of contemporary American liberalism. Conventionally liberal ideals and sentiments have been abruptly called into question by the very objects of those sentiments (the black militants), and the course for the future is still not clear. By definition, liberals ought to remain cognizant of practical realities, but they, like all people, have shown less than perfect ability to do so and thus liberals could become educational conservatives, at least as seen by some radicals.

One thing that does seem to be clear is that the Oberlin black studies program will not become a department. This is perhaps the most significant factor in predicting the impact of this program on the Oberlin of the future, as those who represent black students and black studies often must work from a less than advantageous position in the political structure of the faculty and administration. On the other hand, if Mr. Davis's workshop begins to move into the established curriculum, it may well be that evolutionary change can take place where revolutionary change clearly will not. With the amount of intellectual energy and talent available on the Oberlin campus, such a development would be an exceedingly interesting and hopeful one for all American higher education.

Northern Illinois University was included in this study because of the fact that in a very small number of years it was transformed from a teachers college to a complex and growing university, with specialized graduate departments and all the accoutrements of the modern multiversity. The transition from state college to state university is clearly one which many other institutions will undergo or hope to undergo, and the institution's rapid increase in size and complexity is applicable to a wide variety of institutions.

Established in 1895 by an act of the Illinois General Assembly, the Northern Illinois State Normal School opened its doors in September 1899 to its first class of students. On July 1, 1955, the name of the college was changed from the Northern Illinois State Teachers' College to the Northern Illinois State College. The same legislation authorized the college to broaden its educational services by offering academic work in areas other than teacher education. By action of the 70th General Assembly, Northern Illinois State College became Northern Illinois University on July 1, 1957. Since that time, authority has been granted for the university to offer additional five-year programs leading to the degree of master of arts, master of science, and master of music, in addition to six-year programs and doctoral programs leading to the degree of doctor of education and doctor of philosophy. In 1957 the institution had 4,500 students. The enrollment has quintupled in the short period between 1957 and 1968.

1 *Where did the idea of the change originate?*
According to one administrative official, the change was hard to pinpoint because it was thrust upon the university by the state. According to this view, a senator in the local area was highly influential in initiating the change, which paralleled nationwide movements of teachers colleges to state colleges and then, in some cases, to university status. This change came before most people were ready for it and provoked a great deal of discussion.

Another aspect of the development, consistent with the first, was provided by a faculty member of the institution since 1953, whose view received support from the current president, who arrived on the scene in 1967. According to this view, the enrollment of the institution tripled between 1949 and 1957, so that the growth in population and variety of student and faculty interests which had already occurred was the major contributing factor.

In this view, the critical stage was reached when the liberal arts faculty outgrew the faculty of the department of education—for it was this former group that provided the greatest impetus toward university status. One faculty member, who came in 1947, told us that he was almost not hired because he had no training in education and that he believed himself to be the first faculty member without teacher certification to be hired at the institution.

By the mid-fifties, however, this attitude no longer prevailed, so that a sizable number of faculty members without teacher certification were on hand. At the same time, because of the way in which the state of Illinois bases funding on enrollment, large sums of money were coming into the institution for purposes of development—particularly for graduate programs.

Another vital factor in the change was the creation during the sixties of the Board of Higher Education for Illinois, which laid the groundwork for a more coordinated operating framework for the Illinois system of higher education. As a result of phase 2 of the state's Master Plan, Northern Illinois was identified as one of three "liberal arts universities" in Illinois. As such, Northern was charged with developing relevant programs for the production of teachers at the college and university level. There is little question that Northern Illinois University is an institution "on the move." The faculty is clearly pushing hard for university status, which is interpreted generally on campus as meaning more graduate programs, increased size, and increased research and publication. This push is consistent with the view of the Master Plan of the state. Thus, both inside and outside forces were working in the same direction.

2   *Through what processes did the idea become implemented?*

A document entitled "Historical Development of Administrative Organization" tells part of the story of change. Behind the scenes was a highly interesting political process which had contributed to the written policy. Faculty members at Northern perceived that the governance of the university by the old teachers college board would inhibit development, since apparently this board was perceived by some faculty as being incapable of understanding faculty aspirations toward university status. Its policy demanded that all six institutions in the system be treated equally and identically. Consequently a push for autonomy seemed to dictate the need for Northern's own board, and several faculty members worked directly with the legislature to accomplish this. The major pattern or model for aspiration was Southern Illinois University, which had received its own governing board of trustees in 1949. Such a proposal for Northern passed the Illinois Senate but lost in the House of Representatives. Meanwhile, in 1963–64 a new planning and coordinating body emerged in the state—the Board of Higher Education headed by Lyman Glenny. (Efforts to create such a group had been made since 1961.) Neither a separate board for Northern nor a single board for all public universities in the state seemed feasible, according to the Board of Higher Education. It was believed that the legislators would not agree to place the University of Illinois under a body with the other institutions because so many legislators were University of Illinois alumni.

Faculty members then went directly to the Governor, who promised some reform; and the Board of Higher Education, with his assistance, developed a compromise plan—a separate board entitled the Board of Regents for Northern Illinois University (NIU) and Illinois State University (ISU), leaving Eastern Illinois University, Western Illinois University, and the two Chicago state colleges under the old board. Although this would appear to be chaotic from the outside, it is a compromise system that seems to work. At present there are separate boards for Illinois University and Southern Illinois University, a common board for NIU and ISU, a board for Eastern-Western and the two Chicago schools, and a board for the junior colleges, in addition to the overall planning body entitled the Board for Higher Education!

All these arrangements became effective as a coordinated entity in 1967, which was the time that new presidents were appointed for Northern Illinois University and Illinois State University, so that the meaning of the new system has been in part dependent on the ways the new chief executives have seen fit to use it. Dr. Rhoten Smith, the new president of Northern Illinois University,[3] thinks that it is a good system; it is one of the features which attracted him to the post in the first place. There is a measure of overall order, as in Ohio and California, but it is not as strict a lockstep as in those states—institutional autonomy is preserved in most areas.

The Board for Higher Education has transmitted responsibilities for graduate education to the institutions under the control of the Board of Regents. Northern Illinois thus becomes a unit of the

[3] In the summer of 1971, Dr. Smith left NIU to become president of the University of Pittsburgh.

"liberal arts university" arrangement. The Board of Regents, in turn, has provided for the self-governance of NIU. However, the meaning of these directives is still untested. A new constitution for the total university is in preliminary draft, as well as a committee draft for a university senate. Thus the "idea of the university" is still in the process of reformation. There exists no comprehensive long-range plan for the future of the university beyond enrollment projections and building priorities. The crucial self-measures which the campus uses as bench marks in the push for university status are the expansion of the educational program with its increasing complexity, the development of the graduate school, and the yearning (of some) toward a master planning blueprint for the institution. The increasing "complexity," however, seems to be interpreted on campus largely as a question of increase in size of bureaucratic detail of daily operation rather than any increase in sophistication or complexity of the mission of the institution.

An examination of present rough-draft proposals indicates a university government on the drawing boards with strong faculty power, some student input, and a management system which could be quite effective. All of these represent dimensions of change for the institution, but most represent changes consistent with what other major universities throughout the country are doing. It should be said here that the new president, who seems to enjoy wide rapport with faculty leaders, is committed to the job of humanizing his already large institution. He is a man of obvious compassion and patience with a large job to do. The president sees the management problems of the university as crucial ones, and his major concern seems to be simply to "get on top of the present." A vital step is being taken by dividing the current position of executive vice-president and provost into two senior positions. When the new provost is hired, he will take charge of future planning and development for the academic programs. The vice-president for business affairs plans to reorganize his far-flung operations, since at present 12 separate department heads report directly to him and this he finds unsatisfactory, as can be imagined.

But as we said earlier, the chief initiating factor in changes at the institution is the increasing dominance of the arts and sciences faculty. It is here that the greatest number of graduate programs are being implemented (as suggested in the Master Plan), and of course here that the vast majority of undergraduates receive their instruction. Even though the business school is the largest in the state and one of the largest in the nation, it nevertheless accounts for only a quarter of the undergraduates who still must take their general education courses in the faculty of arts and sciences. Again, using the formula that the state uses, the arts and sciences departments receive the lion's share of the university funds allocated on a per head basis. Thus whatever conception of the university finally emerges victorious, this arts and science faculty will have the major role in its determination.

As in most American universities, aggressiveness on the part of departmental chairmen is rewarded in terms of faculty positions and funds. In discussion with department chairmen it became clear that different departments are at different stages of development, one determining factor being how aggressive and energetic the chairman happens to be. Almost all chairmen have been in office a very short time, primarily because certain persons have been specifically recruited for these positions. If departmental power is a sign of institutional maturity, as some maintain it is (and others would argue the other side), then NIU is certainly approaching maturity at a rapid rate. At the same time the not-as-yet-accepted bylaws for the faculty senate sound a new and more collective note. While agreeing that departmental power is of great importance, the bylaws grant authority to delegated committees which is unusually broad. For example, the personnel committee of the senate is charged not only to measure the performance of men approaching tenure, but also to monitor the performance of deans of colleges and department heads.

This remarkable document takes a rather exclusive stand against the central administration (the presidents and other administrators are not members of the senate). The only function of such exclusion will be to reduce communication, as there have been no apparent major conflicts in point of view or sense of mission and no critical incidents which might have triggered such faculty action. In fact the administration of NIU seems particularly receptive to and sympathetic for faculty prerogative. It appears that the university community, perhaps having read the recent research of Talcott Parsons, David Riesman, and others, is assuming that faculty power is a sign of institutional maturity. Yet the American Association of University Professors (AAUP) is not very active on campus, with 92 local members and 232 national members. The American Federation of Teachers (AFT) unit on campus has about 30 members and is challenging the AAUP slightly. But out of a faculty of 1,200 individuals neither the AAUP nor AFT represents a very significant factor, at least in numbers.

Of course we must also talk about money in that it is increased funding which has propelled NIU on its course of expansion. According to the financial statement, last year's operating budget was over $42 million;[4] and in recent years, NIU, together with other Illinois institutions, has been remarkably fortunate in a fiscal sense, seen in a national perspective. The Board for Higher Education's recommendations have also been the Governor's recommendations to the Legislature. The institution might be classified as having been in the euphoria of rapid growth. A few examples illustrate this point: Five years ago the libraries' book budget was less than $100,000; in 1968–69 it was $600,000 plus federal money amounting to another $170,000. Salaries are high by most standards, with yearly increments being well above national averages. The only problem with buildings has been getting them up fast enough—the money has always been there. This however is changing, with a shift in state administrations and an overall tax squeeze coming up in the state. In order to ease a financial crisis, for example the Governor asked the state universities to return money to the treasury this year, and NIU managed to return $1.2 million in operating funds in addition to money for capital expenditures. (However, some of these funds were already frozen and thus of little current use to NIU.)

The consequences of tighter budgeting only dimly loom on the horizon, and few people are aware of them outside of the central administration; but it is safe to say that there would be no NIU without the relatively great generosity of the state. This generosity cannot continue at present levels, and some retrenchment will occur.

3   *What were the consequences of the change for people in the institution?*

Perhaps the most painful consequence of the change was the "clash of cultures" between the faculty of the older teachers college mentality and the new and more research- and discipline-oriented liberal arts faculty. People who had been "competent" as determined by the old culture were no longer competent as the new

[4] Of this amount, $27 million was appropriated by the state for instructional purposes, and $14 million was put in bond revenue projects and therefore is not available for current instructional costs.

criteria of research, publication, and experience with doctoral work became primary requisites and status symbols for faculty members. Many older faculty simply could not cope with these demands. Some were given leaves to build their competence in a disciplinary area and to find research projects; others were given special tasks such as work in the general education teaching programs (although this is certainly not a mark of high status in the faculty of this institution). Still others left the institution for more congenial surroundings where they could feel at home. By and large, however, most accepted their new status as virtual second-class citizens with surprising ease—according to some of our informants. And although their promotions may have been slowed, salary increments at all levels were coming rapidly enough to keep them relatively comfortable and well fed even if egos may have been bruised.

One dominant fact of this period is growth in faculty personnel. For example, the English department will be adding 20 Ph.D.s to the staff for the coming year. They are mostly replacements, not new positions, but they will be the "new breed." Even if older people were unhappy, their voices would be muted against a constantly changing crowd such as this. It is still relatively easy, according to most informants, to get tenure at NIU and to be promoted to associate professor. Full professor rank, however, is now reserved for those who have "significant publications," or so it is claimed. But the facts of research at the institution do not seem to bear out this assertion. When the sums of money for summer institutes are taken out, the amount of funded research contained in the budget is a rather small $60,000 or $70,000 out of a $45 million total, or $28 million instructional. This might lead one to suspect that quantity of publication is presently more important than quality, at least in the fastest growing disciplines in the institution. This new drive toward academic respectability, which is strong on the campus, means that new programs—especially doctoral programs—will probably be conventional in nature. In fact, the Board for Higher Education of the state has a Commission of Scholars (10 to 12 faculty from the state) which must pass on each proposed program, and it seems to demand conventionality. We got the impression that little energy is expended on innovation, as there is little reward for it within the faculty culture.

There may well be a certain amount of absolutely unavoidable conventionality in the process of starting Ph.D. programs. (Among new institutions, one bit of sage advice frequently heard is, "Do your own experimenting and innovating after you get accredited.") In order to get a Ph.D. program approved, you have to have a faculty of Ph.D. quality. To get a faculty of Ph.D. quality, there has to be the promise of a program at the Ph.D. level, graduate students, library facilities, research facilities, and time to do research. The process limits the options rather effectively. If there is another route to the privilege of granting the Ph.D., few people know of it.

It was indicated that for many people the model for the development of NIU would be Southern Illinois University, which also made an astonishingly rapid move into advanced Ph.D. work and faculty status. This immense growth in size has meant that priorities have placed undergraduate teaching fairly low on the list — especially freshman and sophomore teaching. Consequently, most instruction in these areas is done in huge lecture sections with large numbers of teaching assistants. This has important consequences for undergraduates who are increasing in quality every year, as the ACT scores and class ranks indicate. Students also come from a broader range of socioeconomic and home background, which means that they are probably increasing in sophistication as well. At this point they are fairly docile as a group, but some signs of conflict and rebellion against impersonal instruction are beginning to make themselves known. On the other side, ROTC was approved 2 to 1 by freshmen and sophomore males only two years ago.

During the current phase of building graduate programs, faculty, and students, it seems clear that attention has not been given to undergraduate programs, at least not on a per student basis comparable with that of graduate students. The institution has had large increases in the undergraduate student body which have made the problem even more difficult, but these large freshmen classes are supposed to decrease in size when the junior college system in the state begins taking over more and more of the first two years of college work. By 1970–71, with ceilings on freshmen enrollment, the institution should be in a much better stance with regard to its undergraduates. (In fact, a large number of the new Ph.D.-level appointments for next year are hired in part to upgrade undergraduate instruction, at least in English, which is currently dealing with almost 1,000 undergraduate majors.) Some current changes reflect this new concern, such as a new honors program, a living-learning experience for 1,000 students in two dormitories, a committee on undergraduate curriculum of the College of Liberal Arts and Sciences, etc. But at the moment these are plans, for the most part, not realities, and as funds become tighter, and as faculty may have to choose between allocations to undergraduate or graduate programs, it is not yet clear how they would vote. However, as the size of the undergraduate student body begins to decline, the faculty can do a better job than they now have time for. The logistics of the situation can probably be worked out. The primary question is that of whether or not the faculty, pouring energy and time into the evolution of graduate programs, will be able to manifest a similar interest and incentive in the improvement of undergraduate teaching (and learning).

Active student groups on campus now include the SDS, the Young Socialist Alliance, and the Afro-American Cultural Organization. In the spring of 1969 students picketed against the dismissal of a political science professor who, they said, was being released because of his political views. Some faculty perceived this incident as an indication of increase in institutional status, i.e., if NIU students rebel, it may be seen as a badge of status for the institution, just as Russians are proud of their traffic jams. In any case, efforts to find out from the faculty members what they thought the students were upset about were futile.

The president of the student government (who is an activist on social issues but fairly moderate on student tactics) says he has seen a remarkable change in the temper of the student body in his three years on campus. Although the great majority of students still resist any move toward demonstration or participation in university affairs, the number of genuine activists, he feels, has grown many times over. (One informed observer felt, however, that the radicals could still be outvoted by the conservative students, 15 to 1.) But we were interested to find that the possibility of more genuine confrontations with some of the students does not seem to be a major problem in the minds of faculty or some administrators.

As one would expect, in any institution which has undergone such an increase in size, both formal and informal communication channels between faculty, students, and administration could be improved. Some incidents have occurred because decisions were made without consultation, particularly in the areas of duplicating services, communications, the computer center, and the university press. It has always been easier to get money for faculty than for backup staff. This development is clearly not due to anyone's ill will—there seem to be few Machiavellians within either the administration or the faculty—but simply to the sheer increase in level of complexity, which makes managerial systems obsolete almost at their moment of birth. It seems that in this affluent period a great deal of resources are going to the improvement of academic status. One example of this is the practice of bringing in a few "star" professors at $2,500 per month and up in order to gain approval from the Commission of Scholars for doctoral programs and thereby attract younger faculty who are of exactly the same mold as the senior "star." Few departments have done this, but the "stars" have considerable visibility.

At no time did we discern much serious concern about undergraduate students, undergraduate life, or undergraduate instruction. The talk was of larger sections, audio-visual aids, and more teaching assistants. There appeared to be little visible interest in attempting to measure classroom teaching effectiveness, in reducing class size, in recruiting faculty dedicated to teaching, or in looking again at the nature of the undergraduate curriculum. However, students and some faculty are already beginning to question the system. Black students are asking for black courses, and some whites are asking for drastic revisions of the curriculum and for a larger role for students in the processes of governance. It may be that the current focus on graduate programs is simply masking a latent faculty interest in these areas.

4 *What of the future of the institution?*

There seems to be a wide variety of opinions, ranging from the most euphoric optimism to absolute pessimism on this question. As one faculty member said, "There is no limit to Northern's future potential." But it must be added that we found no very clear sense of what that future potential might be, and several commented on the lack of an academic master plan. Indeed, the usual response to the question was bewilderment or vagueness. As the librarian replied to the question of where the institution will be in five years, "Ask us again in five years." The president himself is vague on this question, primarily because he is preoccupied (and justifiably so) with *present* management problems which are exceedingly difficult. In all likelihood the future holds a greater measure of administrative stability owing to the leveling off of enrollments. Hopefully, the present president will succeed in his mission of humanizing an already overly large institution. There will be more Ph.D. work capitalizing on certain areas of strength already present, such as a Southeast Asian Center, mathematics, and physics. Those persons already on campus who are energetic entrepreneurs and are acquiring money and staff in these and some other academic areas will have a head start.

The president is personally committed to education for disadvantaged students, and there is presently on campus a CHANCE program involving as of fall 1969 about 230 of the university's 700 black students. Apparently this CHANCE program mainly offers special academic counseling services and some remedial work, although a nine-hour communications skills unit is also under development. In terms of community service, there is very little consulting with industry in the area and no contract research. Some coordination with educational institutions, primarily junior colleges, does seem to exist, and will increase as the junior colleges grow. But no one seems very interested in developing additional service orientations. (There is extensive work in the extension and continuing education divisions.)

In terms of the president's desire to humanize the institutional structure he has inherited, it is difficult for us to think of many specific ways in which this could be implemented—indeed, the physical plant of the university is being built on rather conventional and somewhat monolithic lines, with no provision for breaking up the architecture into smaller educational and personal units. Some ideas for altering the nature of undergraduate education have been suggested. It is hoped, for example, that teaching internships will be built into Ph.D. programs in the future, but little is now being done in this way. As money gets scarcer this sort of program may be the first to go, and the university may have to protect its commitment to training college and university teachers.

The evaluation of teaching effectiveness plays a small part in promotion and salary decisions. Class size continues to grow except in arts and sciences where it is already at 36 students per class, and we sensed a rather widespread view that a serious faculty conflict exists between those who want more attention given to undergraduates and those who advocate the building of "strength" —meaning the development of more graduate programs, publication, and research. But at the same time the institution is moving in this direction, the profile of entering students continues to improve, so that NIU can expect in the future a student body which may be more aggressive, demanding better and more relevant undergraduate teaching. Although most students are still interested in getting passing grades, in vocationalism, and in joining Greek letter organizations, the march in the spring of 1969 of several hundred students was viewed by the student body president as a kind of turning point in developing student concern about undergraduate education and teaching. Some of those who were concerned about students seemed to feel that student affairs were simply another administrative problem—if we can put some students on the faculty senate (and they *will* be, in numbers not yet determined), then the problem can be easily solved. It does not seem likely that this move will be enough. Depending upon how militant and coercive the laws which the Illinois Legislature passes dealing with control of student dissidents, it would seem that there is a conflict between the faculty's idea of "making it" in graduate work and the demands of a small percentage of fairly sophisticated undergraduate students. If the university begins to invest large amounts of concern, time, and money in the problems of undergraduate teaching and learning, this situation may change.

In general, however, we found among the faculty and administration a considerable amount of camaraderie and cohesion, particularly in relation to the feelings that Northern Illinois was entering into the select circle of prestige universities and would undoubtedly continue to "move up" on other institutions in this select group. What the institution may be forgetting is that many of the institutions in the select circle are moving up simultaneously.

In its eagerness to embrace the conventional status and prestige criteria of the graduate school mentality, NIU is perhaps the most representative institution of American higher education we have in this series of case studies. One possible source of initiative in providing some alternative to the interest in publication, research, and cognitive rationality to the exclusion of all else is the tiny group of activist students who will undoubtedly gain a few more allies as the quality of the rest of the student body steadily increases. There may be faculty interest and commitment also. On the other hand, it may be that distinctiveness is an institutional quality which can only come after a time of relative stability, and Northern has yet to reach the plateau of relative security in internal organization. But sources of initiative and flexibility must be developed *before* these systems lock into each other in such a way that the institution becomes musclebound in the future.

Yet there is a great deal of restless energy and dynamism to the place, and if some adjustment of the relative value of different levels of teaching can be achieved, NIU could become more clear-cut about its goals and thereby have a better chance of meeting them. The essential paradox of growth was put well by one respondent:

> . . . The real lesson for other institutions is just beginning to emerge. Partly because of fairly generous financing, the institution has grown too rapidly on too many fronts, and, essentially without priorities, has been too many things to too many people. . . . Now that we are faced with a real budget squeeze for a while, indiscriminate growth has caught us short. We are going to suffer for some time the pains of unplanned growth for there are a lot of faculty expectations we will never be able to meet. . . . The lesson, though . . . is that no institution can possibly grow this fast without a master plan for both academic and physical development and a flexible administrative structure.

SOUTHERN COLORADO STATE COLLEGE Southern Colorado State College was selected for this study because it was an institution which had gone from a two-year to a four-year program, offering the B.A. degree. It also has moved from control centered in Pueblo (a city of approximately 100,000) to state control in its new form as a member of the Colorado State College system. Pueblo had no institution of higher learning until 1933, at which time a junior college was formed under a private board of trustees. This institution became public in 1937 and received local tax support.

1 *Where did the idea of the change originate?*

Although the documentation is a little vague, it can be said that almost as soon as Pueblo Junior College was established as a public institution devoted to the community of Pueblo, there began to be discussion of the need for a four-year college. In order to understand this development it should be said that there is a feeling of inferiority in the Pueblo community with regard to Colorado Springs, its neighbor to the north. There is a stong feeling that culture in Colorado ends at the Colorado Springs boundary, and Pueblo is seen from the north as little more than a "dinnerbucket" town, interested largely in manufacturing and manual labor. The college at Pueblo used to be larger than the one at Colorado Springs, although Colorado Springs has had its own four-year institution for a much longer time. The two communities seem to be natural rivals, and this rivalry perhaps spurred the development of the Pueblo institution.

There was general agreement among our informants that the

first open initiation of this change was accomplished by State Senator Vincent Massari. Senator Massari is clearly a direct, forceful, and energetic representative of the interests of Pueblo in the State Legislature. He is a strong advocate of public higher education. Through his instigation, the Pueblo Chamber of Commerce appointed a committee to study the feasibility of the change and make recommendations. There were other Pueblo residents who clearly supported Massari, including Frank Hoag, former president of the junior college board, and Robert Bartley, a local attorney who is now vice-president of the state college board. Mr. Bartley, a Pueblo lawyer, was the chairman of the study committee which recommended that Pueblo have a four-year college and supported the legislation which led to its establishment. Bartley also worked actively with the Legislature to assure passage of the bill which established Southern Colorado State College. Mr. Bartley is a Democrat and presently a member of the Board of Trustees of the State Colleges, the board of control for five institutions, which include Southern Colorado State College.

It is not quite clear how it occurred or who arranged it, but a "ground swell of opinion" in favor of the four-year college movement began to occur in the Pueblo community. Students currently enrolled at Southern Colorado State College told us that as juniors in high school they were encouraged by "representatives of the college" to write letters to the Legislature supporting the proposal. According to the current dean of the college, other four-year colleges in the state supported the change from two- to four-year for Pueblo, with certain restrictions on Pueblo's growth that would mean the new institution would not threaten their own programs. For example, the college was to have no four-year engineering program, no professional education program, etc. Thus, the new institution could grow and develop without endangering the established programs in other institutions.

The primary team, then, seemed to be Mr. Massari, working with the Legislature; Mr. Hoag (a newspaper publisher), representing the leadership in the business community; and Mr. Hartley, chairman of the Pueblo Chamber of Commerce committee, who had active contacts in the business community and in the Legislature. As far as those groups more directly concerned with the junior college as it then was were concerned, they did not seem to be as favorably inclined. The president of Pueblo Junior College was not in favor of the move. The faculty was very quiet initially and took no position for or against. The junior college board seemed ambivalent on the question of Pueblo becoming a four-year institution, although at least one board member, Frank Hoag, did assume leadership in making the change. Part of the faculty's passivity on the question was due perhaps to the fear for personal careers of those members of the faculty who did not hold credentials that would be acceptable for teaching in a four-year college. They also knew that the then president of the college was not in favor of the idea, and this factor may also have contributed to their lack of reaction. The faculty, however, changed their attitude as efforts for a four-year college accelerated and community interest was clearly established favoring the new proposal.

2 *How was the change implemented?*

With growing sentiment in Pueblo favoring the creation of a four-year college out of the existing junior college, there were several decisive acts which led to legislation and final implementation: (1) A local referendum was held, and the vote favored the establishment of a four-year college in the ratio of 17 to 3. (2) Students at the junior college held an all-school assembly and supported the change overwhelmingly. (3) The legislators received letters from the community, even from junior high school pupils, who were encouraged to write in support of the legislation. (4) The three existing state colleges supported the addition of Pueblo to their group.

Pueblo, as the second largest city within the state, had considerable political power. There was energetic leadership both within the Legislature and from civic interests which worked for the appropriate legislation. After extended discussions by Republican and Democratic party forces and the reconciliation of differences between the Democratic Governor and the Pueblo Democratic Senator, Mr. Massari, the Colorado General Assembly, in an act which was signed into law by the Governor on March 24, 1961, created Southern Colorado State College. The college catalog contains a shorthand version of this sequence: "Within the statutory discretion accorded them, the trustees, by resolution, recommended that Southern Colorado State College evolve out of Pueblo County Junior College." This is hardly the whole story, but this board resolution was the vehicle that carried the issue into the State Legislature. In a remarkably short period of time after the Governor signed the legislation, a number of significant events took place:

Southern Colorado became operational under the trustees of the state colleges in Colorado.

The community transferred the Pueblo Junior College campus to the state
and provided the budget for the first year of operation.

Two-year junior college programs, including the extensive vocational-
technical program, were kept intact.

The open-door policy of admissions was maintained, although the policy
has emerged of enrolling high school graduates from the "lowest third"
in high school rank in the two-year division only.

Four-year programs were developed.

Many of the faculty of the junior college were given responsible administrative assignments in the new structure (an important consequence of this
was that high morale among junior college faculty was maintained throughout the transition).

Almost everyone we spoke with about the transitional period
indicated that it was accomplished very smoothly with little personal strife or argumentation. As a junior college the college had
status and high standards in the community and in the state. This
clearly helped in determining the image of the four-year college
and in securing its acceptance in the community. The vision was
to maintain the excellent two-year programs that had been developed, and simply supplement them with four-year programs that
would carry the work further in quality and move into new areas
which had not previously been attempted in the junior college
program.

3 *What are the consequences of the change?*

Probably the most profound consequence of this change is the move
from local autonomy to state control. The 3-mill local levy, which
supported the junior college, was dropped when the school became
a four-year college. The state now contributes an average of $1,500
per student in vocational-technical education, according to the
current president, Dr. Victor Hopper. However, local financial
support of a more general nature has continued. In fact, a "nickel
and dime" campaign conducted locally for television equipment
produced $55,000 in two months, according to Dean Threlkeld,
the current academic dean of the college. In addition to the campaign, use of a 1,000-foot television tower was donated to the
college for educational purposes.

Because Southern Colorado State College is now a member of
the state college system, its budget is reviewed by the Colorado
State Commission on Higher Education. It is this commission

that often seems to set priorities for the college, as the college fits in with needs of the state as a whole regarding higher education. The current academic dean of the college states that it was the junior college philosophy to be responsive to the needs of the local community; but it is harder to make changes now because the Colorado State Commission on Higher Education is "distant from the problem and has to take time to study everything sent to them since they are not as familiar with things as the people on the scene are." Local animosity toward the Colorado State Commission on Higher Education is actually inhibiting the development of the college. These people feel that this commission is but one more layer of administrative-supervisory authority, which also includes the state college trustees, the Legislature, the Governor, and his staff. Administrators comment that they miss the easy access to the president and the board, which was characteristic of the college in its junior college days.

For this reason, budgeting now seems to be a particularly critical problem. For example, one of the strategic dimensions which seem now to have had harmful consequences was the first budget of the new college submitted to the state, which was an absolutely un-inflated budget, giving minimum figures whenever possible. It appears that a custom of institutions in this state is to submit a budget which is slightly inflated as a bargaining position for later negotiations. Because Southern Colorado State College submitted a minimum budget, there was at first some difficulty in dealing effectively with institutions that worked in the other tradition. Compounding the difficulty of that first budget was the fact that it evidently included carryover local funds as revenue items.

The organization of higher education in the state is in considerable ferment. The senior institutions (the University of Colorado and Colorado State University) have their own boards, and the former has constitutional autonomy. This means that it is not subject to the same review by the state Coordinating Commission for Higher Education as other institutions. The five state colleges have their own board of trustees. A state junior college board was recently formed, but all junior colleges in the state are not under it. Some are still controlled and supported by local districts. There does not seem to be much happiness on any level with the commission, which is a coordinating board. In fact, legislation has been introduced by Senator Massari to modify it considerably. Other legislation has been presented to form a single board of higher education in Colorado, and still more to create a single university board, a four-year college board, and a junior college board—each responsible to state authorities. A source of constantly felt local frustration is the fact that the future of Southern Colorado State College lies not with forces on the scene but with forces external to Pueblo—in state politics, in forces forming new alignments for higher education in the state, in the state's economic base and tax structure, in evolving business-industrial-mining and other productive complexes in the state, and finally in the state's manpower needs as interpreted by the Governor and the Legislature. The message of the necessity of statewide coordination is not yet believed in Pueblo.

Students whom we interviewed refer to the need for "a change-over in administration. Administrators are older people who have been here a long time and still have the junior college philosophy." Administrators mention the problem of establishing equivalencies between vocational-technical faculty and academic rank in the conventional professorial structure. The president states, apparently correctly, that most faculty were absorbed by the four-year college and fears were allayed by upgrading some to divisional and departmental chairmen. Also, faculty previously received extra compensation for teaching in the evening program, but now must perform such services as part of their regular teaching assignment.

Administrators feel that there is now more freedom for both students and faculty. It is felt that there are more faculty benefits now (sabbaticals, for example). The college also gained more clerical help, but not in proportion to the growth of the institution in terms of student registrations. When the institution was a junior college, faculty members had to be certified by the state, although this was a perfunctory matter. There is no state certification requirement for four-year faculty.

The institution is currently plagued with enormous logistical difficulties in that it is operating out of two separate campuses. The old campus (the Orman campus) where the junior college was located is still the site of the technical-vocational effort; the new campus (which is a magnificent architectural accomplishment) at the other end of the city is evidently to be the "college" campus. Students point to the difficulty of attending some classes at each campus, despite the inexpensive bus transportation provided by the college. They also point to a loss of the feeling of community as a serious problem caused by having two separate campuses.

More importantly, speculation about the fate of the old campus offers a clue to the likely fate of technical education in the college.

Administrators, students, and the community leaders all refer to the "disposition" of the old campus. There is little mention of keeping it. The old campus, which consists of a handful of relatively new, permanent buildings and several temporary facilities, was the property of the community, but in effect was donated to the state when the institution became a four-year college. Now it appears that the college may give or sell the facility back to the community, perhaps for use as a technical high school to be operated by the Pueblo public school system (other options besides this are possible for the disposition). Technical staff members refer to the possibility of the Orman campus becoming an area vocational high school. The area vocational high school concept has now been approved by the State Control Board of Cooperative Services and by the State Vocational Board. Curiously, there is already some discussion of the possibility of establishing a new junior college at this site, although such talk may be emanating from state junior college staff personnel who are unclear about how to react to the new college, which as a four-year institution with two-year programs is neither fish nor fowl.

In any event, the eyes of the college authorities are obviously focused on the new campus, where an ambitious building program is already well under way. Officials point out, however, that the full extent of the building program has not been eagerly accepted by the state, which provides building funds only from current operating funds and does not issue bonds. There seem to be well-formulated timetables for moving every academic department from the old campus to the new, except for the vocational-technical programs which are in many respects the heart of the old junior college structure. At the moment, it seems that the four-year institution is still maintaining its level of excellence in its two-year programs, as well as adding the four-year programs which make for conventional comprehensive college operation. There is no increase in attrition in the two-year programs, and registration in those areas seems to be as strong as ever.

An extensive report on the two-year programs in the four-year setting was prepared by Management and Economics Research Incorporated (MERI) of Palo Alto, California. Although this report was critical of certain aspects of the college's operation, the criticisms were rebutted rather well by a report which President Hopper issued on March 22, 1968. Just as the comprehensive high school is a model which combines college preparatory, vocational-technical, and general programs under one roof, the comprehensive college which Southern Colorado State is trying to become has a similar mission. Because this new approach is hard to classify and to some extent very hard to evaluate, there is understandable reluctance on the part of junior college networks and four-year college organizations to deal with the new institution. In searching for what the institution is trying to become, we asked for models of emulation. The answer given by the president and by many others was that the college hoped to combine the best of the California junior college system, the best state college, and the best of the California technical college system. While this may sound pretentious, it is not unrealistic, and the institution which is now emerging definitely combines elements of the three in one model; and it seems that the multipurpose philosophy is being implemented with a fair degree of success.

4 *Predictions for the future*
The president reports an anticipated enrollment of 10,000 students by the decade 1975–1985, with about 3 percent coming from outside Southeastern Colorado. Dean Threlkeld states that the faculty "expect to move into graduate programs one by one with the M.A.T. [master of arts in teaching] coming first." The president says that graduate programs are expected to be started in 1970. There has evidently been no public discussion of the possibility that the college might become a university, although students said that "*they* hope it will become a university," without identifying who "they" might be. It was not at all clear from our discussions with faculty or administration that anyone held this view as a goal, but there might be some people in the community who feel that if a four-year college was good, a university could not help but be better. The college has a currently viable philosophy which it expects to sustain for the forseeable future. This expectation is normal for an institution of Southern Colorado State College's stature and history; but there is serious question about whether it can be sustained.

One of the reasons for this is that the future of the college lies not so much with forces internal to it as with forces external—in state politics, in forces forming new alignments for higher education, in the state's economic base, and in evolving business and other structures. In addition, there is considerable reshuffling at the present time between the Colorado Commission on Higher Education; the various governing boards for universities, colleges, and junior colleges; and the offices of Governor and Legislature.

The most important question (and one with important implications for all American higher education) is whether the state college can indeed continue to fulfill the role of a state college and a junior college simultaneously. If one admits that Pueblo College was a good junior college (and that appears to have been the case), then the burden of the new state college will be to continue to perform the services that were performed by a *good* junior college, not just a mediocre one. Otherwise it would be difficult to see the advantage of replacing a good junior college with a second-rate state college. College officials are careful to point out that the state college has a comprehensive goal. The instruction committee indicated that when it became a four-year college it was "charged with being a multipurpose institution."

Administrators and students alike appear to take pride in the comprehensiveness and flexibility of the institution. The catalog (page 12) states that "the demands of a four-year curriculum have not prevented the college from maintaining the basic concept of the former Pueblo College," and lists as goals, "to provide an opportunity for the development or updating of vocational or technical skills so that students may be qualified to seek employment at the end of two years or less" and "to maintain a student life program consistent with the ideals and responsibilities of citizenship in a democratic society."

It is at least possible that when those strong persons now in control of much of the college's administration, who see it as a junior college plus four-year college, retire and are replaced by "a new breed," such new men may have a much different aspiration pattern for the college. As we have seen, current plans call for forming a graduate division and for establishing autonomous professional schools such as business or engineering. In the scramble for resources to do this higher level work (and there are never enough resources to do everything), it is apt to be said more and more, "Let us slough off the two-year subprofessional areas of service to concentrate on the higher areas." As a junior college, Pueblo, it was quite clear, was concerned with providing opportunities for disadvantaged students and for underachievers generally. There are an estimated 13 percent Spanish-American and some other disadvantaged students in the college, according to Mr. Townley, chairman of the humanities division. Townley's comments regarding underachievers suggest that the college will continue, at least for the forseeable future, to provide opportunities for such students by offering special reading courses, mathematics courses, and the like, using a systems approach. Counteracting these fears of declining interest in the minority student is the fact that black studies courses have already been approved for the fall semester. A strong Latin American program has existed as a major for two years.

While the college maintains its open-door policy, the open door refers to admission to the *college,* but admission to various curricula is selective. The question of whether both the open-door philosophy and selective admission to curricula will continue probably depends upon economic factors. Limited resources would force the college to choose between open-door admissions with remedial programs and small upper-division and graduate classes. It is not very likely that the college would choose to remain comprehensive under such economic pressure. Something would have to go.

The most crucial question regarding the future is whether the college will be able to continue to staff vocational-technical areas. It would appear at present that it is doing a more effective job in this area than are many so-called community junior colleges. Its offerings include numerous curricula in engineering-related, industrial-related, business-related, service-related, and health-related areas. The most hopeful development since the change in status to four-year has been the fact that the college has continued to add two-year curricula; for example, in civil technology, mechanical technology, and psychiatric care. The current catalog lists 32 two-year programs, 19 of them in vocational-technical areas. Third and fourth year options for some of the technical curricula have begun to emerge, however, and these may serve in time to change the focus of the two-year terminal degree to such an extent that the two-year programs will dry up and the four-year route will be the one which the vast majority of students will choose.

Another possible cause for optimism is the increase in technical faculty reported by the dean of the vocational-technical division, Mr. Benz. He states that since becoming a four-year college, the full- and part-time vocational-technical faculty has increased from 18 to 70. If the long-range mission of the college were to get out of this area, such increases would hardly be likely. In addition there is some indication that the college will rather obstinately pursue vocational and trade training where it feels this necessary—even in the face of opposition by unions. One example occurred recently when the plumber's union threatened to withdraw support from the apprentice program if a nonunion apprentice was admitted to it. The college admitted the student, and the union withdrew its support.

The statistics since 1965 show a steady rise in the number of A.B. and B.S. degrees granted, with a decrease in the number of A.A. degrees, but a dramatic increase (over 3 times as many) in A.A.S. (technical) degrees. There are those who argue that the community service function of the institution will not be possible because of its change to four-year status. The other side of the argument is that increased faculty size and breadth may even increase the community service function as the institution attempts to reach out and expand its "community." The concern with development of educational television, the allocation of Channel 8 to the institution, and the application to the Health, Education and Welfare Department for funds all suggest that the institution may use television to reach out into a large geographic area without changing its commitment to the local Pueblo community itself.

One of the most important problems in the future will be getting the new faculty members and administrators to understand and absorb the current philosophy of comprehensiveness without invidious status distinctions developing between the two-year and the four-year faculty, students, and programs.

The evidence suggests that the faculty at the junior college before the change were not highly organized, not particularly involved in the governance of the institution, and not involved in social issues in the community; they were, in short, a fairly docile group. On the other hand the commitment of the teachers to teaching, as indicated in several student comments ("The college is personalized, almost like a high school," "The strength of the college is in the availability to lowerclassmen of talented faculty," "At Colorado University faculty are too busy doing research") suggests some good teaching traditions. It must be said, however, that the addition of faculty who will be trained and competent to offer the upper-division courses and advanced seminars for seniors, and ultimately the graduate courses, will bring to the campus a different type of faculty member. The new type is likely to be more aggressive, if not militant, more conscious of disciplinary status in his field, more concerned about research, more likely to demand small teaching loads, less sympathetic toward the open-door philosophy, and less tolerant and willing to work with "those kids who don't belong in college anyway." He also may be less loyal to the institution as such. The rift between vocational-technical and academic faculty is already present to a small extent. It appears to be widening somewhat because of the present separation of the technical and academic functions on the two campuses. The dean of the vocational-technical division has had difficulty in getting academic people to tour the technical facilities to see what is going on there.

In summary there is no doubt that Southern Colorado State College will develop as a state college, perhaps will even emerge as a university at some time in the future. The best prognosis would seem to be that it will be more comprehensive than most state colleges, but increasingly less comprehensive than it is now, as competition for money and shifting faculty sentiment pull the college away from vocational-technical and from remedial education toward a more traditional stance. A reasonable guess might be that the junior college functions will be virtually unrecognizable in another 10 to 15 years.

If a new junior college is established in the community (and this would be enormously difficult to justify in terms of duplication of funding), the junior college function at Southern Colorado State College would probably be lost within five years. The establishment of any new junior college would probably cause the state college to drop its vocational curricula and much of its remedial work, retaining only technical curricula—mostly with baccalaureate degrees as the terminating point. But unless these pressures are brought to bear by establishing new institutions within the area which will compete with Southern Colorado for the technical-vocational function, it is quite clear that Southern Colorado could continue for a number of years serving student needs by offering two-year course sequences as well as four-year ones.

Because the institution to some extent defies the categories which have been established by state coordinating commissions and boards, there is natural pressure for it to give up its two-year program and conform to more normal four-year college configurations. The degree to which the college yields to these pressures will have a significant impact on its future.

CHICAGO
STATE
COLLEGE

Chicago State College was chosen for inclusion in this study because of its long history of service as a city teachers college and because of its recently expanded mission to become an urban university serving the needs of Chicago. Unlike some of the other institutions in our study, Chicago State College has not reached the point of total implementation of its new program, as the president's first two-year report indicates for the years 1966 to 1968. His report, entitled "Two Years of Transition," seems an accurate assessment of what has been going on there, and what the institution may become when it moves to a new site and becomes Chicago State University.

1 *How did the change take place?*

The most important change at Chicago State occurred in 1965 when the college became a state-supported institution, as provided in the *Master Plan for Higher Education in Illinois.* At that time the college was named Illinois Teachers' College South. It became known as Chicago State College only in 1967. Prior to 1965 the college had been under the jurisdiction of the Chicago Board of Education, a period referred to by faculty members not entirely in jest as "the reign of terror." Since 1965 the college has been governed by a state board called, successively, the Teachers' College Board and now the Board of Governors. The most immediate and spectacular results of this change were the adoption of state operating, funding, and evaluative criteria rather than the more provincial Chicago standards which had been used previously when the institution was a teachers college for the city. These new standards applied both to faculty and staff and brought about a structure much more amenable to change. Faculty salaries went up overnight, and it became possible to operate from the framework of a collegiate environment rather than from that of a traditional lower school to train teachers. At Chicago State as recently as five years ago, faculty punched time clocks.

Today, the same instructors seem much more like college faculty — concerned about the quality of their teaching, about the nature of research, and about the role of the administration vis-à-vis faculty power. Much credit for this drastic reorganization must be given to the State Commission on Higher Education, which was largely responsible for producing the *Master Plan for Higher Education in Illinois.* As a consequence of this board and its recommendations, several important decisions were made dealing with higher education in the state: (1) it was decided that a rather large number of junior colleges would be the best answer to certain educational needs throughout the state; (2) a restriction was placed on the number of colleges which would become universities; (3) the establishment of a number of new commuting institutions in urban areas was mandated.

The Commission found Chicago Teachers' College at that time split into Chicago Teachers' College–North and –South, and decided that the state should take over what had been Chicago Teachers' College–South. The faculty of course were delighted with the move in that they wanted to get away from control by the city school board, which had great authority over everyday practices. A new president, Dr. Milton Byrd, assumed the responsibilities of the office in October 1966. Partly because of the change in state-level coordination of higher education, he was remarkably free from imposed policies and plans with regard to the future of the institution. The positions taken by the president in the first two years indicate his commitment to the idea of an urban university:

The new campus must care about the city. The faculty must probe and tap and measure the city until they find the means to improve a thousand conditions. The new campus must send that knowledge to the city through the young men and women she will have educated, to whom she will have given the power of thought and language and the promise of hope.

These are revolutionary words, and it is not at all clear whether the college is currently peopled by individuals who can become active workers in implementing the president's dream. However, he will have great powers of selection of staff in the future; and when he depicts the "new" college personnel as being critical, inquisitive, restless, active, flexible, and enthusiastic, he may well be able to implement these adjectives through the choice of staff in the future.

The president's strategy in fulfilling this mission is to avoid the top of the graduate school pyramid in the form of doctoral and postdoctoral study. The college will concentrate on graduate study which will not be research-oriented but profession- and service-oriented. Graduate work currently involves about 50 percent of all enrollments (3,800 FTE's, with about 5,700 actual people). Along with some graduate work in the traditional disciplines, teacher education is still important (the areas of reading and counseling are well developed), as are social service, paramedical work, and business administration. The president has moved actively and quickly to promote a new organizational structure which will accommodate the kind of diversity and pluralism he has in mind. There are no schools, colleges, or divisions in his plan, although there are 17 or 18 departments.

When Dr. Byrd came in 1966, there were two deans—one of arts and science and one of teacher education. He now has *functional* deans—a dean of the faculty who is responsible for all hiring and faculty evaluation, etc., and a dean of instruction, a curriculum man who will devote most of his time to the development of new programs. There is also a dean of administration who is responsible for physical plant, special services, and so on. The most vital new appointment in his revised administration chart is the executive vice-president, who has access to all reaches of the hierarchy and reports directly to the president. The overall goal of this organization is to allow relatively few intermediate-level organizations above departments—in order to have a valid and active departmental organization from which one can very quickly get to the highest level of administrative authority. This is referred to as a "flat" structure as opposed to the "tall" structures of many institutions which have a great many intermediate levels between the top of the hierarchy and the department.

The president is also interested in the formation of institutes, or interdisciplinary program centers, which can draw on any and all faculty within the entire college. He sees this as a way to combat tendencies toward departmental in-fighting. He also wants only one "faculty" rather than a separate faculty for liberal arts, another for teacher education, etc. The president's reorganization plan seems theoretically very sound and designed to make the college much more of a single, purposeful entity rather than a collection of schools and divisions operating only in their own self-interest. In this model, the executive vice-president will be responsible for most aspects of daily operation, freeing the president for conducting external relations, raising funds, working with the board, and, most important, evaluating the college's present program and helping make the future more interesting and secure.

2 *What must be done to implement the change?*
Although the president's plan for the future seems valid and care-

fully thought through and college publications are cased in a rhetoric which yields a feeling of excitement and promise, change in terms of program and attitude does not yet seem to be widespread. The faculty is, as one might expect, still cut from the cloth of yesterday and reflects a teacher-education mentality (with a few very interesting exceptions). Unlike the more radical and interesting urban-based aspirations of the president, many faculty seem to respond from the classic mold of college evolution—respectable, traditional academic programs operated from a departmental base, eventually moving into conventional doctorate work. There are some exceptions to this, and the exceptions are largely some of the "new men" to whom the president refers. They are, however, in positions of little influence, and their input has yet to be felt in any significant way. The administrative staff is currently bare and efficient. The president has been carrying a terribly heavy load because of his desire to take time in making the key appointments of executive vice-president and dean of instruction. When these appointments are made, his load should certainly be relieved.

The approximately 6,000 students enrolled at the college are 23 percent black and 77 percent white, which does not mirror the immediate community in which the school is currently located—being on the Southside of Chicago, a black ghetto. The faculty of the college are about 10 percent black and 90 percent white, which seems a reasonable distribution by current national standards. There are 280 full-time faculty members.

Students are for the most part first-generation college students, achievement-oriented in a rather conventional sense. The largest number of students major in teacher-education programs. All commute to the campus. The situation is further complicated by the college's present location and facilities. Parker High School and Wilson Junior College, immediately adjacent to the college campus, are now trying to exert more influence on the blacks at Chicago State to develop a vigorous campaign.

As just one example of the problems faced by the president, the first nonnegotiable demand from black students was that the college's racial composition be that of the community. The black militants interpret the community as four blocks around the campus, while President Byrd sees the community as Chicago itself. The Chicago State black students can be characterized as mainly lower-middle class, achievement-oriented, and not interested in violence as a way of life. White students tend to come from blue-collar homes where prejudice against black people is quite openly spoken about. The black students are for the most part eager to learn and perfectly willing to acquire fairly conventional middle-class roles. On the other hand, the white students seemed quite pleased with the president's decision to use the police in one incident and felt it was entirely right that he do so. Social class is perhaps as important as race in interpreting these students' behavior.

Perhaps the most important fact explaining these student characteristics is that 75 percent of all Chicago State students work either in the evening or in the afternoon to support themselves while going to college. This gives them relatively little time and energy for other activities. The American Federation of Teachers has a chapter on campus and attempted a strike last year but was unsuccessful. It claims one-third of the faculty as members. The problem with the AFT-attempted strike was that there was really no central issue to focus people's feelings, and clearly it was a strategic mistake to call a strike without an issue. There is a faculty senate on campus of about 40 members, mostly elected from each department.

There seems to be one coalition within the faculty which is forming rather noticeably under the conventional rubric of the "old guard." These are people, most of them schooled during the Depression, who lived through the "reign of terror" of control by the city board, who came from public school backgrounds as teachers and principals themselves, and who desperately want to maintain positions in a college. This group is unifying as a conservative force and, although it gives lip service to new programs and emphasis on undergraduate education, does not seem committed to either social or academic action.

We found one of the most interesting and hopeful aspects of the institution to be that, although the student body is racially mixed, the black students do not end up at the bottom of the heap. Many in the bottom 30 percent of their class are white. The socioeconomic status of the black student appears to exceed that of many of the white students. Thus the stereotypes about race, social class, and intelligence do not seem to operate on this campus. Of the 42 percent of all students enrolled in primary and secondary teacher-education programs, racial mixing seems to be the rule. On the other hand, in the cafeteria—which is about as close to a social activity center as the campus can now afford—one sees little of black and white students eating together. The pattern of voluntary segregation is very strong.

Probably the single most important obstacle to the president's dream of revitalization is the existing structure of the college. The buildings are old and incredibly decrepit, and it is hard to see how anyone could develop a loyalty to an institution housed in such conditions. The administration seems to be hoping to convince faculty and students of the virtues of the new campus to which they will move, although a number of the students and some of the faculty will not be there to take advantage of it. There seems to be a feeling among some faculty that the administration wishes to "hold the line" on such things as new book purchasing and new equipment (in several years the college will move to the new campus anyway and *that* will be a time for major reform and reordering).

There has been some racial difficulty at the college, although it involves a large number of people who are not attending the institution but who attend the junior college or the high school immediately adjacent to the Chicago State campus. In these situations, the faculty has proved itself to be ineffectual in dealing with the problem. On the question of whether the police should be removed after the president had called them in, the college senate (made up of faculty, except for three students) tabled the motion. They thus pressed the administration for action but were sharply critical of any actions taken by the president. The senate has also been quite ineffectual in dealing with student grievances to the point where many students do not take requests to the senate (where they have representation) but go directly to the president, because they have found that they get faster and more direct action that way.

Although there is the problem of violence on campus, again due partially to outside agitation, there is also the opposite problem of apathy. A large number of students seem very uninvolved in their academic work. They come to school and go home, or they go to their jobs—there is little of the spark of real energy or commitment. There are also rumors that a number of white students may leave the institution (some black students as well) because of fear of physical harm or for other reasons. However, the most important conflict on campus now does not seem to be racial but lies in the fact that the mandate from the Board of Higher Education to develop a state urban university is seen on campus as a mandate to develop such an institution *at the new site.* Hence the heavy allocation of resources and energy to planning that deals with events three years in the future and the dearth of planning for the interim. Many students seem to perceive that the future plans for the institution will not be very relevant to them (the freshman class will be seniors when the new physical facilities are occupied in 1972), and feel for the most part that more concern and planning should be devoted to the interim. This also means more money.

The administration, on the other hand, with its emphasis on the new campus, has been understandably hesitant to devote financial resources to the present facilities. Except for the erection of a temporary office building and the renting of apartment buildings adjacent to the campus for necessary office space, additional present construction would be hard to justify. Yet, by not providing additional resources for faculty now (office space, etc.), they may well lose some of the most valuable instructors to other institutions that can offer far more comfortable accommodations. The strategy of the president in concentrating on an organizational plan which will be fully effective by the time the college moves to its new site has certain costs and casualties as well as benefits. For example, while most students are generally unconcerned about the organizational reshuffling, they do feel that the teacher-education curricula which enrolls the largest number of students should be drastically revised, with much greater emphasis on the problems of inner-city education, "because that's where we'll be teaching." Not many of the current faculty are expert in inner-city educational problems. There seems to be little evidence that such a restructuring of the teacher-education curriculum is taking place. There is also an excellent compensatory education program enrolling about 60 students that could be expanded. Again the program is run on a fairly minimal financial base, and expansion would cost extra dollars.

It is perhaps unrealistic to think that the minute one moves into new facilities, the entire organization will go through a major psychological conversion and people will become suddenly dedicated to the new goals by being in the new buildings. On the other hand, the aspirations the president voices seem to ring hollow in the musty and sagging corridors of the existing structure.

3 *Prognosis*

While President Byrd, an able and forceful man, has a clear view of the future of the institution, it must be said that this view is not yet shared by a majority of his constituents. Transitional periods are never easy, but the next two years look extremely difficult and challenging in terms of what they will do to the ultimate shape of the institution that emerges when the new campus is attained. This transition period must necessarily be a time of holding and planning actions for the administration, with the president essentially in a reactive position in dealing with present conflicts in order to maintain his position in dealing with future matters on the new campus. Unfortunately for the administration this posture places the present initiative in the hands of the faculty and the students; demands will be made and bargains must be struck by the administration. The effect of these bargains on long-range plans is at the present unclear, but it is likely that they will create some changes in President Byrd's scenario for the future of Chicago State College.

In strategic terms, the president probably took the best approach possible in the circumstances by establishing an organizational plan toward which he can build staff in the future. He gave himself time in the area where time is most essential—the acquiring of additional faculty and administrative personnel. An inspiring, visionary attack on the problems of the central city, including poverty and the improvement of urban teacher education, is probably impossible given the present incredibly gloomy and disreputable facilities. During the next two or three years the institution will most likely lose some faculty members who would not fit well into its incarnation; but it also will lose some who are most interested in achieving the intellectual goals the president has set forth and who are therefore impatient at the two- or three-year delay. Whether the loss of the latter is worth the loss of the former can only be speculated upon.

The students' demands are necessarily going to be couched in "now" terms; the administration cannot invest much money in "now," and must be concerned with the future. Thus deep conflict along a time dimension seems inevitable. The president, who has been virtually a one-man administration in his first two years, has now recruited a very able and energetic administration. However, he is used to doing things by himself, and considerable delegation of authority to the new administrators will have to be a major task of the next year or two.

In its present struggling, poverty-ridden condition, the institution represents an almost direct analogy to the slum. In its future incarnation (although still in the city) its affluence, interesting architecture, and reasonably expensive construction will make an analogy not to the slum but perhaps to the suburb or to urban renewal at its best. If the institution is to be truly dedicated to the city, it will be interesting to see whether the facilities will mirror that dedication and will enhance the new programs which have not yet been developed. It does not seem at the moment that the college has the personnel and staff to accomplish a truly creative curriculum innovation, and yet this will have to be done if the new campus is—in the president's own words—to:

. . . wrap itself around the new program. The instructional enterprise must dictate the form and flow of enclosed space. That space must encourage the student and the faculty member and produce a setting of stimulating exchange. Other spaces must provide for private, independent, contemplative effort. The emphasis of the new architecture must be its sensitivity to scale and its attractive and inviting character.

This can only be accomplished architecturally if the new curriculum is ready almost immediately, due to the necessary lead time of architectural planning over actual building construction. It does not seem that this lead time is possible. One has only to talk a minute or so with the president to realize his energy and the integrity of his vision for the college. But he may be banking too heavily at the moment on the ability of new architecture to convert human personalities. Certain conversations and new academic programs must be started now if they are to manifest themselves when the new facilities are ready. If this is accomplished successfully, Chicago State College (or Chicago State University as it will become known) could well become one of the most exciting and innovative institutions in the United States—the beginning, perhaps, of a new breed of urban-oriented universities which have the mission of training people not in research techniques which are useful in a scholarly sense only, but of teaching them specific skills of inquiry and service which will help to make the city a better place. We usually think of junior colleges when we think along this line. It will be extremely interesting to see what a truly urban university looks like.

Part Three

Special Analyses of Questionnaire Results

6. Rankings of Most Significant Change and How Accomplished

In the questionnaire sent to the presidents we asked each respondent, after completing the rather elaborate list of *all* change that had taken place at his institution in the last decade, to list the *one* change which in his opinion was the most significant. We thus have responses from a thousand or so institutions in terms of what the president feels is the most significant event in the institution's recent past. These data will be presented in terms of totals for the whole sample and then in terms of various breakdowns, including size of institution and type of control as well as highest degree offered. We then will look at some interesting data on how the major change was brought about.

OVERALL TOTALS Some presidents apparently found this question difficult to answer, as we received 1,022 responses out of the 1,230 total questionnaires received. It may be that the more a person knows about an institution the harder it is to isolate a phenomenon in the institution's recent history. At any rate here are the totals for the 1,022 responses we did receive in terms of the major area in which the change took place.

It is quite clear from these data that the largest single category of institutional change reported by presidents has to do with changes of internal authority and the governance structure of the institution. One would have suspected that most of the 331 presidents who responded to this item as the most significant change would have been referring to increased faculty control in internal governance. Although 126 responses did indicate an increase in faculty authority, 100 institutions reported an increase in student control. Because these data were gathered during the early part of the academic year 1968–69 before news of increases in student participation in governance had been hitting the papers with great

	Number of presidents responding
Kinds of change most often reported	
Changes in internal authority (increases in faculty authority, 126; increases in student authority, 100)	331
Changes in academic programs (updating curriculum, 55; special programs, 43)	173
Changes in composition of student body (increased diversity of background, 29; quality of admissions, 46)	115
Institutional concerns (growth of institution, 33; recruitment of staff and students, 20; changes in calendar, 12)	95
Changes in faculty (interest in teaching, 20; diversity of faculty, 19; interest in research, 12)	89
Changes in administration	77
Finances	60
Changes in physical plant	45
Changes in external authority	37
TOTAL	1,022

TABLE 24
Most important changes as reported by presidents, listed by frequency of response

SOURCE: Author's questionnaire.

regularity, they point to increased student participation now and in the future. The next most important area nominated, well over 100 nominations behind, is academic program changes. Interestingly enough, the category of special programs is spread out over a remarkable number of areas. Only two institutions listed new programs for disadvantaged students, and no responses indicated special ethnic programs for black students or black studies as the most significant change, even though a large number of institutions were involved in black studies and special programs for black students during that academic year. A cynic might suggest from these data that in the minds of presidents ethnic studies programs and special programs for disadvantaged youth are not central to the mission of the institution at the present time, but are peripheral or transitory matters to be kept at arm's length so that they do not interfere with the basic structure or workings of the institution. (For example, there are a large number of black studies *programs* in the United States but relatively few black studies *departments*. Politically, faculty authority works through the departmental structure, and if black studies have no departmental base, they cannot be a threat to the political structure of the faculty.)

The next most important major change, as reported by the

presidents, is in the character of the student body, primarily in diversity and quality of admissions. From here the nominations begin a gradual decline in numbers through institutional concerns, changes in faculty, changes in the administration, etc. The perception of the presidents of increased internal authority given to students and faculty is interesting in that other sources in the data indicate a widespread decrease in the authority of the central administration. This could be interpreted to mean that the presidents see power as a "zero-sum" game like poker, in which if one player wins $5 the others must lose the same amount. Internal authority could also be seen as a multiplier phenomenon in which increased responsibility of students or faculty represents an increase in the *total* influence pool available—and thus everybody including the institution could be seen to gain. The presidents clearly do not perceive the change in that way and seem to see a necessary decline in administrative authority because of increased participation on the part of students and faculty.

TABLE 25
Most important change by type of control

Changes in	Public (441 institutions)	Sectarian (342 institutions)	Nonsectarian (203 institutions)	Total
Internal authority	139 30.95%*	104 30.4%*	41 20.19%*	284 28.6%*
Academic programs	65 14.5%	57 16.7%	42 20.7%	164 16.5%
Students	53 11.8%	35 10.2%	26 12.8%	114 11.5%
Institutional concerns (growth, calendar, etc.)	19 4.2%	38 11.1%	24 11.8%	81 8.14%
Faculty	41 9.1%	24 7.0%	14 6.9%	79 7.9%
Administration	22 4.9%	30 8.8%	12 5.9%	64 6.4%
Finances	19 4.2%	9 2.6%	13 6.4%	41 4.1%
Physical plant	13 2.9%	10 2.9%	10 4.9%	33 3.3%
External authority	13 2.9%	4 1.2%	1 0.5%	18 1 8%
TOTALS	441 45.1%	342 34.4%	203 20.4%	994

* This figure represents the percent of the total sample taken for each column.
SOURCE: Author's questionnaire.

On another level it is perhaps interesting that although 29 presidents report the most significant change as an increase in the diversity of the background of students, only two presidents feel that *programs* for these more diverse students, particularly those from disadvantaged elements, are the most significant change. One could conclude from this that the admission of new kinds of students to higher education has not been matched by development of programs designed specifically to meet their needs.

The data could also be said to indicate that several aspects of presidential activity are not seen in their proper perspective—that is, one usually thinks of a college or university president as spending most of his time dashing around after funds and putting up buildings; yet changes in the physical plant and changes in finance (where one would expect the presidents' egos to be) rank near the bottom of the list. This would seem to indicate that although presidents put a great deal of time and energy into these activities, they have a broader sense of their importance than faculty and students might suppose. The presidents seem to be aware of the fact that buildings and money are important to the academic program, but not as important as the people and the programs.

SIGNIFICANT CHANGE BY TYPE OF CONTROL For the most part the changes indicated here in public, sectarian, and nonsectarian institutions occur in approximately the same number of cases in each type of institution.

There are, however, several differences that are interesting. First, shifts in internal authority are nominated as the major change in public and sectarian institutions more often than in nonsectarian institutions. On the other hand, shifts in the academic program are nominated by presidents of nonsectarian institutions more often than by presidents of either public or sectarian. It also seems that the interest in institutional concerns as the major change occurs far less often in public institutions than in either sectarian or nonsectarian institutions. But with these few exceptions, the major changes listed by presidents seem to have occurred in approximately equal numbers in the various types of institutional control.

MAJOR CHANGE BY HIGHEST DEGREE Once again the predominant tendency is for major changes to take place in all institutions regardless of highest degree awarded.

But here again there may be a few discrepancies that are worth pointing out. First, changes in the student body are listed less often

TABLE 26 *Most important change by highest degree*

Changes in	Less than B.A. (292 institutions)	B.A. (263 institutions)	M.A. (206 institutions)	Ph.D. (121 institutions)	Total
Internal authority	111 38%*	80 30.4%*	72 34.9%*	22 18.2%*	285 32.3%*
Academic programs	42 14%	60 22.8%	34 16.5%	34 16.5%	170 19.2%
Students	33 11.3%	37 14.0%	24 11.6%	12 9.9%	106 12.0%
Institutional concerns (growth, calendar, etc.)	19 6.5%	27 10.2%	25 12.1%	11 9.09%	82 9.3%
Faculty	25 8.5%	21 7.9%	22 10.6%	12 9.9%	80 9.7%
Administration	24 8.2%	20 7.6%	13 6.3%	9 7.4%	66 7.5%
Finances	14	8	3	16	41 4.6%
Physical plant	16	7	8	3	34 3.8%
External authority	8	3	5	2	18 2.04%
TOTALS	292 33.1%	263 29.8%	206 23.4%	121 13.7%	882

* This figure represents the percent of the total sample taken for each column.

SOURCE: Author's questionnaire.

in Ph.D. institutions than in the other three degree-awarded categories. Changes in academic program occur more often in the B.A.-granting institutions than any other level as the major change listed by the president. Changes in internal authority are seen most often in the less-than-B.A.-granting institutions, then the M.A. level, then the B.A. level, and least often of all the Ph.D.-granting level. Institutional concerns are nominated by presidents of less-than-B.A.-granting institutions half as often as they are in M.A.-awarding institutions. However, these differences by highest degree are slight, and the predominant mood again is one of consistency across institutional types rather than marked discrepancies.

MAJOR CHANGE BY SIZE OF INSTITUTION When the institutions are split as in Table 27, it must be realized that there are relatively few institutions in categories 4 and 5 by size.

TABLE 27
Most important
change by size
of institution

Changes in	Under 1,000 students (376 institutions)	1,000–5,000 students (366 institutions)	5,000–15,000 students (90 institutions)
Internal authority	122 32.4%	121 33%	30 33.3%
Academic programs	67 17.8%	68 18.5%	14 15.5%
Students	45 11.9%	43 11.7%	12 13.3%
Institutional concerns (growth, calendar, etc.)	35 9.3%	35 9.6%	2 2.2%
Faculty	38 10.1%	33 9.0%	9 10%
Administration	35 9.3%	24	8
Finances	17 4.5%	14 3.8%	6 6.6%
Physical plant	10 2.6%	20 5.4%	4 4.4%
External authority	7	8	1
TOTALS	376 43.6%	366 42.4%	90 10.4%

SOURCE: Author's questionnaire.

Thus the percentages should not be considered too seriously. However, it must also be remembered that institutions in these two categories consist of a large number of students, and therefore variations are often quite significant in terms of the total numbers of people involved. Although the number and percentage of institutions reporting major shifts in the student body are quite common across the size categories, the individual breakdowns within that student category show that nominations for increased *diversity* of student background occur almost entirely in the first and second categories of size only (27 of the 29 institutions that indicated increased student diversity as the major change are in the first two size categories). As the size category gets larger, the percentage of institutions reporting changes in the academic program increases. Changes in internal authority, however, are seen as the most important change more often in the smaller institutions than

15,000–25,000 students (24 institutions)	Over 25,000 students (7 institutions)	Total
7 29.1%	0	280 32.4%
7 29.1%	2 28.4%	158 18.3%
3 12.5%	1 14.2%	104 12.0%
1 4.1%	1 14.2%	78 9.0%
2 8.3%	1 14.2%	83 9.6%
0	0	67 7.8%
2 8.3%	2 28.4%	41 4.7%
0	0	34 3.9%
2	0	18 2.0%
24 2.8%	7 .8%	863

in the larger ones. Changes in the physical plant are mentioned as the major concern in the first two size levels rather than in any other size dimension.

From this analysis it is quite clear that although there are some differences in major changes listed by size, type of control, and highest degree awarded, major changes have taken place in American higher education regardless of size, highest degree, or type of control. This means that the rank ordering of major changes is not influenced by the kind of institution in which the change takes place. In all higher education, changes in internal authority occur most often, academic programs next, changes in student body next, etc. The only conclusion we can possibly draw from this is that although there are unique factors in each institution's life, there are also very common response patterns by which all institutions can be grouped, regardless of their control, highest degree awarded, or size. Once again the heralded diversity of higher education can be called into question from these figures.

HOW THE CHANGE CAME TO BE

It should be said at the outset that this section represents a limited attempt to deal with a very complex problem—the analysis of *how* change happens. This investigation is hardly the final answer, but it does shed some light on problems of fact and method.

The model we used was a very simple one. Changes are based on new ideas. These are initiated by individuals and/or groups, who then try, through a variety of means, to spread their ideas to others. The latter either agree with the notion and become advocates or at least neutrals, while others disagree and oppose the idea and the advocates. Presumably, only the "fittest" ideas survive in this Darwinist arena. This conception of change is activist, is adversary in nature (advocates versus opponents), and has a "force field" (ideas that have "stronger" support than opposition will survive; "weaker" ideas will not). It is also probably very American.

We do know that not all changes come about this way. Often a new idea is not championed by specific individuals or groups; it just seems to appear. There is no particular battle over a policy. But we have found out a little about that process as well.

WHO INITIATED THE IDEA?

In our questionnaire, after the president had stated the one change which in his opinion had the greatest impact on the institution, we then asked him to indicate the individuals and/or groups that had initiated the change. A large number of presidents found this very difficult to answer; in fact, 385 could not. They often wrote in some comment like "It just seemed the right time" or "It just happened." But this is not equally true for all types of change. For example, if a change must become codified in the form of a written policy, it is much more likely to occur (or fail) in an adversary model, with supporters and opponents. On the other hand, changes which represent a gradual shift of attitudes without formal policy are called *accretion* (a gradual shifting, such as the faculty's becoming more interested in research, less loyal to the institution). Certain changes require both, in some settings anyway. For example, the establishment of programs for minority groups in higher education required a considerable period of "gestation" in which attitudes were slowly changed, followed sometimes directly by the establishment of policy and its implementation, but usually followed first by the adversary battle of the arena of ideas. But a fair number of presidents *could* respond, and we were able to code their responses, as indicated in Table 28.

The vision of presidents may be myopic, but as they see life, they and other individuals in the administration (not always deans, but often) have initiated most of the major changes. (Although this may be a biased judgment on the part of the president, the case studies in this report do tend to support it, albeit in a small number of cases. The author's experience generally would agree.) In 55 cases, the initiating move came from an off-campus individual or group, particularly community and state government agencies, businesses, and alumni. Neither the faculty nor students show up as being skilled champions of new and important changes for the institution.

It is also interesting to observe that the process of "team initiation"—a person or group working directly with another—accounts for only about 157 of the major changes. Of these, 45 come from the president working with other administrators, and 53 come from the faculty working with other administrators. The team of president and trustees has produced only 14 major changes, which suggests some interesting things about the nature and nurture of innovation in higher education coming from the "top."

Did different major changes have different initiators? Table 29 can give us some answers.

We have to conclude that the change initiators remain about the same as we vary the major changes—for example, in most changes, the president and other administrators combined amount to somewhat less than half of the initiators of the change. There

TABLE 28   *Who initiated the major changes?*

		Combinations	
President	215	*Other administrators and faculty*	53
Faculty	91	*President and other administrators*	45
Trustees	43	*President and faculty*	20
Other administrators	150	*President and trustees*	14
Students	39	*Other administrators and students*	8
Other internal groups	4	*Trustees and faculty*	7
Other external groups	55	*President and students*	6
No groups of individuals mentioned	40	*Trustees and other administrators*	4
		No answer	385

SOURCE: Author's questionnaire.

are some differences in patterns of initiation; for example, the faculty were not overwhelmingly strong in initiating changes in the academic area (14 institutions), nor was the president working alone (35 institutions). Other administrators, mostly academic deans, initiated change at 6 institutions. However, they also worked better with the faculty in teaming up to create academic change (17 institutions), while the president worked with the faculty in initiating academic change at only 3 institutions! It is also interesting to note that apparently faculty and students have been much more interested in gaining power (changes in internal controls) than they have been in changing the nature of the students or the faculty. This can be explained by the classic political science notion: one first must acquire power; then one can change one's constituency and program.

This analysis also suggests that the president who wishes to initiate major change should pay particular attention to his selection of administrative staff, as they, working with the president and with the faculty, were able to initiate many changes by working together (they started 53 major changes with the faculty, while the president started only 20 with the faculty). Looking just at changes in academic programs, other administrators worked with faculty to initiate this change in 17 institutions, while presidents and faculty worked together in only 3.

It would be hard to contend from these figures that trustees have been a major source of the initiation of change. Even the president-trustee combination produced the major change in only 14 institutions (Table 28), although we hear much of the rhetoric of the team of president and board.

It also seems that we have isolated the change agents on campus fairly well, but "other external groups" were listed as primary initiators of change in 55 institutions by Table 28. They appear in every major change described in Table 29, and are quite strong in changes in finance and in external authority. They may be churches, town governments, alumni groups—we simply don't know.

The general pattern in Table 29 is one of consistency. It is not true, apparently, that change agents are "issue-bound"; they seem to be equally effective in producing a variety of types of major changes. Presidents seem to lead the pack in terms of single change agents, but in academic changes the other administrative staff is the best combination ingredient one could add to create major change.

1. Changes in internal controls (331 institutions)

		Combinations	
President	84	*President and faculty*	11
Faculty	34	*President and other administrators*	16
Trustees	8		
Other administrators	52	*President and students*	6
Students	32	*Other administrators and faculty*	17
Other external groups, individuals	12	*Faculty and students*	6
No groups or individuals mentioned	7	*Other administrators and students*	6

2. Changes in academic programs (173 institutions)

		Combinations	
President	35	*President and faculty*	8
Faculty	14	*President and trustees*	2
Other administrators	6	*President and other administrators*	11
Other external groups or individuals	5	*President and other external groups*	2
No groups or individuals mentioned	6	*Other administrators and faculty*	17
		Other administrators and students	2

3. Changes in students (115 institutions)

		Combinations	
President	14	*President and faculty*	2
Faculty	7	*President and trustees*	3
Trustees	5	*Faculty and trustees*	2
Other administrators	12	*Trustees and administrators*	2
Students	5		
Other external groups or individuals	4		
No groups or individuals mentioned	17		

4. Institutional concerns (95 institutions)

		Combinations	
President	23	*President and trustees*	7
Faculty	12	*President and other administrators*	5
Trustees	6		
Other administrators	13	*Faculty and president*	2

TABLE 29
(cont.)

Other internal groups or individuals	1	Faculty and other administrators	4
Other external groups or individuals	4	Faculty and trustees	2
No groups or individuals mentioned	2	Trustees and other administrators	2

5. Changes in faculty (89 institutions)

		Combinations	
President	20	President and faculty	2
Faculty	10	President and other administrators	4
Other administrators	10	Faculty and other administrators	6
Students	1		
Other external groups or individuals	4		
No groups or individuals mentioned	2		

6. Changes in administration (77 institutions)

		Combinations	
President	19	President and trustees	2
Faculty	8	President and other administrators	2
Trustees	6	Faculty and trustees	3
Other administrators	7	Faculty and other administrators	2
Students	1		
Other external groups or individuals	2		

7. Changes in finances (60 institutions)

		Combinations	
President	6	President and other administrators	2
Faculty	1	Faculty and other administrators	2
Trustees	4		
Other administrators	7		
Other external groups or individuals	9		
No groups or individuals mentioned	1		

8. Changes in physical plant (45 institutions)

		Combinations	
President	9	President and other administrators	3
Faculty	1		

Trustees	6
Other administrators	2
Other internal groups or individuals	1
Other external groups or individuals	7
No groups or individuals mentioned	2

9. Changes in external authority (37 institutions)

		Combinations	
President	5	*President and other administrators*	2
Faculty	4		
Trustees	2	*Faculty and other administrators*	5
Other administrators	7		
Other internal groups or individuals	2		
Other external groups or individuals	8		
No groups or individuals mentioned	2		

HOW DID THE INITIATION TAKE PLACE? The data in Table 30 will help to answer this question.

It would appear from the second line of Table 30 that the successful initiator not only enunciates the idea, but carries through the idea as well—this seems true for presidents and faculty, other administrators, and trustees, although presidents seem to do more of it. (These data come again from an open-ended question in which we asked the president to describe simply the interaction of individuals and groups in the major change and his own role in the change. The answers were quite difficult to code, and a number were excluded to avoid erroneous coding.)

The presidents seem to split about evenly among strategies of supporting and approving ideas initiated by others, initiating and helping to carry ideas out, and playing the mediator between groups or individuals in conflict. We have no evidence as to which of these strategies is most effective; perhaps it varies with the president, the campus, and the issue. It does appear, however, that presidents seldom play a veto role in change. Indeed, the written documents of most campuses make it difficult for the president to do so. But two groups do show up as being opposers of change

TABLE 30 *Role played in major changes**

	President	Other administrators	Faculty	Trustees
Initiated only	15	7	3	4
Initiated; helped to carry out	80	22	14	6
Mediator, conflict involved	63	3	1	
Mediator, apathetic environment	21	1		
Resisted, opposed change	7	10	22	15
Supported, advocated, approved	95	50	78	36
Neutral, not involved	6	2	3	
Not present when changes occurred	42			

* Scores for "students" and "other groups" were insignificant. Response to this open-end item was small. In 142 cases, respondent indicated "general consensus on campus, no roles involved."
SOURCE: Author's questionnaire.

more often than the others—they are the faculty and the trustees. The written comments often indicate that the *style* of opposition used by faculty and trustees was the veto. And on many campuses, these are the two groups that can use the veto and survive, as those who object to the veto have no, or sketchy, opportunities for retribution. Faculty or trustee resistance comes rather seldom, and in the comments made by presidents, these groups were mentioned as supporting, advocating, and approving the majority of new ideas.

At least, these data tend to support the notion that the president is no longer the imperial autocrat, issuing orders from on high that are instantly, automatically obeyed. (Indeed, only a few may ever have done that.) Our presidents—the relatively small number who filled in the write-in section—seem to work hard at supporting the ideas of others, mediating across factions, and working to implement their own ideas ("seeing them through"). Given the amount of veto power invested in trustees and faculty, at least in 1968–69 when these data were taken, these three seem the most pragmatic approaches for the president, as well as the most effective. For every educational giant today, there seems to be an educational giant-killer.

DIFFERENT PATTERNS OF SUPPORT AND RESISTANCE We also asked the president to describe the actions of a number of individuals and groups in relation to the change he considered most important to the campus. This question was in the form of a checklist, and the response rate was rather good (Table 31).

Overall, the patterns of "support," "neutral," "resistance," and "don't know" remain quite constant for each reference group, regardless of issue. But there also appeared *some* differences that made each issue unique, as well as certain patterns of individuals and groups that held across the issue. First, let us look at the total pattern of interaction by role, putting all the major changes together.

Looking at the resister column, it is clear that the largest number of checks for resisting the major change come from the tenured faculty (a minority of them), with 185, followed by a minority of the nontenured faculty (116) and a minority of the student body (83). Then come the alumni, with 69 resister checks, and the majority of the tenured faculty, with 51. The external groups that showed the most resistance were other colleges and universities (44); religious groups (32); and then state government agencies, local businesses and public and private schools, and all at about the same level.

Some things follow from these data. Most of the resistance to the major changes has come from on-campus sources rather than off-campus. A minority of tenured and nontenured faculty contribute most heavily, accounting for 301 resistance checks out of about 900 on-campus resistance checks in all. In fact, although a minority of both tenured and nontenured faculty have resisted change most, a majority of the tenured faculty have done fairly well also. It is also interesting to note that academic departments, supposedly hotbeds of academic conservatism, do not score very high as resisters of major change. One reasonable inference to be made from these data is that on crucial, major changes, faculty alliances develop *across* departmental lines rather than within them. This might be particularly true in smaller colleges in which the departmental unit is too small to be politically effective. But both faculty and students seem, at least from these data, to be better at resisting change than they are at initiating it. Please note that we are not making moral judgments about those who have resisted change. On some campuses, certain changes (greater student participation in decision making, allowing more diversity of the student body and endangering "standards," and changing the curriculum to meet the needs of these new students) could have been resisted with a clear conscience. But when we see that a minority of the tenured and nontenured faculty and of the student body are the major resisters on almost *every* major change, then one begins to wonder.

TABLE 31 *Supporters and resisters to most important change—totals for all major changes combined*

	Supporter	Neutral	Resister	Don't know
Factors internal to institution:				
President	926	29	32	5
Board of trustees	715	184	47	21
Deans	825	62	49	9
Other administrators	712	123	39	23
Alumni groups	363	252	69	173
Faculty senate or executive committee	648	106	49	31
Other faculty committees	607	112	43	60
Tenured faculty:				
Minority	260	118	185	50
Majority	671	82	51	44
Nontenured faculty:				
Minority	274	165	116	80
Majority	716	94	22	68
Student body:				
Minority	243	221	83	112
Majority	624	188	20	92
Departments	557	109	29	73
Student newspaper	538	185	22	79
Student political activist groups	275	167	19	214
Student government	594	168	15	87
Teaching and/or research assistants	250	118	3	180
Dormitory groups	309	143	5	177
Fraternities, sororities, eating clubs	193	114	9	179
Factors external to institution:				
National government agency or power (NSF, AEC, NIMH)	185	209	5	251
State government agency or power	314	204	28	147
Regional agency or power	211	215	8	193
City agency or power	174	240	15	193
Local community governments	203	233	20	183
U.S. Office of Education	229	205	4	215
Military	57	231	4	283
Professional groups (learned societies)	225	185	3	217

TABLE 31 *(cont.)*

	Supporter	Neutral	Resister	Don't know
American Council of Education, AAUP, NEA, AFT	253	172	8	196
Research institutions or centers	123	198	1	252
Foundations (Ford, Carnegie)	167	194	3	251
Civil rights groups	146	190	5	237
Business or fraternal groups (Rotary, Lions)	193	220	18	189
Industry (IBM, Xerox)	238	185	6	205
Local businesses	303	184	24	152
Religious groups	229	202	32	183
Medical groups	132	212	10	230
Public or private schools	225	184	25	177
Other colleges and/or universities	302	168	44	139
News media	345	153	15	123
Others (please specify):				
Legislature	10	4	6	
Community	4	1	7	

Did Patterns of Support and Resistance Vary with the Type of Change?

This question can be answered in two ways—first with a summary of all the checks of "support," "neutral," "resistance," and "don't know," as in Table 31, but broken down by type of major change, as in Table 32. We made a division here between internal and external sources, even though on some issues the external forces were so small as to be negligible. The top half of the table gives the raw score, or total number of checks, per type of major change. The bottom half shows the same data in simple ratio form, dividing the total number of checks, as given in the top half, by the number of presidents who listed that change as the most important to take place at their institutions.

It is interesting to note how consistent the ratios are across the kinds of change, particularly the *internal* forces of "support," "neutrality," and "resistance," where the numbers are larger. This means that the patterns of internal dynamics in terms of change have been remarkably similar, *whatever the major change.* For each change, the support forces had a factor of 10, the neutral forces about 2.7, the forces of resistance about .9, and unknown about 1.6. We cannot translate these factor numbers into either number

	(331) *Internal authority*	(173) *Academic programs*	(115) *Composition of student body*	(95) *Institutional concerns*
TABLE 32*				
Total checks from *internal* sources				
Support	3,410	1,771	1,116	1,001
Neutral	869	495	245	257
Resist	275	141	122	86
Don't know	662	260	167	169
Ratios—*internal* sources				
Support	10.30	10.23	9.07	10.53
Neutral	2.62	2.86	2.13	2.70
Resist	.83	.81	1.06	.90
Don't know	2.00	1.50	1.45	1.77
Total checks from *external* sources				
Support	544	105	296	91
Neutral	875	4	153	59
Resist	80	15	33	14
Don't know	890	40	137	31
Ratios—*external* sources				
Support	1.64	.60	2.57	.95
Neutral	2.64	.23	1.33	.62
Resist	.24	.08	.28	.14
Don't know	2.68	.23	1.19	.32

The label to the left of the table reads: **TABLE 32*** / *Total support and resistance, all sources by major change*

* The ratios used in the second and fourth major columns of this table are established by dividing the total number of checks for the "support," "neutral," "resist," or "don't know" areas for each change by the number of presidents who list that change as most important for this institution, as in Table 24. (Thus, the ratio for "Internal support on changes in internal authority" is 10.30, dividing 3,410 by 331.)

of individuals involved or number of groups involved, but the numbers do indicate a general pattern of change forces which is surprisingly consistent across kinds of major change. The exact meaning of this consistency can only be hinted at, but would seem to merit further inquiry.

The second way to answer the question is to break the data down by the major changes, and also by the major internal and external individuals and groups that we mentioned in Table 31. This more comprehensive analysis is contained in the Appendix of this section, Tables 1 through 7 (one table for each major change). From these tables, it is clear that the consistency of the patterns of support

(89) Changes in faculty	(77) Changes in administration	(60) Changes in finance
817	756	554
265	200	201
94	36	62
180	127	75
9.17	9.81	9.23
2.97	2.59	3.35
1.05	.46	1.03
2.02	1.64	1.25
49	34	50
62	28	10
9	6	8
36	18	15
.55	.44	.83
.69	.36	.16
.10	.07	.13
.40	.23	.25

and resistance per issue also seems to hold for individuals and groups — in each of the major changes, the highest resistance comes from two minorities of the faculty: tenured and nontenured. Next come the minority of the student body on almost every major change. The alumni show up as strongly resisting some changes, especially in Table 3 of the Appendix, changes in the composition of the student body. (One could theorize that alumni would object to "lowering standards" and accepting students from a variety of racial and socioeconomic backgrounds on the basis that it might lessen the prestige of their own degree from the institution. For example, trustees generally feel that higher education is a right, while attendance at *their* institution is a privilege, to be given to a carefully limited few.) The faculty also show resistance to the changes in composition of the student body, as did a minority of the students themselves. These student and faculty minorities may have argued from the same premises as the alumni—changes in the student body also threaten faculty and student self-interest. It is unfortunate that we do not know more about these minorities in the faculty and student body. However, there was a limit to the amount of time we could honestly ask the presidents to take in filling out our questionnaire, and this would have meant another open-ended write-in, with low response rate and coding problems.

Perhaps the greatest shock from these tables, as well as from Table 31, is the very small amount of resistance offered by the academic departments to the major change. Much of the literature suggests that the department is the "bad boy" of the current academic scene, yet we find little resistance to the *major* change. It is possible that the president is simply unaware of their subtle forms of resistance, or that departmental resistance increases as highest degree and size increase (although if this were true, we would expect much more resistance from our approximately 420 institutions in the sample which award the M.A. and/or Ph.D.), or that departments spend all their time obstructing minor changes rather than the big ones, *or* that departmental resistance to change has been overemphasized in the literature and in the folklore of academe.

Also surprising was the small resistance to the major changes indulged in by the student newspapers. Neither are they listed in spectacular numbers as supporters of the major change. The same could be said of student political activist groups, teaching assistants, and fraternities and sororities, all of which are often accused of impeding change—considering that over 300 institutions in our sample reported that they had seen an increase in student activism in accomplishing or impeding their major change. One likely possibility is that many of the major changes in internal control, curriculum, and student body composition had already been accomplished *before* the upsurge in student protests which seemed to begin during 1967.

Looking at the role of internal and external forces in accomplishing the change, it would seem that two changes caused more extensive involvement of outside forces than the others—these were in internal controls and in the composition of the student body. In almost all the changes, the most active groups were religious, other colleges and universities, and state government agencies, but their roles seemed to be those of general support.

There was, however, considerably more external *resistance* to the changes in internal controls and changes in the composition of the student body than there was to curricular changes. (This may be due to the fact that external agencies are not concerned with curricular matters, but it may also be that they get little information about these changes until they have been implemented.)

SUMMARY   In this section we have discovered what changes were considered to be of the greatest importance to the campus by our presidents, as well as a few things about how these major changes were brought about. It is clear that the changes listed as most important have occurred in about equal numbers in different types of institutions, providing some support for our thesis that institutions of higher education in America are becoming more alike. We also learned that these major changes are produced by individuals and/or groups working in combination with other individuals and/or groups. The other administrators seem to work well with other groups, and the president-trustee combination does not seem to work very well in producing changes. It is also clear from this analysis that looking at change simply in terms of who makes the decision to go the new route is not as important as looking at the process of implementation and decision making. He who initiates only is not as successful as he who initiates *and* helps to carry it through. Few of our presidents are playing their role in an autocratic fashion—they characteristically mediate, initiate and carry through, and support the actions of others. They do not veto, although faculty and trustees seem to be in a position to do so and on occasion do. The major changes that have come about in higher education have done so with remarkably similar patterns of support and resistance from the various groups. Those who have assumed that curricular changes are accomplished with very different patterns of individual and group interaction from changes in governance, for example, will not find much support from these data. A minority of the faculty and student body consistently resist change of whatever sort, while the traditional enemies of change, such as departments, do not show up as playing any important roles in change.

Recently, much attention has been given to the argument that higher education is unable to change—that resistance to change is genetic, inbred in the structures of higher education. To the contrary, over three-fourths of our presidents were able to isolate a major change that had significant impact on the institution, and could deal knowledgeably with questions of how the change came about. More can be learned about the nature of these change processes. Even though the changes are reducing the heterogeneity of higher education by moving all of it in the same directions, the fact remains that significant changes *have* taken place in our colleges and universities. By finding out how, we may some day be able to control the processes of change.

Appendix to Chapter 6

TABLE 1 *Changes in internal controls (331 institutions)*

	Supporter	*Neutral*	*Resister*	*Don't know*
Factors internal to institution:				
President	293	13	14	2
Board of trustees	179	104	18	12
Deans	258	29	17	4
Other administrators	209	55	18	10
Alumni groups	82	90	17	81
Faculty senate or executive committee	227	23	16	10
Other faculty committees	211	27	15	17
Tenured faculty:				
Minority	102	27	59	23
Majority	221	20	19	21
Nontenured faculty:				
Minority	108	45	33	31
Majority	245	22	7	28
Student body:				
Minority	78	68	18	42
Majority	204	55	4	37
Departments	181	35	8	30
Student newspaper	189	49	6	26
Student political activist groups	110	48	3	67
Student government	218	43	2	27
Teaching and/or research assistants	73	36	0	69
Dormitory groups	108	46	0	58
Fraternities, sororities, eating clubs	57	34	1	67
TOTAL*	3,410 (10.30)	869 (2.62)	275 (.83)	662 (2.00)

TABLE 1 *(cont.)*

	Supporter	Neutral	Resister	Don't know
Factors external to institution:				
State government agency or power	57	85	7	64
Regional agency or power	47	81	3	77
City agency or power	18	91	3	81
Local community governments	31	84	8	78
Business or fraternal groups (Rotary, Lions)	36	71	8	80
Industry (IBM, Xerox)	35	73	3	82
Local businesses	48	68	9	75
Religious groups	59	62	14	70
Medical groups	21	73	4	88
Public or private schools	45	66	6	76
Other colleges and universities	75	55	10	62
News media	72	66	5	57
TOTAL*	544 (1.64)	875 (2.94)	80 (.24)	890 (2.68)

* Number in parenthesis is a ratio of total checks and the number of institutions calling this the major change, e.g., "Internal support" equals 3,410 to 331 (10.30). This ratio will be used in appendix Tables 1 through 7, as in Table 32.

SOURCE: Author's questionnaire.

ACCOMPLISHING THE MAJOR CHANGE II:

TABLE 2 *Changes in academic programs (173 institutions)*

	Supporter	*Neutral*	*Resister*	*Don't know*
Factors internal to institution:				
President	160	5	3	
Board of trustees	137	26	2	2
Deans	148	3	5	1
Other administrators	125	18	1	3
Alumni groups	70	43	11	24
Faculty senate or executive committee	107	17	8	3
Other faculty committees	103	13	12	9
Tenured faculty:				
Minority	38	24	38	6
Majority	122	14	6	7
Nontenured faculty:				
Minority	46	29	23	12
Majority	121	17	3	10
Student body:				
Minority	41	43	18	14
Majority	111	36	1	13
Departments	98	17	6	5
Student newspaper	91	37	1	12
Student political activist groups	41	36	1	36
Student government	88	41	1	16
Teaching and/or research assistants	44	20		29
Dormitory groups	47	29		29
Fraternities, sororities, eating clubs	33	27	1	29
TOTAL*	1,771(10.23)	495 (2.86)	141(.81)	260(1.50)
Factors external to institution:				
State government agency or power	64	22	6	23
Other colleges and universities	61	19	9	17
TOTAL*	105 (.60)	4 (.23)	15 (.08)	40(.23)

SOURCE: Author's questionnaire.

TABLE 3 *Changes in students (115 institutions)*

	Supporter	Neutral	Resister	Don't know
Factors internal to institution:				
President	99	5	1	2
Board of trustees	81	9	8	3
Deans	92	7	5	1
Other administrators	87	10	1	2
Alumni groups	48	18	15	14
Faculty senate or executive committee	63	13	6	4
Other faculty committees	55	16	4	8
Tenured faculty:				
Minority	26	13	21	4
Majority	70	9	7	3
Nontenured faculty:				
Minority	25	15	15	9
Majority	73	10	4	7
Student body:				
Minority	30	14	14	12
Majority	71	14	4	8
Departments	52	16	2	9
Student newspaper	58	19	5	6
Student political activist groups	29	16	4	24
Student government	58	14	2	9
Teaching and/or research assistants	29	9		20
Dormitory groups	38	12	2	7
Fraternities, sororities, eating clubs	32	6	2	15
TOTAL*	1,116 (9.7)	245 (2.13)	122 (1.06)	167 (1.45)
Factors external to institution:				
State government	46	20	4	15
City agency or power	26	25	5	19
Community government	33	24	3	8
Business or fraternal groups	31	21	5	19
Local businesses	49	12	6	15
Religious groups	39	15	4	21
Public or private schools	36	13	3	22
Other colleges and universities	36	23	3	18
TOTAL*	296 (2.57)	153 (1.33)	33 (.28)	137 (1.19)

SOURCE: Author's questionnaire.

TABLE 4 *Changes in institutional concerns (95 institutions)*

	Supporter	Neutral	Resister	Don't know
Factors internal to institution:				
President	92	1		
Board of trustees	77	12	3	1
Deans	81	5	3	1
Other administrators	75	9	4	8
Alumni groups	40	27	3	8
Faculty senate or executive committee	64	11	3	5
Other faculty committees	61	11	6	4
Tenured faculty:				
Minority	17	11	21	5
Majority	64	10	3	5
Nontenured faculty:				
Minority	17	19	12	9
Majority	68	9	1	8
Student body:				
Minority	23	18	9	12
Majority	58	21	3	8
Departments	55	11	6	5
Student newspaper	47	18	3	6
Student political activist groups	30	14	1	19
Student government	60	18	1	4
Teaching and/or research assistants	26	11	1	17
Dormitory groups	28	13		23
Fraternities, sororities, eating clubs	18	8	3	21
TOTAL*	1,001(10.53)	257 (2.70)	86 (.90)	169 (1.77)
Factors external to institution:				
Religious groups	32	20	3	14
Public or private schools	26	20	4	11
Other colleges and universities	33	19	7	6
TOTAL*	91 (.95)	59 (.62)	14 (.14)	31 (.32)

NOTE: Most external sources had 0 as "resisters."

SOURCE: Author's questionnaire.

TABLE 5 *Changes in faculty (89 institutions)*

	Supporter	Neutral	Resister	Don't know
Factors internal to institution:				
President	80	1	5	2
Board of trustees	62	12	5	3
Deans	68	7	5	1
Other administrators	54	13	6	1
Alumni groups	29	27	4	10
Faculty senate or executive committee	54	10	8	5
Other faculty committees	52	10	1	9
Tenured faculty:				
Minority	21	8	15	3
Majority	54	7	7	1
Nontenured faculty:				
Minority	20	14	15	6
Majority	64	9	2	3
Student body:				
Minority	16	23	9	11
Majority	46	21		10
Departments	49	6	2	7
Student newspaper	38	22	3	10
Student political activist groups	13	18	5	25
Student government	39	20	2	12
Teaching and/or research assistants	21	13		15
Dormitory groups	25	12		19
Fraternities, sororities, eating clubs	12	13		17
TOTAL*	817 (9.17)	265 (2.97)	94(1.05)	180(2.02)
Factors external to institution:				
Religious groups	10	25	3	12
Public or private schools	15	21	3	12
Other colleges and universities	24	16	3	12
TOTAL*	49 (.55)	62 (.69)	9 (.10)	36 (.40)

SOURCE: Author's questionnaire.

TABLE 6 *Changes in administration (77 institutions)*

	Supporter	Neutral	Resister	Don't know
Factors internal to institution:				
President	69		4	
Board of trustees	60	8	3	2
Deans	63	1	5	2
Other administrators	56	3	1	4
Alumni groups	29	19	4	13
Faculty senate or executive committee	46	13		1
Other faculty committees	40	13		3
Tenured faculty:				
Minority	17	11	8	4
Majority	48	7		3
Nontenured faculty:				
Minority	17	17	3	3
Majority	50	9		3
Student body:				
Minority	16	16	3	9
Majority	45	10	1	8
Departments	44	8		4
Student newspaper	39	14		4
Student political activist groups	16	12	1	14
Student government	47	9	2	4
Teaching and/or research assistants	19	8	1	11
Dormitory groups	28	13		23
Fraternities, sororities, eating clubs	7	9		12
TOTAL*	756 (9.81)	200 (2.59)	36 (.46)	127 (1.64)
Factors external to institution:				
Religious groups	16	15	3	8
Other colleges and universities	18	13	3	10
TOTAL*	34 (.44)	28 (.36)	6 (.07)	18 (.23)

SOURCE: Author's questionnaire.

TABLE 7 *Changes in finance (60 institutions)*

	Supporter	Neutral	Resister	Don't know
Factors internal to institution:				
President	53	2	1	
Board of trustees	47	5	2	
Deans	48	3	3	
Other administrators	43	7	3	
Alumni groups	26	17	5	6
Faculty senate or executive committee	38	7	5	1
Other faculty committees	33	8	2	2
Tenured faculty:				
Minority	11	13	8	1
Majority	39	7	4	1
Nontenured faculty:				
Minority	8	14	4	6
Majority	36	7	2	6
Student body:				
Minority	11	18	4	4
Majority		19	3	2
Departments	36	4	3	3
Student newspaper	28	13	2	5
Student political activist groups	12	14	2	9
Student government	31	12	2	5
Teaching and/or research assistants	18	10		7
Dormitory groups	23	7		12
Fraternities, sororities, eating clubs	13	14	5	6
TOTAL*	554 (9.23)	201 (3.35)	62 (1.03)	75 (1.25)
Factors external to institution:				
State government agency or power	29	3	4	8
Other colleges and/or universities	21	7	4	7
TOTAL*	50 (.83)	10 (.16)	8 (.13)	15 (.25)

SOURCE: Author's questionnaire.

7. A Special Analysis of Student Protests

As one might suspect, there is an increasing amount of research literature on the assessment of student protest and demonstrations on college and university campuses across the country.[1] For example, Peterson, of Educational Testing Service, has done a replication of his earlier study of 1964–65 of 849 institutions of higher education in America. His study and the replication in 1967–68 (859 institutions) deal almost entirely with the types of issues which initiated student protest. His respondents were deans of students (it is quite common knowledge, however, that deans of students do not always take an active or central role in dealing with student protest on most campuses). Also, Peterson did not include junior and community colleges, where student protests seem to be increasing. Astin reported at the American Psychological Association meeting in September 1969 on a project assessing student protest at 200 institutions. Again a great deal of the analysis was devoted to the type of issue involved, although some attention was given to the institution by control and by highest degree.

One of the questions asked of the presidents of the 1,230 institutions in this study was whether they had experienced an *increase* in student protest and demonstrations during the last 10 years. (Responses came in during the 1968–69 academic year.) The purpose of the analysis which follows is not to discuss the issues involved in student protest and demonstrations (indeed there is much evidence from within the student protest movement itself that issues are often devised on the spot in order to have maximum effectiveness in the political arena of the student demonstration). Our concern here is with the *institutional characteristics* which distinguish those

---

[1] Material in this chapter was published as "Student Protest—A National and Institutional Profile." (See Hodgkinson, 1970.)

institutions reporting increased student protest from those which do not. There is a wealth of data within the IIT project for making these comparisons. In the study as a whole the president was given the options of saying whether student protest had increased, whether it had remained unchanged, whether it had decreased, or whether no student protest at all had been experienced.

Leaving out multiple responses in our sample of 1,230 institutions, we see that 355 reported that they had had an increase in student protest and demonstrations, 535 reported that they had had no change, 20 reported that they had had a decrease in student protests, and 270 reported that they had had no protests at all. In the sample then, about 30 percent reported increased protest, 44 percent reported no change, 1½ percent reported a decrease, and 22 percent reported no experience with student protest. In that our sample of 1,230 institutions is a fairly close approximation of 50 percent of the full national complement of institutions of higher education, we can hypothesize that approximately 700 institutions of higher education have had an increase in student protest and demonstrations in the last 10 years.

In our study we have to rely on the perceptions of presidents, whereas Peterson relied on the perceptions of deans of students. One could argue that the president, as the senior administrative officer of the campus, is the person who is most likely to be embroiled in student protest and demonstrations. And thus when he reports an increase in student protest and demonstrations, it is most likely something he himself has personally experienced. We will now analyze how the 355 institutions that reported an increase in student protest differ from those institutions in the sample of 1,230 which did not.

LOCATION   By separating the reporting institutions into regions of the country, it is very clear from our data (Table 33) that although some areas have had more student protest than others, there is no "safe" region of the country.

The highest areas are the Far West (36 percent of the institutions there reported an increase in student protest), the Mideast (35.7 percent), and the Great Lakes (33.2 percent). The lowest areas are the Southwest (19.2 percent) and the Southeast (22.3 percent). The differences in protest by region are not very great, although the regions with high population density seem to have more student protest, not only in real numbers but on a percentage basis. It

	Increased student protest	No change	Decrease	No protest
New England	33 29.7%	54 48.6%	3 2.7%	17 15.3%
Mideast	80 35.7%	84 37.5%	2 .9%	50 22.3%
Southeast	49 22.3%	170 48.6%	3 1.4%	58 26.4%
Great Lakes	69 33.2%	91 43.7%	4 1.9%	39 18.7%
Plains	38 24.2%	77 49.0%	2 1.3%	36 22.9%
Southwest	15 19.2%	34 43.6%	2 2.6%	22 28.2%
Rocky Mountains	9 23.7%	21 55.3%	1 2.6%	6 15.8%
Far West	62 36.0%	66 38.4%	3 1.7%	40 23.3%
TOTALS	355 29.3%	535 44.2%	20 1.7%	270 22.3%

TABLE 33
Student protests and demonstrations by geographical area: number of institutions reporting

SOURCE: Author's questionnaire.

certainly seems to be true that the 20 percent of institutions in the Southwest and Southeast have not received nearly as much national publicity about their student protest as those in the Far West and the Mideast. One could argue that the mass media have assisted in the notion that student protest is occurring primarily on the East Coast and the West Coast. Our data indicate that all regions of the country have had student protest at approximately the 30 percent level of institutions reporting.

When the institutions are broken down by state, more significant differences can be noted (see Table 42 for complete breakdown by state). These cannot be explained on population basis alone. The states with the highest incidence of student protest are New York (50 percent of the reporting institutions), Iowa (48 percent), Michigan (43 percent), Massachusetts (40 percent), California (36 percent), and Illinois (30 percent). The lowest states (ranging from 16 percent to 27 percent reporting increased protest) include Florida, Georgia, Kansas, Minnesota, Missouri, Ohio, New Jersey, Oregon, Pennsylvania, and Texas. There are some hypotheses which might explain these differences. With the exception of

Iowa, the high-protest states tend to be urban, while the low-protest states tend to be rural. The data provide some support for the hypothesis that the crisis on campus is a parallel to the crisis of the city. This does not mean that protest occurs only on campuses located in big cities, but simply that the students must be close enough to a city that the culture and conflict of the city become a part of the way students see the campus. The students may, from contact with ghetto residents, come to see themselves as similarly powerless and oppressed in the campus setting (e.g., very high density housing; residents having no say about food, or rent, etc.). However, even this urbanity hypothesis does not explain the differences by state in every case between the high and the low, in that a number of the low-protest states such as Ohio, New Jersey, and Pennsylvania have significantly high population densities. The urbanity hypothesis explains increased protest in the high states but does not work to explain the relatively low protest in the states mentioned above.

INSTITU-TIONAL CHAR-ACTERISTICS There is no significant effect of public versus private control on student protests. Of the 355 institutions reporting an increase in protest 162 are public (46 percent) and 182 are private (51 percent). In the whole study 42 percent of the institutions are public and 55 percent of the 1,230 are private. Thus there seems to be no significance in whether an institution is controlled by public or private forces. There is a significant increase, however, by whether or not the institution is accredited; of the 355 institutions reporting increased student protest, 93 percent have accreditation. It should be clearly pointed out, however, that if an institution wishes to avoid student protest, dropping its accreditation will not be a particularly helpful device. These are relationships only between factors, and we assume no causal relationship between one factor and student protest. The *association* of factors, however, may help institutions in providing some patterns for their own development.

The age of the institution has absolutely no effect on increased student protest. We have nine categories of age of founding of the institution, and there is absolutely no difference in any category in the amount of student protest or whether there has been an increase or not. There is, however, a definite relationship between highest degree awarded by the institution and the percentage of institutions reporting increased student protest.

It is clear, however, that the community colleges awarding lower

Type of institution	Increased protest, percent
Less-than-B.A. awarding	24.8
B.A.-awarding	33.5
M.A.-awarding	50.0
Ph.D.-granting	67.1

SOURCE: Author's questionnaire.

degrees than the B.A. have not been immune from student protest even though they have few of the characteristics usually attributed to protest-prone institutions, such as a residential student body, large numbers of teaching assistants who teach courses, a remote administration, etc. In that most of the public community colleges do exist in cities, it tends to further the urbanity hypothesis about student protest. It does seem, however, that as "quality" (number of Ph.D.s on faculty, SAT scores of entering freshmen, selectivity, size of library, etc.) increases, the incidence of student protest also increases. This is so because "higher quality" students perhaps may be more aware of the more political aspects of campus governance, more deeply involved in the intellectual side of campus life, and less malleable and less easily led around by the nose, as well as less impressed with authority which comes from position rather than competence.

It is also possible that in the community colleges the vocationalism of the students and the small preoccupation with research which characterizes the faculty and perhaps a concomitant increase in teaching hold down the protest level. It is also difficult for students to argue about "absentee landlords" when the board which governs the community college is usually right in town and quite accessible to students or faculty who wish to ask questions about institutional policy.

Although highest degree awarded does predict increased incidence of student protests and demonstrations, in this study institutional size is a better predictor of the incidence of student protest than is highest degree. Regardless of highest degree awarded, as the size of the student body increases, the percentage reporting student protest also increases.

Note that the Ph.D. institutions with increased student protest average 12,000 students, while the Ph.D. institutions which have not reported an increase in student protest have a mean student size of 5,300 students. At all degree levels, the increased-protest in-

TABLE 35
Mean size of institution by highest degree awarded

Degree	Increase in protest		No change	
	Mean size	Number of institutions	Mean size	Number of institutions
Less-than-B.A.	3,282	(66)	1,707	(198)
B.A.	1,197	(79)	1,147	(161)
M.A.	3,987	(102)	2,708	(105)
Ph.D.	12,014	(90)	5,360	(45)

SOURCE: Author's questionnaire.

stitutions are larger than the institutions that report no change in protest. This is particularly true at the Ph.D.-granting-institution level and at the less-than-B.A.-degree-awarding level. In both of these categories, the high-protest institutions are twice as large as the institutions that have not reported an increase in protest. If one neglects highest degree awarded and lumps all the institutions in the study by size alone, increasing size of student body dramatically increases the likelihood of increased student protest in all size categories (Table 36).

The variable of size also functions effectively when we break the institutions down by type of control (Table 37).

Note that in this analysis that the public institutions which report an increase in protest have a mean size of almost *triple* the public institutions which report no change in protest. The nonsectarian institutions that have reported increased protest are more than twice the size of the nonsectarian institutions that report no change in protest. (It is also interesting to observe that the sectarian institutions have not been immune from the phenomenon of increased student protest, 96 institutions in that category reporting

TABLE 36
Institutions reporting student protest by size

Enrollment	Increase in protest		No change	Total number of institutions in sample
	Number of institutions			
Small (under 1,000)	72	(14%)	234	501*
Medium (1,000–5,000)	154	(32%)	223	468
Large (5,000–15,000)	75	(58%)	43	128
Giant (15,000–25,000)	24	(75%)	4	32
Super (25,000 and over)	8	(88%)	1	9

*A large number of "small" institutions have had *no* student protest, and could not therefore report any change.

SOURCE: Author's questionnaire.

TABLE 37
*Institutions
reporting
protest by
control of
institution*

Type of Control	Increase in protest		No change	
	Mean size	*Number of institutions*	*Mean size*	*Number of institutions*
Public	8,282	(161)	3,005	(242)
Private sectarian	1,894	(96)	1,109	(169)
Private nonsectarian	3,770	(77)	1,319	(94)

SOURCE: Author's questionnaire.

increased student protest.) As further investigation of the phenomenon of size, we broke the institutions down by regions of the country in terms of size of institutions reporting increased protest (Table 38). Once again the institutions that report increased protest are significantly larger than those which do not.

The regional breakdowns are particularly impressive in the increased size of the increased protest institutions. Notice, for example, that in the Great Lakes area the institutions reporting increased protest have a mean student body of 7,125 students against a mean of 1,994 for the institutions reporting no change in protest. The Far West is also extreme in having a mean student body of 7,000 for institutions with increased protest compared with a mean size of 2,000 for institutions reporting no change in protest. In every region of the country the high-protest institutions are at least twice as big as the institutions reporting no significant change. With regard to student protest the data do not seem to reveal any kind of "critical mass" beyond which size the institution is more likely to have increased protest. Mean sizes of student body were

TABLE 38
*Student
protest by
mean size
and region*

Region	Increased protest		No change	
	Mean size	*Number of institutions*	*Mean size*	*Number of institutions*
New England	3,312	(32)	1,432	(53)
Mideast	4,122	(75)	2,085	(80)
Southeast	3,954	(45)	2,390	(104)
Great Lakes	7,125	(68)	1,994	(89)
Plains	4,087	(38)	1,261	(75)
Southwest	5,833	(15)	3,349	(33)
Rocky Mountains	5,684	(9)	1,905	(21)
Far West	7,174	(60)	2,118	(66)

SOURCE: Author's questionnaire.

recorded for each of the institutions reporting an increase in protest, and these were compared with the means of institutions that have reported no increase. There seems to be no single point at which the curve jumps sharply toward increased protest; rather it is a steady increase in protest as the enrollment of the institution increases.

The variable of size seems to be worth some consideration in that it holds for whatever analytical category we wish to put in opposition to it. If as America grew we had simply increased the number of governing units, we would now be a nation of 200 million Americans, each living in a small town of about 2,000 people. We would probably have 150 states and 10 presidents; but we have not chosen that path and can never choose it now, as urbanization and high population densities are obviously here to stay. In fact, we now have a new term, megalopolis, which suggests that what used to be a city is now taking over hundreds of square miles to form a "city" which is even larger than a state. In terms of governing huge and expanding populations with a structure designed for one-hundredth of the present numbers, one can equate the problem of Mayor John Lindsay of New York and the president of any major public university. In the early days of this country a representative of the federal legislature probably had 4,000 constituents to serve. Today, the same individual must be responsive to the needs and interests of 400,000 people.

It is highly unlikely in a situation like this that any sort of personal visibility can be accomplished. Individuals are bound to feel that they are part of a supersystem and that they have little power in relation to it. There is some research evidence on the question of size which perhaps could be mentioned here. Children of large families tend to have poorer self-concepts and self-evaluations by age 12 than do children of smaller families who have easier and more frequent access to parental attention. Also, any teacher knows the frustration of trying to provide meaningful rewards for individual children in a class of 35 or more students. Although large schools are supposed to provide more options for individual participation, the facts of the matter can be summarized from a recent study as follows: (1) students in small schools hold an average of 3.5 responsible positions per student (members of play casts, members of organizations, athletic teams, etc.); students in large schools average 0.5 responsible positions per student, or every other student in the large school has but one responsible role; (2)

students in small schools exceed those in large schools in having satisfying experiences relating to developing confidence, to being challenged, and to participating in important activities; (3) students in small schools receive twice as many pressures to participate or to meet the expectations of the schools as those in large schools.[2]

There are also a great many studies of size of work groups in factories, public agencies, discussion groups, task forces, and training encounter groups, all of which indicate a negative relationship between size and individual participation, involvement, and satisfaction. As the group gets larger, no matter what the activity, more highly developed specialization will take place. Contrast, for example, the typical pickup sandlot baseball game with the little league game of today. In the pickup game there were just enough players, and everybody had to continue if the game was to be played at all; everybody played every position. On the little league teams, however, typically 30 or 40 boys are trying out for the team, so that at any given moment more people are watching than playing. Specialization develops; some people do nothing but pitch; others play first base or catch; nobody has the experience of playing all the positions. Most are glad if they have a chance to play at all.

It is not the function of this paper to go into this matter, but one might consider possible alternatives in order to provide a feeling for small-sized organizations even on a large campus. Something on the order of *selective decentralization* will probably have to take place in the next few years. Indeed, we can begin to see the outlines of such a movement on the horizon at the present time with the interest in cluster colleges, etc.

We also have information on institutions by calendar. Forty percent of institutions on a semester system report an increase of protest, thirty-six percent of the institutions on the quarter system report increases, fifty-one percent of institutions in the trimester system report an increase, and forty-five percent of the institutions on a four-one-four work experience program report increases in student protest. There seems to be a fairly significant increase in the trimester institutions compared with the others, while the four-one-four and other experimental curricula also seem to be a high area. It is conceivable that experimental calendars tend to attract experimentally oriented students and that this accounts for

[2] This material is summarized in Chickering (1969).

the relatively high incidence of student protests on the trimester and four-one-four calendars. But this is speculation at this point.

**STUDENT
CHARACTER-
ISTICS** There are some very interesting differences between students in the increased protest institutions and in the institutions that report no change (Table 39).

It is clear that the institutions reporting an increase in student protest have a far more open and heterogeneous student body than the national average. In every one of our factors of student diversity the high-protest group of institutions has greater diversity in the student body than the national norms (although national norms also show significant increases in these areas of student diversity). These factors suggest a shifting, transient student body with few local ties which might serve as a deterrent to protest. In support of an urban theme pursued in an earlier section of this report, one of the highest relationships with students involves the number of

TABLE 39
*Comparison
of student
characteristics*

Item	High-protest institutions		National sample, percent
	Percent	*Number of institutions*	
Increased heterogeneity of students — age	29	(105)	25
Increased heterogeneity of socioeconomic background	54	(192)	45
Increased heterogeneity of ethnic composition	69	(248)	55
Increased proportion of out-of-state students	65	(203)	48
Increased student participation in community volunteer programs	79	(281)	66
Increased proportion of transfer students entering institution	62	(223)	53
Decreased authority of central campus administration	32	(114)	18
Decreased degree to which institution controls student behavior	66	(237)	40
Increased underground publications and films	40	(143)	17

SOURCE: Author's questionnaire.

students who participated in community volunteer programs. In the 355 high-protest institutions, 79 percent (281) reported increased participation in community volunteer programs, while 66 percent of the national sample reported an increase in student participation in community volunteer work.

Another sharp and striking difference involves the frequency of underground publications and films. In the high-protest group, 40 percent reported an increase in this material, while in the whole sample less than half that many institutions (17 percent) reported that many increases. Most administrators would like to control underground student activities if they could, but they obviously can't. Support for the inability of institutions to govern student behavior is obvious in these particular data. In both the item of decreased authority of central campus administration and the item of decreased degree to which the institution controls student behavior, the high-protest institutions show much more decrease in authority over the students than is true of the national sample.

FACULTY CHARACTER-ISTICS There is some evidence from our study that faculty have taken a part (not always knowingly) in student protest (Table 40).

TABLE 40
Comparison of faculty characteristics

	High-protest institutions		National sample, percent
Item	*Percent*	*Number of institutions*	
Increased hours *of faculty time spent in research*	55	(197)	34
Decreased hours *of faculty time spent in teaching*	63	(227)	49
Increased commitment *of faculty to research*	53	(189)	34
Decreased faculty commitment *to the institution*	47	(169)	27
Increased faculty support of students who oppose administrative policies	60	(216)	31
Increase in faculty who publicly advocate positions on national policy	72	(256)	41
Increased proportion of budget based on federal support	68	(243)	56

SOURCE: Author's questionnaire.

Faculty at high-protest institutions have increased the hours spent in research far more than the national sample and have decreased the hours spent in teaching far more than the national sample. In addition to hours spent, the high-protest institutions also report a greatly increased faculty commitment to research compared with national figures. All this tends to suggest a decreased faculty loyalty to the institution and an increased faculty loyalty to the discipline, and indeed that evidence is clear. Almost twice as many of the high-protest institutions report decreased faculty commitment to the institution than is true of the national sample.

Two of the highest relationships in the faculty sector concern increased faculty support of students who oppose administrative policies and the number of faculty who publicly advocate positions on national policy. On both of these items the high-protest institutions have a percentage double the national norms for those items. Perhaps the most striking fact is that 60 percent of the high-protest institutions report increased faculty support of students who oppose the administration, while nationally only 31 percent of the institutions report that increase.

The faculty picture, then, is quite consistent: interest in research, lack of interest in teaching, lack of loyalty to the institution, and support of dissident students. Indeed, at some institutions the faculty status system (emphasizing as it does the discipline and the rewards of research; the feeling that institutional loyalty is unintellectual and corny, beneath them as professionals) may create a kind of superman mentality. There are so few counterforces to the prevailing faculty culture that at some institutions faculty may begin to assume that their right to complete academic freedom is to be kept entirely separate from any discussions of academic responsibility. In support of our assessment that the high-protest institution tends to be research-oriented and "on the make," in which the student is frequently lost in the struggle to acquire as much research support as possible, we cite the figure of 68 percent of the high-protest institutions reporting an increased proportion of the budget based on federal support compared with 56 percent reporting such an increase in the national sample.

CONCLUDING REMARKS AND ANALYSIS   Most of the current thinking about student protest suggests that the answer is to open up the governance structure of the institution to student participation. This should make most students feel that the institution cares about them (or at least about their legally elected representatives). We have fairly clear evidence in our study that this is not the case, that the roots of protest are deeper than simply being allowed to elect a student who will then "speak for the student body" on various committees of the institution. Interestingly enough, we decided to find out what the relationship was between incidents of student protest on campus and the amount of student control in institutional policy making, with the following results (Table 41).

As can be seen, 284, or 80 percent, of the institutions reporting an increase in student protest also report an increase in student control in institutional policy. There is a slight chicken or egg problem here in that we cannot tell from our data whether the increase in student protest came before or after the increase in student control in institutional policy making. The most likely guess is that they occur contiguously. Certainly the other hypothesis that increased student control in institutional policy making would result in a *decrease* in student protest is not supported by our data at all. The reverse would seem to be more likely. Thus while the national sample of 1,230 institutions reports increased student control in institutional policy making in 64 percent of the institutions, the high-protest sample of 355 institutions reports 80 percent also having an increase in student control in its institutionwide policy making.

One gets the impression from all this that these high-protest

TABLE 41
Student control in institution-wide policy making by on-campus student protests

	Student control				
Student protest	*Increase*	*No change*	*Decrease*	*Not applicable*	*Total*
Increase	284	69	0	0	355
	80.0%	19.4%	0.0%	0.0%	
No change	331	191	3	8	535
	61.9%	35.7%	.6%	1.5%	
Decrease	15	2	0	2	20
	75.0%	10.0%	0.0%	10.0%	
No protest	131	95	1	38	270
	48.5%	35.2%	0.4%	14.1%	
TOTALS*	775	367	4	48	1,230
	64.0%	30.3%	.3%	4.0%	

*Totals do not add due to incomplete responses.
SOURCE: Author's questionnaire.

campuses are simply superactive places in which people are more intense, more active, and more involved in *something,* although that something may not necessarily be the welfare of the institution itself. One assessment that could be made from this study is that tinkering with structures may not be any long-term solution to problems of student protest. Oftentimes there may be a "hidden agenda" in which students say that they are protesting issue A while actually something much deeper is involved. There are quite clearly protest-prone students and protest-prone faculty. They also are, for better or worse, some of the most intelligent and most able students and faculty in the United States.

The next few years in higher education will undoubtedly show increased factionalism; increased use of the styles of collective negotiation rather than collegial and professional trust; increased intrusion into on-campus activities from "outside" agencies, particularly state departments of education; and declining budgets for higher education. It also is quite likely that in addition to these factors there will be a continued disillusionment of the young in the ability of governmental structures to solve any of the urgent social problems we now face at any *level* of government. That will probably include disillusionment with faculty senates (local and statewide) as much as with city managers and state senators.

Our data do not give any easy answers to the problems, but clearly some way must be found whereby individuals can participate more meaningfully in decision making that governs their own lives. Electing one representative to speak for a student body of 20,000 students will not make the 19,999 students satisfied in very many institutions. It may be that the concept of selective decentralization mentioned earlier is a possible model for future change. In this model, those activities which directly touch the lives and futures of individuals should be handled with the smallest possible decision-making machinery, while those matters which are purely logistical and have little reference to individual lives should be handled in the largest possible network. Thus the curriculum, student advising, faculty evaluation, and all aspects of student life should probably be handled in the smallest and most intimate groups possible, while service, maintenance, and other logistical concerns should be handled on the largest possible network. This is hardly a panacea, but it points out a direction in which most institutions would probably gain more than they would lose.

TABLE 42 *Student protest by state, number of institutions, and percentages*

State	No answer	Increased protest	No change	Decrease	No protest	Total
Alabama	1 10.0%	2 20.0%	3 30.0%	0 0.0%	4 40.0%	10
Alaska	0 0.0%	0 0.0%	0 0.0%	0 0.0%	2 100.0%	2
Arizona	0 0.0%	2 22.2%	4 44.4%	0 0.0%	3 33.3%	9
Arkansas	0 0.0%	3 25.0%	6 50.0%	0 0.0%	3 25.0%	12
California	1 9%	43 36.8%	48 41.0%	0 0.0%	25 21.4%	118
Colorado	1 6.7%	4 26.7%	9 60.0%	1 6.7%	0 0.0%	15
Connecticut	0 0.0%	5 26.3%	7 36.8%	0 0.0%	7 36.8%	19
Delaware	0 0.0%	1 33.3%	0 0.0%	0 0.0%	2 66.7%	3
District of Columbia	0 0.0%	5 62.5%	2 25.0%	0 0.0%	1 12.5%	8
Florida	0 0.0%	6 23.1%	13 50.0%	0 0.0%	7 26.9%	27
Georgia	0 0.0%	4 18.2%	13 59.1%	1 4.5%	4 18.2%	22
Hawaii	0 0.0%	2 66.7%	0 0.0%	0 0.0%	1 33.3%	3
Idaho	0 0.0%	2 33.3%	3 50.0%	0 0.0%	1 16.7%	6
Illinois	3 5.0%	18 30.0%	29 48.3%	1 1.7%	9 15.0%	63
Indiana	1 3.3%	10 33.3%	11 36.7%	0 0.0%	8 26.7%	30
Iowa	0 0.0%	12 48.0%	7 28.0%	0 0.0%	6 24.0%	26
Kansas	0 0.0%	4 16.0%	15 60.0%	1 4.0%	5 20.0%	25
Kentucky	0 0.0%	3 18.7%	10 62.5%	0 0.0%	3 18.7%	16
Louisiana	1 12.5%	4 50.0%	3 37.5%	0 0.0%	0 0.0%	8
Maine	0 0.0%	2 14.3%	6 42.9%	1 7.1%	5 35.7%	14

TABLE 42 *(cont.)*

	No answer	Increased protest	No change	Decrease	No protest	Total
Maryland	0 0.0%	4 19.0%	11 52.4%	0 0.0%	6 28.6%	21
Massachusetts	1 2.0%	20 40.0%	24 48.0%	1 2.0%	4 8.0%	50
Michigan	0 0.0%	16 43.2%	15 40.5%	0 0.0%	6 16.2%	38
Minnesota	2 6.7%	6 20.0%	16 53.3%	0 0.0%	6 20.0%	30
Mississippi	1 9.1%	1 9.1%	7 63.6%	0 0.0%	2 18.2%	11
Missouri	2 5.3%	9 23.7%	17 44.7%	0 0.0%	10 26.3%	38
Montana	0 0.0%	2 25.0%	5 62.5%	0 0.0%	1 12.5%	8
Nebraska	0 0.0%	4 25.0%	10 62.5%	1 6.3%	1 6.3%	16
Nevada	0 0.0%	1 100.0%	0 0.0%	0 0.0%	0 0.0%	1
New Hampshire	0 0.0%	4 40.0%	6 60.0%	0 0.0%	0 0.0%	10
New Jersey	1 4.5%	5 22.7%	10 45.5%	1 4.5%	5 22.7%	22
New Mexico	0 0.0%	2 33.3%	3 50.0%	0 0.0%	1 16.7%	6
New York	4 4.2%	47 49.5%	29 30.5%	0 0.0%	14 14.7%	96
North Carolina	0 0.0%	12 32.4%	15 40.5%	0 0.0%	10 27.0%	37
North Dakota	0 0.0%	3 27.3%	4 36.4%	0 0.0%	4 36.4%	11
Ohio	1 1.9%	14 26.9%	24 46.2%	3 5.8%	10 19.2%	53
Oklahoma	1 9.1%	1 9.1%	6 54.5%	0 0.0%	3 27.3%	11
Oregon	0 0.0%	5 19.2%	8 30.8%	2 7.7%	11 42.3%	27
Pennsylvania	1 1.3%	18 24.0%	32 42.7%	1 1.3%	22 29.3%	77
Rhode Island	1 14.3%	2 28.6%	3 42.9%	0 0.0%	1 14.3%	7

	No answer	Increased protest	No change	Decrease	No protest	Total
South Carolina	0 0.0%	2 10.0%	8 40.0%	1 5.0%	9 45.0%	21
South Dakota	0 0.0%	0 0.0%	8 66.7%	0 0.0%	4 33.3%	12
Tennessee	0 0.0%	2 12.5%	7 43.7%	0 0.0%	7 43.7%	16
Texas	4 7.7%	10 19.2%	21 40.4%	2 3.8%	15 28.8%	53
Utah	0 0.0%	1 16.7%	3 50.0%	0 0.0%	2 33.3%	6
Vermont	2 18.2%	0 0.0%	8 72.7%	1 9.1%	0 0.0%	11
Virginia	0 0.0%	5 18.5%	14 51.9%	1 3.7%	7 25.9%	30
Washington	0 0.0%	11 47.8%	10 43.5%	1 4.3%	1 4.3%	24
West Virginia	0 0.0%	5 33.3%	8 53.3%	0 0.0%	2 13.3%	15
Wisconsin	0 0.0%	11 37.9%	12 41.4%	0 0.0%	6 20.7%	29
Wyoming	0 0.0%	0 0.0%	1 33.3%	0 0.0%	2 66.7%	3
Special services	0 0.0%	0 0.0%	0 0.0%	0 0.0%	1 100.0%	1
Other	0 0.0%	0 0.0%	1 50.0%	0 0.0%	1 50.0%	3
TOTALS	29 2.4%	355 29.3%	535 44.2%	20 1.7%	270 22.3%	1,230

SOURCE: Author's questionnaire.

8. Academic Preparation and Mobility of Presidents

In the questionnaire we asked each president for a considerable amount of information about himself: his highest degree, the area in which it was obtained, his age, etc. We can give here only a brief look at the presidents of American colleges and universities under some of the categories available in the data.

PRESIDENT'S AGE AND YEARS AT INSTITUTION It was interesting to notice that the presidents in our sample ranged through the spectrum of years from recent postgraduate work to well over retirement, in approximately equal numbers, although there is a sharp drop below age 35 and an equally sharp drop over age 65. In the categories from age 40 to age 64 the numbers are approximately equal. The median age for the presidents in our sample is 50:

Age	Number
Less than 35	18
35 to 39	74
40 to 44	165
45 to 49	235
50 to 54	277
55 to 59	243
60 to 64	139
65 and over	49
No response	30

NOTE: Median age 50; range 28 to 78.

We also were interested in how many years the president had been on the job as president, and how many years he had been at the institution. The largest number had been president of the

Number of years served as president	Number of presidents
Less than 1	119
1 to 2	115
2 to 5	369
5 to 10	293
10 to 15	143
15 to 20	79
20 to 25	42
25 or more	20
No response	10

NOTE: Range 1 month to 35 years; median 4 years.

SOURCE: Author's questionnaire.

institution between 2 and 10 years, with a rather sharp drop in the number of presidents who had survived the presidency for over 15 years (see Table 43.)

For a large percentage of our presidents, this was the first time they had been president of a college or university. The stereotype of the mobile president running from institution to institution taking presidencies in a long string does not seem to be borne out by our data.

President of another campus	Number
Yes	168 (14%)
No	1,054 (86%)

We also were interested in whether or not the president had "worked his way up" through the ranks of faculty or administrative positions and received the presidency from the same institution. Our data seem to indicate that this is not the case. Although 10 percent of the sample had held one other administrative position on the campus and 14 percent had held some combination of one administrative and one or more faculty positions, the vast majority of the 739 (60 percent of the sample) had held no previous positions on the campus where they were president. This suggests that most presidents do not work their way up through the hierarchy but indeed are imported from outside; rather than vertical mobility the direction seems to be horizontal.

TABLE 44
President's
highest
degree

Degree	Number	Percent
B.A.	57	5
M.A.	264	21
Ph.D.	576	47
Ed.D.	245	20
Law	30	2
Medicine	13	1
Others	35	2
No response	10	1

SOURCE: Author's questionnaire.

We were interested in the study in what highest degree various presidents had attained, in what area they had attained it, and what sort of institution they were now working in. The figures run as in Table 44.

It is clear from this that a little less than half of the presidents in our survey earned the highest academic degree, the Ph.D. If one adds the Ed.D. to that figure, it means that about 30 percent of the presidents attained less than the conventional terminal degrees. We also broke the data down by the area in which the presidents earned their highest degree (Table 45).

It is clear that the presidents in our sample did their work primarily in the areas of education, humanities, and social science. The number of education area degree earners is higher than the number of Ed.D.'s awarded, which means that a considerable number probably took the Ph.D. in education.

TABLE 45
Area of
president's
degree

Area	Number	Percent
Administrative, business, legal	87	7
Education	416	34
Applied and technical sciences	57	5
Humanities	310	25
Natural science	89	7
Social science	204	17
No response	67	5

SOURCE: Author's questionnaire.

TABLE 46
Number of presidents during last decade

Number of presidents	Number	Percent
One	430	35
Two	565	46
Three	162	13
Four	51	4
Five or more	10	1
No response	12	1

NOTE: Range 1 to 11; median between one and two presidents during the 10-year period.
SOURCE: Author's questionnaire.

We were interested in the number of presidents, including the respondent, the institution had had during the last 10 years, to get some rough measure of the stability of the position. The figures suggest a slightly greater stability than had been previously expected (Table 46).

Thus approximately 71 percent of our institutions had no more than two presidents during the previous decade; this suggests some stability, but as with our earlier findings, gives a presidential "life expectancy" of only four to five years.

CONTROL AND HIGHEST DEGREE BY AGE OF PRESIDENT

We were interested in determining whether younger presidents could be found in certain kinds of institutions offering certain degree levels or whether they were scattered rather uniformly throughout the system (Table 47).

TABLE 47
Age of president, highest degree and control of institution

| | | | | | | | *Control* | |
| | | *Public* | | | | *Private sectarian* | | |
	Less than B.A.	B.A.	M.A.	Ph.D.	Less than B.A.	B.A.	M.A.
President's age:							
Under 35	9				1	2	1
35–39	21	6	7	1	7	12	6
40–44	68	5	10	4	7	25	12
45–49	57	13	23	18	12	42	23
50–54	66	8	21	27	11	47	22
55–65	79	19	45	36	27	71	33
TOTALS	300	51	106	86	65	199	97

SOURCE: Author's questionnaire.

Both M.A.- and Ph.D.-granting institutions tend to have more presidents in the older brackets, while the public two-year colleges have a much greater age range. Indeed, it may be that "young" institutions have a preference for youthful administrators, who can represent aspirations of growth, while the "established" university seeks a presidential image suggesting maturity and stability.

PRESIDENT'S ACADEMIC AREA We were interested in investigating whether presidents who took their degrees in certain academic areas became presidents of particular kinds of institutions more often than not. There are some significant differences, as shown in Table 48.

Several things emerge from Table 48. First of all, the vast majority of presidents of less-than-B.A.-degree-granting institutions are presidents whose own academic work was in education (67 percent). The next highest is social science, with 8 percent of the less-than-B.A.-degree-granting institutions. In similar fashion, the B.A.- and M.A.-granting public institutions tend to have presidents whose academic work was also done in the field of education, although at the master's level social science emerged with almost 25 percent of the presidents. At the doctoral level for public institutions we see the emergence of social science as the major area in which presidents did their work, and a major decline of education. This strength in social science is unique to the public institutions and is not shared by the presidents of private-sectarian or private-non-sectarian Ph.D.-granting institutions. Note the small number of presidents of Ph.D. institutions whose work was in education.

| | Private nonsectarian | | | |
Ph.D.	Less than B.A.	B.A.	M.A.	Ph.D.
	1	1	2	
1	2	6	2	1
1	8	9	9	3
5	5	10	4	7
8	11	21	12	13
14	23	39	28	22
29	50	86	57	46

TABLE 48
President's
academic area
by highest
degree offered
in public
institution

Level	Academic area				
	No area	*Business/ legal*	*Educa- tion*	*Tech- nology*	*Human- ities*
Less than B.A.	18 6.0%	15 5.0%	202 67.3%	12 4.0%	17 5.7%
B.A.	1 2.0%	6 11.8%	21 41.2%	4 7.8%	8 15.7%
M.A.	6 5.7%	8 7.5%	41 38.7%	2 1.9%	17 16.0%
Ph.D.	2 2.3%	7 8.1%	8 9.3%	13 15.1%	11 12.8%
No response	0 0.0%	0 0.0%	6 66.7%	0 0.0%	0 0.0%
TOTALS	27 4.9%	36 6.5%	278 50.4%	31 5.6%	53 9.6%

SOURCE: Author's questionnaire.

The emphasis on education and social science in the public institutions may indicate a certain pragmatic outlook of these campuses and a desire on the part of presidents to receive training which is directly relevant to their role as administrators.

If we look at private-sectarian institutions (Table 49), we find that a number of these trends have been altered.

Here we see that although a considerable number of presidential

TABLE 49
President's
academic area
by highest
degree offered
in private-
sectarian
institution

Level	Academic area				
	No area	*Business/ legal*	*Educa- tion*	*Tech- nology*	*Human- ities*
Less than B.A.	6 9.2%	4 6.2%	17 26.2%	2 3.1%	25 28.5%
B.A.	9 4.5%	7 3.5%	43 21.6%	2 1.0%	81 40.7%
M.A.	6 6.2%	5 5.2%	5 5.2%	3 3.1%	54 55.7%
Ph.D.	1 3.4%	4 13.8%	2 6.9%	0 0.0%	16 55.2%
No response	0 0.0%	0 0.0%	0 0.0%	0 0.0%	2 66.7%
TOTALS	22 5.6%	20 5.1%	67 17.0%	7 1.8%	178 45.3%

SOURCE: Author's questionnaire.

	Natural science	Social science	Total
	11 3.7%	25 8.3%	300
	3 5.9%	8 15.7%	51
	6 5.7%	26 24.5%	106
	16 18.6%	29 33.7%	86
	1 11.1%	2 22.2%	9
	37 6.7%	90 16.3%	552

degrees at the less-than-B.A. and B.A. levels are in education, it is clearly the humanities which provides the academic background for the largest number of the presidents. (Note also that the area of social sciences, which amounted to 34 percent of the presidents in Ph.D. public institutions, is reduced to only 3 percent of the total in the private-sectarian category.) One would suspect that most of the denominational colleges have presidents whose work has been in

	Natural science	Social science	Total
	2 3.1%	9 13.8%	65
	18 9.0%	39 19.6%	199
	8 8.2%	16 16.5%	97
	5 17.2%	1 3.4%	29
	0 0.0%	1 33.3%	3
	33 8.4%	66 16.8%	393

the areas of religion and the humanities generally, and that it is the denominational colleges and universities which are being measured here.

The smallest number of institutions is in the category of private nonsectarian (there are 552 public institutions in the sample, 393 private sectarian and 240 private nonsectarian). When we look at the president's area of academic competence for the private-nonsectarian institution, we see that the humanities dominance declines (Table 50).

Although our sample of institutions is somewhat smaller here, it is nevertheless quite clear that a large number of the less-than-B.A.-degree-granting institutions have presidents who have done their academic work in the field of education, with a significant number in social science. At the B.A. and M.A. level of highest degree, there is a large number of presidents who have taken their work in humanities; while at the Ph.D. level the presidents seem remarkably evenly distributed in the academic areas.

One gets the impression from this summary of materials that presidents of public institutions are by and large more pragmatically trained and perhaps should have developed skills more directly relevant to their administrative tasks in the presidency. On the other hand, the private institutions — particularly in the sectarian

TABLE 50
President's academic area by highest degree offered in private-nonsectarian institution

Level	Academic area				
	No area	*Business/ legal*	*Education*	*Technology*	*Humanities*
Less than B. A.	5	6	19	2	6
	10.0%	12.0%	38.0%	4.0%	12.0%
B.A.	6	10	16	4	28
	7.0%	11.6%	18.6%	4.7%	32.6%
M.A.	3	5	9	4	25
	5.3%	8.8%	15.8%	7.0%	43.9%
Ph.D.	0	7	8	8	8
	0.0%	15.2%	17.4%	17.4%	17.4%
No response	0	0	1	0	0
	0.0%	0.0%	100.0%	0.0%	0.0%
TOTALS	14	28	53	18	67
	5.8%	11.7%	22.1%	7.5%	27.9%

SOURCE: Author's questionnaire.

area—have presidents whose academic work in the liberal arts should have inculcated in them a higher degree of responsiveness to humane values, to tolerance, and to understanding. A separate study would be needed to check this assumption out on the basis of direct evidence, but it is an interesting hypothesis.

The presidency seems to be a slightly more stable institution than some reports would have us believe. (Most presidents have been in office for four years and are the second president the institution has had during the decade, which suggests a rough presidential mortality rate of four to five years.) Although presidents are well scattered as to age, it does seem that the younger men are in the institutions that offer the lower degrees, and the M.A.- and Ph.D.-granting institution tends to select a man somewhat closer to retirement for the presidency.

As we have indicated, "working your way up" doesn't seem to be terribly appropriate as a goal for a presidential aspirant. It would probably be better for him to go out, take an advanced degree—probably in education or perhaps in social science—and then seek a position in a public institution, particularly in a community college. In the private-sectarian area, the presidential candidate should perhaps take work in the humanities with particular emphasis on religion and theology, and keep his fingers crossed.

	Natural science	*Social science*	*Total*
	2	10	50
	4.0%	20.0%	
	4	18	86
	4.7%	20.9%	
	4	7	57
	7.0%	12.3%	
	7	8	46
	15.2%	17.4%	
	0	0	1
	0.0%	0.0%	
	17	43	240
	7.1%	17.9%	

(Parenthetically, it is interesting that very little is known about the way in which presidents are selected, even though it is one of the major decisions an institution makes.)

The lack of presidents of public institutions whose academic work was in the humanities area is perhaps the most striking conclusion in this analysis. One gets the impression that social science training is becoming the "academically respectable" prerequisite for the public presidency that the humanities are and always have been for the private institutions. (Training in education seems inappropriate for presidents of all Ph.D.-granting institutions, regardless of public or private designation, due in no small way to the lack of respectability within academic circles, especially in universities, of the study of education per se. It is far better, apparently, to have the degree awarded in social science, which will maintain one's respect from the faculty over a longer period of time.)

9. A Look Ahead

This study has taken us a very small way down the road of institutional assessment. We have looked at change from a variety of perspectives, from institutional to national, from the kinds of changes that have taken place to some of the dynamics of institutional life that have made the changes possible. The general conclusion emerges with some clarity that institutions of higher education respond to stimuli in very similar ways. This is partly what makes them often rather dull as *institutions,* although they may be full of brilliant, interesting people. Ask anyone in higher education to list some truly interesting campuses (not departments or subunits), and he will be hard-pressed to mention more than a handful.

There is a bitter irony here, as one of the main forces that resists needed change in higher education is institutional uniqueness — "what happened at X is interesting, but of course it has nothing to do with us — we have a different heritage" — and institutional uniqueness is a myth. Often one finds two institutions within a mile or so of each other, so much alike they could have been stamped out of the same cookie cutter, yet denying each other's existence. It must be said, however, that the private colleges are beginning to pool their resources in 1971, and consortia and merger arrangements are being forced by one of the most innovative agents around — the threat of going out of business. But although there are traces of collaboration and cooperation, the primary mode of interinstitutional relations is still competitive.

The case studies also reveal that one of the major threats people on campus feel when a major change is proposed is some diminution of institutional autonomy, even though that autonomy is seldom used for productive alteration of program or mission. Autonomy is interpreted often as the right to do nothing.

One of the reasons that each institution tends to play the game by itself is the lack of any single comprehensive information network for higher education in America. The information network which would be truly useful would be a resource directory, covering everything from research data, to lists of other institutions which have had experience in some new programs, to access to knowledgeable individuals who can give good advice. At the moment, no national organization is providing this kind of leadership, and although national conferences praise the virtues of cooperation for *institutions,* there are few previous examples of the national higher education *associations'* working together on anything—although the major reason for their moving to One Dupont Circle in Washington was to make sure that cooperation was achieved.

The processes of change can be speeded up by the easy availability of facts, expert opinion, and personal consultation. As we have seen, not all change is caused by administrators—the information network we speak of here should be available to any qualified person on any campus, from student to trustee. To make such a service available only to presidents, as often happens, is to misread the nature of higher education, as we have seen.

Another conclusion, arising out of our data, is that, in addition to the network already described, a series of federally financed "model colleges" is needed, somewhat akin to the Model Cities program, to try out promising innovations in a variety of institutional settings, with a sophisticated research-and-evaluation component designed into each model college. This is one way to lick the current passivity of institutional responses to new needs —the research and evaluation must be conceived from the ground up as an essential program function. At the moment, research is usually seen as an outside intervention from the perspective of the program staff, while program may be seen by the research people as a contaminating dimension. They must get together within the parameters of an ongoing institution, in this case, the model college. The idea is really not too radical—schools of education have run laboratory or demonstration schools for a long time, both to try out new ideas and to provide student-teaching experience for future elementary and secondary school teachers. At the college level, Shimer College was for years a "farm school" for the University of Chicago, just as Bard College was for Columbia University. If the model colleges were carefully designed to be representative of the major types of institutions in the country (and we have seen that this would not be too difficult), and if the new programs, together with "quality control" and performance evaluation, could be fed to the institutions represented by the model college through the network already described, providing facts, opinions, and people knowledgeable about the new program, then the incentives for change would be greatly increased. The problem with existing experimental colleges as models for the rest of higher education is their lack of representativeness—they are intended to be "uncommon" and thus no institution needs to consider adopting their programs (indeed, the current rash of popularity of independent study, seminar, tutorial, and work-experience programs comes about 40 years after the experimental colleges first put them into operation). In his Education Reform Message of March 1970 President Nixon advocated the establishment of experimental schools along with the proposed National Institute of Education. The notion of a model colleges program would be entirely consistent with the goals of the Nixon proposal, and six model colleges would be a tiny item in the massive HEW budget.

If there is a single weak area in higher education, it is probably the curriculum of the first two years of undergraduate programs. The freshman year is often a disaster, resulting in very high attrition rates in all types of institutions. These programs are very difficult to change, largely because the faculty, for reasons of the monolithic status system mentioned earlier, is really not very interested in them. Freshman English is a course that everybody wants taught, but which no one wants to teach. It is hereby proposed that the junior college take seriously its role as a "bridging institution," as the junior high school did during the years when America began accepting the idea that everyone should have 12 years of schooling. The junior high school produced innovations— the core curriculum, the project method of teaching, differentiated staffing, block scheduling, etc.—which are still exciting today. One reason they were successful was that junior high schools were often newly built institutions with no inheritance to perpetuate. Similarly, the public junior colleges are basically relatively new (we build a new one every week) and represent the "bridge" to a normal expectation of four years of higher education for all. At the moment, their transfer curricula are terribly conservative, designed to get the approval of colleges and universities for the award of two years of credit. This is undoubtedly one reason why the attrition rates in public community colleges are so high. One of the most helpful changes would be a policy of *providing automatic acceptance in state four-year colleges and universities of all graduates of community colleges within the state.* This would free the community college to do some creative work in undergraduate education, an area in which new thinking is vitally needed, particularly in the first two years. If the community college could make some of the same contributions to curriculum and teaching that the junior high school has made, then higher education will unquestionably be stronger as a result.

Finally, a great deal of attention needs to be paid to the role of the educational "periphery," as contrasted to the educational "core" —a distinction we mentioned in the first chapter. Just as institutions have tended to ignore each other, so has the educational core ignored the thousands of proprietary institutions, industrial training programs, and other organized educational programs which characterize the periphery. Yet a great deal of very successful teaching and learning goes on in the periphery, institutional objectives are admirably clear, and teachers are very interested in their teaching and students in their learning. Serious thought needs to be given to the possibility of *legitimizing parts of the periphery* through accreditation and other devices. If this were done, a number of alternative institutional paths could be opened up, each with its own definition of excellence, allowing the student to choose the route that seems best for him. He would not have to select a conventional four-year liberal arts course just for its prestige value, as each alternative route would have its own standard of excellence. The country might save vast sums of money if, rather than building large numbers of new conventional colleges, we simply legitimized some of the peripheral institutions. In fact, the person who wants to learn to develop the qualities of the artisan—the cabinetmaker, jeweler, tailor—need not face a life of financial hardship in an era in which the label "custom made" is beginning to appeal to large sectors of our dominant middle class. This is not the end of the conception of excellence in education, but simply the admission that excellence is a word that has applicability in many areas, some of them not currently linked to the bachelor's degree. A great deal of the dissatisfaction of the young with higher education probably stems from the fact that they are often herded into one kind of institution, rewarding one kind of excellence only. Anything else is now "second rate," even though a really good tool-and-die craftsman can earn much more than the typical college graduate, and probably gets more fun out of doing his work. To recognize other standards of excellence is not to downgrade the collegiate notion of excellence—indeed, if other kinds of educational institutions were providing meaningful alternative notions of excellence, higher education in the conventional sense could concentrate more on its own version of quality than is now possible.

Of course, none of these changes will appear overnight, nor should they. But the essential problem indicated by this research dealing with change is the limited perspective of educational practitioners in terms of *what is possible,* and the even more limited notion of what is desirable. There are not enough good alternatives floating around in the collective consciousness of American higher education. The Carnegie Commission has enlarged our consciousness of alternatives by a good bit, but more needs to be done before higher education comes of age.

Commentary

"Institutions in Transition" is a title that conjures up moving and dynamic operations occurring from the time of the garden of Eden, when Adam turned to Eve (or should it be the other way around in these days of Women's Lib?) and said, "We are in a transition state," to the present, and extending into the future in which may exist the type of society that Alvin Toffler warns us is almost here in *Future Shock*. The findings of Dr. Hodgkinson's study are, in one dimension, much less exciting than one would have hoped would have been the case, but, in a second dimension, they offer much hope that a basic transition has, indeed, taken place.

Perhaps its saddest theme is that the various levels of higher education and the myriad institutions are not "moving in different directions. . . ." The model of the great universities permeates many of the thousands of other institutions, and it is no idle statement to say that there is a pecking order based on this model where the compacts strive to be family cars, the family cars to be deluxe models, and the deluxe to be Cadillacs.

In our anxiety over the lack of diversity, however, we should not skip quickly over some of the major conclusions of the study. They indicate basic social changes which may not have had time to permeate the fabrics of many institutions, but well could. Some really fundamental changes have occurred. They show up statistically, and, I venture to say, many are deep in importance and will be long lasting.

We are in a period of mass education—the first the world has known at the higher education level, and one that is still not completed. Professor Hodgkinson concludes from his research data that students are "much more diverse in terms of social and economic background." Doesn't this fulfill our American Dream that the right to benefit from the American society, in this case to benefit from higher education, should not be limited by social class or economic condition or by race or religion? Has not the Carnegie Commission on Higher Education called for a continuation in this direction and for additional funds to make it a reality? The study shows that more students from more socioeconomic groups are attending our colleges—and are staying longer, that more are graduating and more are going on to graduate school. With federal programs encouraging this trend, we may expect the change to continue; and we will come closer to seeing higher education open to all who can benefit, regardless of color, class, or financial status of their parents.

This change in the nature of the students attending may be the one most important finding of the Hodgkinson study and the one which holds the most hope for change in curriculum and organization. These students are typically first-generation students, and it will be some years before large numbers enter graduate schools and, it is hoped, return to teach at various institutions. Their values and their concerns about higher education may well differ from those of their predecessors, and future changes in higher education may well have been born in this fundamental change of the 1960s.

Along with this basic finding of change in the nature of the students, consideration should be given to the projected surplus of holders of doctoral degrees, who will reach a significant number by 1980. The impact of education without employment is one which our society must be prepared for, and steps must be taken to provide additional employment opportunities not only in the traditional fields for Ph.D. employment but also in those fields that have not previously tapped such individuals and in new careers which will burgeon in the next decades.

Within higher education, special efforts will have to be made to employ a mix of the new social and economic classes in instruction and research. Additional efforts will have to be made to employ representatives of these social and economic groups, which include minority groups, in special services not well provided in higher education today. Special services should include appropriate counseling, special seminars, and community college relationships. They should also include special campus activities in non-class hours which are generally accepted by academics as recreational rather than instructional but may well be related to the roles these students may occupy in society and which may take the place of the fraternities of an earlier age in the socialization process.

The case studies of the five institutions in transition are helpful in describing the major changes of those institutions and in providing an understanding of the transition other institutions might, or might not, enjoy. All five institutions seemed to me to be institutions moving from "good" to "better," and I wondered what five institutions moving from "poor" to "poorer" would have looked like beside the five described. These poorer institutions are rarely described except in financial terms. Whether because of finances, leadership of presidents, failures of governing boards, geographical location, or a combination of events, there are institutions, both public and private, which are moving more and more out of the mainstream of changes in higher education. Someday, some brave soul will rush in and name and describe them, having his bags packed and having resolved to emigrate to Australia the day the work is published. Canada is too close.

Yet as one considers institutions of higher learning in the light of this study, one has to come away with a feeling that institutions are most difficult to describe in quantitative terms. A college is not a college is not a college. There is a quality, there is a spirit that comes through as one visits and talks to faculty, administration, and students on one campus that does not come through on another. How big is a college or a university? For every document that reports economies through size, a truly great institution disproves the thesis or at least allows that the exception proves the rule.

Could it be that education remains a highly qualitative and highly personal matter even when projected through the most modern of media? Perhaps we would do well to recall the point of view of students regarding the impersonality of higher education. The report of the *President's Commission on Campus Unrest* (Scranton Commission) states:

... We do think it can be said that some of the causes of student unrest are to be found in certain contemporary features of colleges and universities. It is impressive, for example, that unrest is most prominent in the larger universities; that it is less common in those in which, by certain measures, greater attention is paid to students and to the needs of education, and where students and faculty seem to form single communities, either because of their size or the shared values of their members.

One of Professor Hodgkinson's conclusions that should not be passed over without a concrete recommendation for action relates to "the lack of any single comprehensive information network for higher education in America." Why is it that whenever you want to find out an answer to a specific question in higher education, the only answer is another research study or another questionnaire? Professor Hodgkinson has also put his finger on the place from which this information should come, namely, from the various associations which represent higher education on an institutional basis. If labor negotiations had to be conducted by the labor unions with the current information available to higher education, the unions would collapse. It is only because higher education has been, to a large degree, sacrosanct for many years that it could survive even though the "information network" has operated at such a slow, casual pace. The last decade has seen some change, as information on higher education became front-page and night-beat news on television. Even in this regard, one reason why the occasional event or situation became accepted as the norm may have its roots in the lack of a comprehensive national information network. Objective information needs to be available to everyone on the campus, as Professor Hodgkinson advocates, but this information should also be available to the public beyond the campus — and I would extend this network to them so that the reasons for change may be seen and the changes themselves supported.

The great challenges for institutions in the future revolve around developing a truly unique conception of their role in American higher education. One can make a case for copy catting the best within a particular type, as, for example, the major research university, the community college, the liberal arts college, and the state college — although even here one would hope for some uniqueness. One can make no case for each of these models trying to be all things to all people; and since persuasion, educational plans, and even boards of regents' policies have often failed to control aspirations for commonality, then fiscal controls unfortunately seem to be the route left. They are disastrous to the autonomy and, in the long run, to the uniqueness of institutions.

Within the uniqueness of institutions and models, each college or university should be encouraged to give detailed examination to:

1   Its relationship to its local environment, including responsibility to the community in the broadest sense with due regard for cultural, ethnic, and ecological aspects.

2   Its validity for existence, including the nature of its essential character and of the forces that demand a college in this place and at this time.

3   Its commitment to research or teaching, research and teaching, and the extent to which boundaries are drawn around these responsibilities.

4   Its qualitative role in admissions and graduation, with a clear understanding of what it strives to do with open admissions and its relation to graduation, "open" or "not-so-open."

5   Its requirement of everyone taking the same time to complete undergraduate college, with evidence available that many come better prepared than others from high school and that students learn at vastly differing rates. The Carnegie Commission recommendations for the three-year baccalaureate degree should be carefully examined.

6   Its aspirations, and the extent to which the faculty and curriculum are consistent with these aspirations. The projected oversupply of Ph.D.'s could enhance the model of the research university further into the state colleges and even into the community colleges. Thus, the employment of faculty consistent with the institution's role is fundamental, and the recommendation of the Carnegie Commission for an alternative to the research degree in the doctor of arts is important for those institutions whose mission is at the doctoral level. Institutions whose mission is primarily an instructional one should consider the employment of individuals with the doctor of arts degree, and community colleges and other institutions should give less consideration to paper credentials and more to the competence of individuals to undertake the unique task of the institution. It is hoped that the accrediting associations will take a new view toward evaluation of faculty competence.

7   Its responsibility toward encouraging and discouraging students from attending particular institutions. Guidance counselors and prospective students often know altogether too little about institutions when decisions for or against attendance are made. Proximity may mean lower cost economically, but it also may mean higher academic and social malfunctioning because student and institution are incompatible.

8   Its transfer and acceptance policies, with a view to making the loss of time and energy through transfer as slight as possible.

9   Its power structures on campus, viz., the faculty, students, administration, committees, rumor mill, and the like, with a view to ascertaining the obstacles to developing a unique mission appropriate to the institution and to instituting necessary change.

I wish that I could disagree with Professor Hodgkinson's observation of the dullness of so many institutions and with his further observation that there are really very few "truly interesting campuses." But even without the benefit of his thorough study my own observations would lead me to suspect that he is quite correct. In fact, many of our students would observe that getting an education is indeed a very dull experience. In another decade, or sooner, someone will say that our institutions of higher education are in transition. The hope I would have is that Professor Hodgkinson's study of transition, taken with the recommendations of the Carnegie Commission for change in higher education, might play a part in making higher education much more exciting. I have faith, too, that the students will play a major role in this task. The university will benefit from such influences, so that when the next study of institutions in transition is undertaken, the diversity of American higher education to which we all give lip service to, and most among us truly want, will have moved from mythology to fact.

Stanley J. Heywood

References

Byrnes, James G.: "The Quality of Instruction Today and Tomorrow," *Notes on the Future of Education,* vol. 1, no. 2, Syracuse University, February 1970, p. 3.

Chandler, Marjorie O.: *Opening Fall Enrollment in Higher Education, 1968: Part A—Summary Data,* U.S. Government Printing Office, February 1969.

Chickering, Arthur: *Education and Identity,* Jossey-Bass, San Francisco, 1969.

Hodgkinson, Harold: "Student Protest—A National and Institutional Profile," *Teachers College Record,* vol. 71, no. 4, May 1970.

Moses, Stanley: "Notes on the Learning Force," *Notes on the Future of Education,* vol. 1, no. 2, Syracuse University, February 1970, p. 7.

Nisbitt, Robert: "The Year 2,000 and All That," *Commentary,* pp. 60–66, June 1968.

Organization for Economic Cooperation and Development: "Planning New Structures of Post-Secondary Education," *Directorate for Scientific Affairs,* Paris, February 10, 1970 (mimeograph prepared by the Secretariat as a working paper).

Schultz, R., and W. H. Stickler: "Vertical Extensions of Academic Programs in Higher Education," *Educational Record,* summer 1965, pp. 231–241.

U.S. Office of Education: *Education Directory,* various years.

Bibliography

Astin, Alexander: *The College Environment,* American Council on Education, Washington, 1968.

Astin, Alexander: *Student Protest,* American Council on Education, Washington, 1969.

Barker, Roger, and Paul Gump: *Big School, Small School,* Stanford University Press, Stanford, Calif., 1964.

Cartter, Allan: *An Assessment of Quality in Graduate Education,* American Council on Education, Washington, 1966.

Chickering, Arthur: *Education and Identity,* Jossey-Bass, San Francisco, 1969.

Clark, Burton: *The Open Door College,* McGraw-Hill Book Company, New York, 1960.

Dunham, Alden: *Colleges of the Forgotten Americans,* McGraw-Hill Book Company, New York, 1970.

Gleazer, Edmund: *This Is the Community College,* Houghton Mifflin Company, Boston, 1968.

Gross, Edward, and Paul Grambsch: *University Goals and Academic Power,* American Council on Education, Washington, 1968.

Hartnett, Rodney: *College and University Trustees,* Educational Testing Service, Princeton, N.J., 1969.

Hefferlin, J. B. Lon: *The Dynamics of Academic Reform,* Jossey-Bass, San Francisco, 1969.

Jencks, Christopher, and David Riesman: *The Academic Revolution,* Doubleday & Company, Inc., Garden City, N.J., 1968.

Kerr, Clark: *The Uses of the University,* Harvard University Press, Cambridge, Mass., 1963.

Organization for Economic Cooperation and Development: "Planning New Structures of Post-Secondary Education," Paris, February 10, 1970 (mimeograph prepared by the Secretariat as a working paper).

Syracuse Educational Policy Research Center, occasional papers and monographs.

Peterson, Richard: *The Scope of Organized Student Protest in 1967–68,* Educational Testing Service, Princeton, N.J., 1968.

Veysey, Lawrence: *The Emergence of the American University,* The University of Chicago Press, Chicago, 1965.

Index

*This book was set in Vladimir by University Graphics,
Inc. It was printed and bound by The
Maple Press Company. The designers were Elliot Epstein
and Edward Butler. The editors were Herbert Waentig and
Cheryl Allen for McGraw-Hill Book Company and Verne A.
Stadtman for the Carnegie Commission on Higher Education.
Frank Matonti and Alice Cohen supervised the production.*